The Really Useful Physical Education Book

Learning and teaching across the 7–14 age range

Edited by Gary Stidder and Sid Hayes

Routledge
Taylor & Francis Group

LONDON AND NEW YORK

First published 2011
by Routledge
2 Park Square, Milton Park, Abingdon, Oxon, OX14 4RN

Simultaneously published in the USA and Canada
by Routledge
270 Madison Avenue, New York, NY 10016

Routledge is an imprint of the Taylor & Francis Group, an informa business

Typeset in Palatino by Keystroke, Tettenhall, Wolverhampton
Printed and bound in Great Britain by MPG Books Group, UK

British Library Cataloguing in Publication Data
A catalogue record for this book is available from the British Library

Library of Congress Cataloging-in-Publication Data
The really useful physical education book / edited by Gary Stidder and Sid Hayes.
       p. cm.
    Includes index.
  1. Physical education and training—Study and teaching—Great Britain.
  2. Physical education and training—Great Britain—Curricula.   I. Stidder, Gary,
  1962– II. Hayes, Sid, 1964–
  GV363.R43 2010
  613.7′071041—dc22   2009033213

ISBN13: 978–0–415–49827–2 (pbk)
ISBN13: 978–0–203–85813–4 (ebk)

The Really Useful Physical Education Book

The Really Useful Physical Education Book provides training and practising teachers with guidance and ideas to teach physical education effectively and imaginatively across the 7–14 age range. It is underpinned by easy-to-understand theory and links to the curriculum and presents a wide range of high quality, fun lessons alongside engaging teaching examples and methodologies.

With practical advice to ensure pupils exercise safely and enjoyably, it is a compendium of ideas for learning and teaching a range of activities:

- games
- gymnastics
- dance
- swimming and water-based activities
- athletics
- on-site outdoor and adventurous activities
- exercise and healthy lifestyles
- thematic learning and teaching through physical education
- using ICT in physical education.

The Really Useful Physical Education Book is for all secondary school physical education teachers responsible for the new Key Stage 3 (11–14 age range) curriculum as well as those working with primary and junior schools within school sport partnerships, providing them with ideas and advice to help all pupils participate in and enjoy physical education lessons. Primary and junior school teachers will also find a range of relevant and innovative ideas for making their physical education lessons more appealing and engaging for their pupils at Key Stage 2 (7–11 age range).

Gary Stidder is Senior Lecturer in Physical Education and PGCE Physical Education Course Leader at the University of Brighton, UK, as well as the co-founder of the Football4Peace Project in Israel.

Sid Hayes is Senior Lecturer in Physical Education and Learning and Teaching Co-ordinator at the University of Brighton, UK.

The Really Useful Series

This book is dedicated in memory of Andy Sibson – physical education teacher and deputy head teacher.

Andy Sibson died on 18 January 2009 aged 51. He had the attributes that every teacher needs: he was very knowledgeable, had a natural rapport with young people and knew how pupils learn. He was a master of his trade and will be remembered as a much loved professional, friend and colleague by so many.

Contents

Photos

Figures

Tables

Boxes

Contributors

Gary Stidder is Senior Lecturer in Physical Education at the University of Brighton's Chelsea School and route leader for the postgraduate (PGCE) physical education secondary initial teacher training course. Gary is the co-editor (with Sid Hayes) of *Equity and Inclusion in Physical Education and Sport* (2003) published by Routledge and is the co-founder of the pioneering Football4Peace project in Israel. In 2008 Gary received an award from the Association for Physical Education (AfPE) for his contribution to research and scholarship in physical education. His main academic interests include gender issues, outdoor education and mentoring.

Sid Hayes is Senior Lecturer in Physical Education, Learning and Teaching Co-ordinator at the University of Brighton and a former secondary school head of physical education. His present position includes responsibility for learning and teaching at the Chelsea School, University of Brighton, as well as contributing significantly to the teacher education programmes in physical education. His areas of expertise include games teaching, mentoring, ethnicity, teacher training and special educational needs.

Debra Barrett is Senior Lecturer in Physical Education at the University of Brighton and a former secondary school physical education teacher.

Jonathan Binney is Senior Lecturer in Physical Education at the University of Brighton and a former secondary school advanced skills teacher in physical education.

Joanna Gardiner is a newly qualified secondary school physical education teacher and the *Sunday Times* 2007 sportswoman of the year (Helen Rollason category for inspiration). She is also leader for the Football4Peace girls' project in Israel.

Adrian Haasner is Senior Lecturer at the Deutsche Sporthochschule (German Sports University), Köln, Germany and leader for the Football4Peace project in Israel.

Jackie Hannay is Senior Lecturer (Primary) at the University of Brighton.

Robert Harley is Principal Lecturer in Sport and Exercise Science at the University of Brighton.

Sue Keen is Senior Lecturer in Physical Education at the University of Brighton.

John Lambert is Senior Lecturer in Physical Education at the University of Brighton and a former secondary school head of physical education. He is also leader and director of coaching for the Football4Peace project in Israel.

Lucy Pocknell is Senior Lecturer at the University of Brighton and route leader for the Postgraduate (PGCE) Dance secondary initial teacher training course. She is also a former secondary school advanced skills teacher in Dance.

Fiona Smith is Principal Lecturer in Dance and Physical Education at the University of Brighton.

Andrew Theodoulides is Principal Lecturer in Physical Education and course leader for the BA QTS PE degree course at the University of Brighton. He is also a former secondary school head of physical education.

James Wallis is Senior Lecturer in Physical Education at the University of Brighton, a former secondary school physical education teacher and college lecturer in A-level physical education. He is also a leader for the Football4Peace project in Israel.

Preface

When we decided to embark upon the production of this book it was our intention to edit this publication as a textbook that can be used by daily practitioners involved in the learning and teaching of school physical education, as well as by physical education students enrolled on undergraduate and postgraduate teacher-training courses.[1] It is not an academic text in the sense that it is grounded in research and theory nor is it related to competitive school sport.[2] In this respect we have drawn upon the definition of 'physical education' from the Association for Physical Education (AfPE 2008).

> Physical education is the planned, progressive learning that takes place in school curriculum timetabled time and which is delivered to all pupils. This involves both 'learning to move' (i.e. becoming more physically competent) and 'moving to learn' (e.g. learning through movement, a range of skills and understandings beyond physical activity, such as co-operating with others). The context for the learning is physical activity, with children experiencing a broad range of activities, including sport and dance.
>
> (AfPE 2008: 3)

Our impetus for editing this text is that few books currently exist that specifically address the secondary National Curriculum for Physical Education (NCPE) (QCA 2008)[3] and the UK government's focus in primary junior schools on understanding physical development, health and wellbeing (QCA 2009).[4] Moreover, it is our intention to give the teaching of physical education in primary schools a prominent position within the curriculum proposed by the Rose Review and to highlight the concerns expressed by the AfPE.[5] In addition, a number of significant policy initiatives have been introduced to schools over the past five years that have implications for the way in which physical education is taught in primary junior and secondary schools. *The Physical Education School Sport Club Links Strategy* (PESSCL) aimed to provide new opportunities in physical education as part of an overall national strategy (DfES 2003). Part of this strategy saw the increase and development of specialist sports colleges and the school sport co-ordinator programme which aimed to provide a broader balance of activities to young people outside of traditional games activities. Specialist sports colleges were established in 1997 by the UK Labour government. These are state-maintained secondary schools that receive increased funding from central government for the purposes of raising standards in physical education within their own schools as well as in a cluster of schools within the local community known as a school sport partnership (SSP). In January 2008 PESSCL was replaced by the Physical Education and Sport Strategy for Young People (PESSYP) which aims to improve the quantity and quality of physical education and ensure that all 5- to 16-year-olds have access to two hours physical education and three hours beyond the curriculum. Collectively, this is referred to as the 'Five Hour Offer' (DCFS 2008).

The school sports co-ordinator programme aims to promote opportunities for young people through an arrangement with primary schools working across the Key Stage 2 and Key Stage 3 curriculum within a school sport partnership. Within this partnership, a partnership development manager (PDM) typically based at a specialist sports college (SSC) is responsible for supporting the partnership and up to eight secondary school sports co-ordinators. School sports co-ordinators (SSCos), who are experienced specialist physical education teachers, are released from their secondary schools for up to two days a week to support their local feeder primary schools. However, not all primary schools benefit from the school sport partnership and in this respect research suggests that in the United Kingdom only 9 per cent of primary schools have a full-time physical education specialist, whilst 93 per cent rely upon classroom teachers or other staff to teach physical education (Green 2008: 49). Moreover, the Association for Physical Education (AfPE 2008) estimate that the time spent on physical education training in primary teacher education is very limited, with as little as six to twelve hours on some one-year courses.

More recently, Ofsted (2009) stated that the situation had not changed significantly in primary schools.

> The subject knowledge of primary teachers was less secure than that of secondary teachers, often because they had entered the profession inadequately prepared to teach the full range of physical education activities and this had not been fully compensated for by professional development.
>
> Ofsted (2009: 5)

In addition, Ofsted (2009) have provided evidence from primary and secondary schools which suggests that there is a need to manage the provision of physical education more efficiently across the junior and primary sectors. In this respect, the report states that 'the schools visited did not promote continuity of learning across points of transition effectively' (Ofsted 2009: 6). Consequently, one of the recommendations from Ofsted (2009) relates specifically to developing subject knowledge in physical education for primary and junior schoolteachers and in this context the report states that

> The Training and Development Agency for Schools (TDA) and providers of primary initial teacher education should review the time allocated to physical education during primary initial teacher education to ensure teachers are better prepared to teach all aspects of the subject.
>
> Ofsted (2009: 7)

The central theme of this book, therefore, revolves around Key Stages 2 and 3 (ages 7 to 14) and the learning and teaching of physical education in its numerous forms, in order to support both non-specialist physical education teachers and school sports co-ordinators. Hence, this publication should assist teachers in the primary and secondary sector with ideas for physical education lessons as well as developing a coherent approach to the subject in line with the NCPE (2008). It will be of interest to those in managerial positions responsible for implementing the NCPE (2008) such as physical education specialist teachers, school sport co-ordinators, and heads and aspiring heads of physical education and dance departments. The book will also appeal especially to day-to-day practitioners, giving them both practical ideas and a theoretical underpinning to their teaching, and to those currently being trained for future positions in schools.

Green (2008: 42) refers to the physical education curriculum as the 'meat in the sandwich' (the what) that sits between the nature and purpose of physical education (the why) and the actual delivery of the physical education curriculum by teachers (the how). In this context, what goes into the sandwich (the physical education curriculum) and the means through which it is made (the management of the physical education curriculum) depend upon individuals and groups within and beyond the immediate policy network of physical education. We acknowledge the fact that there will be different interpretations of the recipe and ingredients between teachers, departments and schools, who are invariably the final link in a chain between policy and practice. In this modest text we have attempted, therefore, to provide teachers with practical teaching ideas based upon our own interpretation of a broad and balanced physical education curriculum that will appeal to pupils across the 7–14 age range. It is by no means a prescriptive or definitive version of what *ought* to be or *should* be included, but merely what *could* be included.

We have secured a representative group of authors, who have provided a range of material to support learning and teaching in physical education. The contributors are experienced physical education practitioners. In Chapter 1 Sid Hayes, Gary Stidder and Jackie Hannay outline some of the possibilities that the revised NCPE (2008) may offer junior and secondary school physical education. Here, we also examine some of the potential philosophical differences offered by the NCPE (2008) in terms of a reduced dependence on prescribed activity areas towards the teaching of key concepts and processes. The chapter identifies how the suggested range and content for physical education in the NCPE (2008) may be effectively delivered covering the areas of:

1. Outwitting an opponent.
2. Accurate replication of actions, phrases and sequences.
3. Exploring and communicating ideas, concepts and emotions.
4. Identifying and solving problems to overcome challenges of an adventurous nature as in life saving and personal survival in swimming and outdoor activities.
5. Performing at maximum levels in relation to speed, height, distance, strength or accuracy.
6. Exercising safely and effectively to improve health and well-being.

(QCA 2007: 194)

In Chapter 2 we have provided advice on how to develop professional attributes, knowledge and skills in the context of physical education. It is our intention to help all teachers involved in teaching of physical education to improve their practice through effective learning and teaching strategies so that all pupils can progress and develop to their full potential.

In Chapter 3 we address the key health and safety issues in physical education. This considers the guidance from AfPE (2008) 'safe practice in physical education' and relates to the issues associated with the teaching of physical education at Key Stage 2 and Key Stage 3.

Chapters 4 to 10 identify the range and content of activities and how they may contribute towards meeting aspects of the NCPE (2008). These chapters discuss pertinent issues in relation to teaching of those activities. Each chapter includes teaching method-ologies along with ideas and examples of tasks and activities for physical education lessons. In addition, these chapters focus on the inclusion of the key processes and concepts within physical education.

In Chapter 4 John Lambert provides examples on learning and teaching through games activities. Practical examples and educational discussion are included with respect to aspects of the NCPE (2008) through the delivery of games activities from a learner's and teacher's perspective. This chapter discusses methods of teaching including a games for understanding approach as well as issues and ideas on how to condition and progress games activities.

Jon Binney and Debra Barrett discuss learning and teaching through gymnastics in Chapter 5. This chapter provides advice and commentary on how to structure gymnastic activities within the framework of the NCPE (2008).

In Chapter 6 Fiona Smith and Lucy Pocknell provide guidance on learning and teaching through dance activities. This chapter will highlight methods of inclusion and delivery of dance activities to engage all pupils across the 7–14 age range.

In Chapter 7 Gary Stidder and Adrian Haasner provide ideas for learning and teaching through outdoor and adventurous activities. This chapter provides pedagogical debate surrounding the teaching of specific on-site outdoor and adventurous activities through trust games, problem-solving activities, joint decision-making and team building without the need for any specialised equipment or resources.

James Wallis and Jon Binney have outlined ways of learning and teaching through swimming and water-based activities in Chapter 8. This chapter includes ideas for lesson planning and how to structure a water-based activities curriculum across the 7–14 age range.

Andy Theodoulides and Sue Keen have outlined learning and teaching through athletic activities in Chapter 9. This chapter provides advice on how to challenge traditional approaches to teaching athletics through a sequence of related lessons as opposed to event-based teaching.

In Chapter 10 James Wallis and Rob Harley discuss ways of learning and teaching through health-related exercise. This chapter includes practical advice on how to develop pupils' knowledge and understanding of health-related exercise and how to motivate young people to engage in healthy lifestyles.

In Chapter 11 John Lambert and Joanna Gardiner provide examples of learning and teaching citizenship through physical education. Case study examples of how physical education may contribute to the whole-school concept of citizenship from a learner's and teacher's perspective are included.

In Chapter 12 we have indicated ways in which learning and teaching through cross-curricular themes in physical education may contribute to the whole-school concepts of literacy and numeracy from a learner's and teacher's perspective.

In Chapter 13 Gary Stidder draws attention to the range of information and communications technology available to teachers and how it may be applied to physical education in order to support learning and teaching.

The combination of each of the areas covered, drawing on the ideas and examples of all the contributors, highlights how teachers can best address teaching physical education to all pupils.

Gary Stidder and Sid Hayes
University of Brighton, Chelsea School

Postscript

The previous UK Labour government accepted recommendations put forward by Sir Jim Rose to implement a new primary curriculum from September 2011. In May 2010 a new UK coalition government was elected and subsequently announced that they do not intend to proceed with the 'new' primary curriculum proposals from Sir Jim Rose. The new coalition government now intend to give schools more freedom from unnecessary prescription and bureaucracy. They have indicated that the focus will be on the basics and providing teachers with more flexibility. The Government intends to return the National Curriculum to its intended purpose – a minimum national entitlement organised around subject disciplines. In the meantime, the existing primary curriculum will continue to be in force in 2011/12 and schools have been advised that they should plan on that basis.

Notes

1   The term 'physical education' is often abbreviated to 'PE'. Other secondary school subjects are also referred to in an abbreviated form such as RE (religious education) and CDT (craft, design and technology). We believe this reinforces the marginal status and value of these subjects compared to other curriculum areas. We have, therefore, chosen not to abbreviate 'physical education' but to use the term in its entirety throughout this book.

2   Throughout this book we have deliberately avoided the use of the term 'school sport'. The term 'school sport' has been increasingly used in government policy documents alongside 'physical education' in the title of the subject, thus giving the impression that school sport is synonymous with physical education. We believe that to refer to 'school sport' alongside 'physical education' is potentially misleading and may cause some confusion amongst our readers. Our use of the term 'physical education', therefore, refers specifically to the UK government's intended offer of at least two hours of high quality physical education in the curriculum to all 7- to 14-year-old pupils.

3   A fourth national curriculum for physical education in England was published by the QCA in 2007 and implemented in September 2008 for all pupils beginning their compulsory secondary schooling at the age of 11.

4   The UK government published its proposals on the primary curriculum in April 2009 in a report led by Sir Jim Rose. Physical education as a curriculum subject has been included within an Area of Learning referred to as 'Understanding physical development, health and wellbeing'. Together with the personal, social and emotional aspects of the Essential Skills for Learning and Life, this area of learning contributes to the personal development framework. Social and emotional aspects of learning (SEAL) are also included in this area of learning. Aspects of economic and business understanding are also included in historical, geographical and social understanding. The physical activities in this area of learning contribute to the five-hour offer per week of physical activity. This should include at least two hours of high quality physical education (QCA 2009: 1).

5   The Association for Physical Education (AfPE) press release dated 30 April 2009 read as follows:

> Physical Education is the only school subject which is expected to make major contributions to national strategies in education, health and sport. It is therefore disappointing that the Rose Review has failed to recognise the distinctive value of physical education, and has reduced both its visibility and its importance within this proposed primary curriculum.
>
> The lack of visibility and lower profile of physical education in these proposals constitute a direct threat to its continuing place in the primary curriculum. Right across the world, where physical education has been subsumed under an umbrella curriculum title, it has all but disappeared. At a time when the UK should be seen to be delivering on its commitment to a lasting Olympic legacy for children and young people, it is sad that the future of their physical education, the basis for lifelong participation in sport and physical activity, apparently is at risk.
>
> The Association for Physical Education (AfPE) welcomes the opportunities for physical education to lead children's learning in health and wellbeing, but believes that a golden opportunity has been lost to place physical learning and achievement at the heart of an area of learning which could have made a major contribution to education and health strategies. With one in five primary aged children currently overweight or obese, it is regrettable that the area of learning 'Understanding Physical Development, Health and Wellbeing' should be diluted by disparate elements like 'economic wellbeing'.

It is also disappointing that the integrity of physical education has been undermined by the removal of dance, which is a vital physical activity to meet the needs of children and young people whose interests do not include competitive sport. While dance is included in the Arts area of learning, and may be delivered within physical education, clear progression from generic movement education through to dance in the secondary physical education curriculum has been lost. This also means that the government's own ambition for all children to enjoy five hours' physical education and school sport within the Physical Education and School Sport strategy is less likely to be achieved.

During the consultation process, AfPE will be making strong representation to restore physical education to the central position in the primary curriculum which it, and the nation's children, deserve (www.afpe.org.uk accessed 18 November 2009).

References

AfPE (Association for Physical Education) (2008) *Health Position Paper,* September 2008. Retrieved from http://www.afpe.org.uk/public/downloads/Health_Paper08.doc

Department for Children, Family and Schools (DCFS) (2008) *Physical Education and Sport Strategy for Young People (PESSYP)* (Ref. 00131-2008LEF/EN). DCSF.

Department for Education and Skills and Department for Culture, Media and Sport (2003) *Learning through Physical Education and Sport: A guide to the Physical Education, School Sport and Club Links strategy (PESSCL)* (Reference: LTPES), DCSF. Available at www.teachernet.gov.uk/_doc/5062/LTPES.pdf

Green, K. (2008) *Understanding Physical Education,* London, Sage.

Ofsted (2009) *Physical Education in Schools 2005/08: Working towards 2012 and beyond,* April, Reference number: 080249. Available at www.ofsted.gov.uk

Qualifications and Curriculum Authority (QCA) (2007) *Physical Education Programme of Study Key Stage 3.* Available at www.qca.org.uk/curriculum

Acknowledgements

We would like to acknowledge the help and support of our contributing authors and thank Professor Jo Doust, Head of Chelsea School, for his encouragement in pursuing this venture.

Gary Stidder would like to thank Karen, for continuing to take an interest in the progress of the book. Also, Oliver and Lily for providing the motivation and inspiration.

Sid Hayes would like to thank Elaine and Ethan for making everything worthwhile.

Abbreviations

AFL	Assessment for Learning
AfPE	Association for Physical Education
AOL	Assessment of Learning
ASA	Amateur Swimming Association
DAP	Digital Audio Player
DCFS	Department for Children, Families and Schools
DCMS	Department for Culture, Media and Sport
DfEE	Department for Education and Employment
DfES	Department for Education and Skills
ECM	*Every Child Matters*
EVC	Educational Visits Co-ordinator
HRE	Health Related Exercise
HRF	Health Related Fitness
HSE	Health and Safety Executive
ICT	Information and Communications Technology
IMT	Internet Media Tablet
ISDN	Integrated Services Digital Network
KS	Key Stage
LEA	Local Education Authority
NCPE	National Curriculum for Physical Education
OFSTED	Office for Standards in Education
PDM	Partnership Development Manager
PESSCL	Physical Education School Sport Club Links
PESSYP	Physical Education Sport Strategy Young People
PLTS	Personal Learning and Thinking Skills
PMP	Portable Media Player
PSA	Public Service Agreement
PSHE	Personal Social and Health Education
PT	Physical Training
QCA	Qualifications and Curriculum Authority
QTS	Qualified Teacher Status
SSC	Specialist Sports College
SSCo	School Sports Coordinator
SSP	School Sports Partnership
SWBA	Swimming and Water-Based Activities
TDA	Training and Development Agency for Schools

TGFU   Teaching Games For Understanding
UK   United Kingdom
VLE   Virtual Learning Environment

1 Introduction

Sid Hayes, Gary Stidder and Jackie Hannay

Our aims in this introductory chapter are to examine changes to the National Curriculum for Physical Education (NCPE), predominantly at Key Stage 3, and to suggest how teachers may wish to present their lesson content material in the short, medium and long term in order to ensure that the requirements for the National Curriculum (2008) are being met at a minimal level. It should be noted at this stage that changes at Key Stage 2 are yet to be finalised; however, the QCA's aim is to create a seamless progression in pupils' learning across all age ranges. This chapter will outline some of the possibilities that the proposed primary curriculum may offer school physical education. We have, therefore, included guidance and teaching ideas for those professionals who work within the primary sector (Key Stage 2) and school sport co-ordinators who work in partnership with cluster schools. The chapter will also examine some of the potential philosophical differences offered by the 2008 curriculum in terms of a reduced dependence on strict activity area delivery towards the teaching of key concepts and processes.

Physical education is an integral part of the core curriculum and a foundation subject in all secondary and junior schools. The aim of physical education is to enable young people to participate competently in a range of activities that will become a part of their lives as they grow older. A high quality physical education curriculum enables all pupils to enjoy and succeed in many kinds of physical activity, in which they develop a wide range of skills and the ability to use tactics, strategies and compositional ideas to perform successfully.

When they are performing, pupils think about what they are doing, analyse the situation and make decisions. They also reflect on their own and others' performances and find ways to improve them. As a result, they develop the confidence to take part in different physical activities and learn about the value of healthy, active lifestyles. Discovering what they like to do, what their aptitudes are at school, and how and where to get involved in physical activity helps them make informed choices about lifelong physical activity. Physical education helps pupils develop personally and socially. They work as individuals, in groups and in teams, developing concepts of fairness and of personal and social responsibility. They take on different roles and responsibilities, including leadership, coaching and officiating. Through the range of experiences that physical education offers, they learn how to be effective in competitive, creative and challenging situations.

Key Stage 3 curriculum

Since the curriculum at Key Stage 3 has been finalised we thought we would deal with this stage of learning first. The Key Stage 2 review process will be discussed in this chapter later because the review process is on-going and changes may occur.

The curriculum has a number of over-arching aims at Key Stage 3 with regard to learners' development. These aims should be borne in mind when teachers are developing specific programmes of learning for specific activity areas. These general aims of the Key Stage curriculum for 2008 include the development of:

- successful learners
- confident individuals
- responsible citizens.

These generic aims for all curriculum areas should then be coupled with the *Every Child Matters* agenda, which outlines the concepts of:

- being healthy
- staying safe
- enjoying and achieving
- making a positive contribution
- achieving economic wellbeing.

Clearly these aspirations are rather unspecific and global in nature, but they are worth bearing in mind when practitioners turn to more subject-specific planning, to ensure their pedagogic approach to the subject matches up to these aspirations.

With the previous points in mind we now examine the specific nature of the school physical education and sport programmes in terms of the 2008 curriculum requirements. Each curriculum area at Key Stage 3 has an 'importance statement' which clearly identifies the essential role of the subject. It may be a worthwhile task to look at the 'importance statement' for physical education, which has been reproduced in Box 1.1 with selected words removed. Teachers may wish to attempt to fill in the spaces themselves from their own vocabulary to see if their own ideas and philosophies fit in with the curriculum statement for 2008. Equally, they may wish to use the list provided, the idea being that it will encourage teachers to think and identify what are the essential characteristics of physical education.

Box 1.1 The importance of physical education statement Key Stage 3

PE develops pupils' _____ and confidence to take part in a range of physical activities that become a central part of their lives, both in and out of school.

A high-quality PE curriculum enables all pupils to _____ and succeed in many kinds of physical activity. They develop a wide range of _____ and the ability to use tactics, _____ and _____ to perform successfully. When they are performing, they think about what they are doing, _____ the situation and make decisions. They also reflect on their own and others' _____ and find ways to improve them. As a result, they develop the confidence to take part in different _____ and learn about the value of _____, active lifestyles. Discovering what they like to do, what their aptitudes are at school, and how and where to get involved in physical activity helps them make informed choices about _____ physical activity.

PE helps pupils develop _____ and _____. They work as individuals, in groups and in teams, developing concepts of _____ and of personal and social responsibility. They take on _____ and responsibilities, including leadership, coaching and _____. Through the range of experiences that PE offers, they learn how to be effective in_____, _____ and challenging situations.

From the list of words complete the previous paragraph. Try this first without referring to the official statement then check your response to see how many you achieved.

Skills, officiating, physical activities, lifelong, personally, socially, competence, enjoy, healthy, different roles, competitive, strategies, creative, compositional ideas, analyse, performances, fairness.

(www.qca.org.uk)

Following on from the 'importance statement' are four *key concepts*. These are:

1. competence
2. performance
3. creativity
4. healthy, active lifestyles.

More detailed explanations of the four key concepts can be found in the national curriculum document where these key concepts are significantly elaborated upon. Building upon this the curriculum then highlights five *key processes* that learners should develop whilst engaged in physical education lessons. These include:

1. (2.1) developing skills in physical activity
2. (2.2) making and applying decisions
3. (2.3) developing physical and mental capacity
4. (2.4) evaluating and improving
5. (2.5) making informed choices about healthy, active lifestyles.

Again, further details of the meaning and interpretation of these key processes can be found in the actual documentation.

In order to develop learners' understanding of the key concepts and processes teachers will need to select appropriate activities from the range and content section of the curriculum. This is an area where teachers will be able to, within reason, select content which both suits the learners in the school and accords with the school's own resources and philosophy of what is an appropriately broad and balanced physical education curriculum. In other words, colleagues' professional interpretation and philosophy will determine the nature of the learners' curriculum experience. Teachers may select content from the following areas identified in the 2008 curriculum. This includes the areas of:

*   outwitting an opponent
*   accurate replication of actions, phrases and sequences

- exploring and communicating ideas, concepts and emotions
- identifying and solving problems to overcome challenges of an adventurous nature as in life saving and personal survival in swimming and outdoor activities
- performing at maximum levels in relation to speed, height, distance, strength or accuracy
- exercising safely and effectively to improve health and wellbeing.

(QCA 2007: 194)

During Key Stage 3 a number of other opportunities are identified as being central to the learner's physical education and engaging them more fully with the key concepts, key processes and range and content of the subject. In the curriculum at Key Stage 3 these are categorised under the heading of 'Curriculum Opportunities'. As outlined below, learners have opportunities to:

- get involved in a broad range of different activities that, in combination, develop the whole body
- experience a range of roles within a physical activity
- specialise in specific activities and roles
- follow pathways to other activities in and beyond school
- perform as an individual, in a group or as part of a team in formal competitions or performances to audiences beyond the class
- use ICT as an aid to improving performance and tracking progress
- make links between PE and other subjects and areas of the curriculum.

(QCA 2007: 195)

Figure 1.1 outlines the inter-connectedness of the curriculum at Key Stage 3 and how the different aspects of it link together. The importance statement lies at the centre of the curriculum activity area and the key concepts, processes and opportunities emanate from the statement to develop a physically educated pupil. When teachers are planning in the short, medium and long term, referring to the conceptual idea will be useful in enabling them to enhance and meet the curriculum requirements.

Key Stage 2

It is important to recognise that the teaching of physical education in primary schools is going through a significant transitional stage and that teachers in both the primary and secondary sectors need to be aware of the stages of pupils' development. Although the Key Stage 2 new primary curriculum is not due to be introduced until September 2011, the *Independent Review of the Primary Curriculum: Final Report* carried out by Jim Rose recognises the importance of both subject content and extra-curricular teaching. Rose states that pupils should continue to be taught 'the essential knowledge and skills . . . through visible subject disciplines, such as . . . physical education' but acknowledges that 'there are times when it is right to marshal content from different subjects into well planned, cross curricular studies' (Rose 2009: 11, 25). This means that there will be ample opportunity to teach 'essential content both discretely and directly' (2009: 4) and that teachers should base their selection of pedagogy on the method that potentially maximises pupils' learning. For example, pupils may engage in a dance lesson where the learning objective is for them to gain an understanding of choreography. Then they may use their choreographic knowledge to explore an historical concept such as 'the Egyptians'.

Figure 1.1 The physical education curriculum at Key Stage 3

The Rose review recommends that the primary curriculum be organised into six areas of learning:

1. Understanding English, communication and languages.
2. Mathematical understanding.
3. Scientific and technological understanding.
4. Historical, geographical and social understanding
5. Understanding physical development, health and wellbeing.
6. Understanding the arts.

(Rose 2009: 31)

It is anticipated that the teaching of the physical education curriculum can still centre around the current six areas of learning: gymnastics, dance, games, swimming, outdoor and adventurous activities, and athletics. However, within the report Rose states that teachers will 'have more freedom to decide upon the range of activities pupils should participate in to promote physical development both inside and outside the classroom' (2009: 2.18). Further to this, teachers may opt to develop other skills through the physical education curriculum. For example, within the area of 'Understanding English, communications and language', pupils can be provided with opportunities to develop their communication skills when they engage in one of the QCA's four strands of learning: 'evaluating and improving performance' through peer assessment of a movement pattern in dance, a gymnastics sequence, or a defence or attack strategy in a game.

The new primary 5–11 curriculum will need to link the six early years areas of learning in the foundation stage with the fourteen subjects delivered at Key Stage 3. Therefore, within the physical education curriculum, pupils in the 5–11 age range will continue to build on physical development and the physical education skills nurtured during the early years foundation stage. Here pupils are encouraged to explore a range of physical movements and equipment through structured and exploratory play in order to develop and master key motor skills. Through careful planning, transition into Key Stage 1 should continue to consolidate skills learnt and provide opportunities for pupils to develop new skills on their own, with a partner and in two-versus-one game situations, for example 'Piggy in the Middle'.

A natural progression should continue into Key Stage 2, with pupils continuing to master key generic skills that will allow them to engage successfully in a range of sports and become proficient dancers and/or gymnasts. The teaching of games at Key Stage 2 should continue to focus on developing generic sport skills such as tracking, throwing and catching, and gaining knowledge of attacking, and defending strategies through regular physical participation. In gymnastics and dance pupils should consolidate and develop new movement ideas. There should be a progression through developing longer sequences, working in pairs and small groups, and ensuring that compositions include a change in direction, speed and levels (as outlined in the Physical Education National Curriculum). It is vital that pupils develop generic skills in preparation for invasion, striking and fielding and net/wall games through engagement in small-sided games to maximise individual participation. This will provide them with the opportunity to develop the skills required to play adult versions of sport activities in Key Stage 3.

Successful skill development will only occur through regular, structured engagement, so that pupils have the opportunity to develop from the initial, elementary and finally the mature skill stages outlined by Gallahue (2002). Therefore, it is essential that teachers ensure that regular and sufficient time is allocated to practical activity in the primary curriculum.

Making sure that pupils engage in active learning is essential, and a physically active programme will provide pupils with opportunities to gain understanding in many of the key areas of learning. For example, through a vigorous warm-up pupils will experience changes to their bodies, thereby gaining some understanding of the body's physiology. Further to this, when teachers plan lessons using the QCA schemes of work to develop skills and understanding through the four strands of learning – acquiring and developing skills, selecting and applying skills, tactic and compositional ideas, evaluating and improving their skills – pupils may also develop their social skills as they are required to:

- listen and observe
- take the lead
- make decisions
- problem solve
- peer assess
- give feedback
- share ideas
- negotiate.

Teachers may want to assess pupils against these criteria.

There is a growing trend in schools for coaches to cover PPA (Planning, Preparation and Assessment) time in Key Stage 2, but the role of the primary teacher should not be underestimated in the development of pupils in *all* curriculum areas. Primary teachers are in the prime position of teaching a class the whole curriculum for the majority of the school day and therefore are able to build unique relationships with the individual pupils. It is this information that allows teachers to plan lessons that maximise learning for the individual pupil. Coaches are not in this position and although they have sport expertise, sport is only one facet of the curriculum. Through physical education there are also opportunities for pupils to develop socially, morally, spiritually and culturally.

In physical education, teachers should focus on pupils learning generic physical skills, sharing ideas, working together, and on maximum participation and differentiated tasks to optimise learning for each individual. Coaches, on the other hand, will be more concerned with teaching skills that are sport-specific and with individual/team performance; the sole purpose will be for competition, winning at all cost – being the best – and this can be exclusive. Furthermore, a team sport tends to focus on the team rather than on individual needs and can be predominantly concerned with promoting excellence. Therefore, sport taught by coaches often has desired outcomes that may not be congruent with those of the teacher in physical education lessons.

We believe that teachers are in the best position to deliver the physical education curriculum and within this book we aim to show how a bank of ideas can provide you with the starting point and how to progress your professional development.

Physically literate learners

We would expect that the implementation of the physical education curriculum (2008) should help to make a significant contribution towards the development of a physically educated child who is prepared to interact effectively with many facets of their environment. As identified by Whithead (2007) this should include ability to:

- utilize movement potential
- move with poise, economy and confidence in a variety of physical environments
- anticipate changes to a physical learning environment and react appropriately.

(www.physical-literacy.org.uk/)

The concept of physical literacy is an important one and should form part of any curriculum implementation, especially at Key Stage 2/3 where physical movement life-skills are being formed and developed. For many pupils play and physical movement are a natural part of their everyday lives, and it is hoped and expected that the curriculum and its design will foster such instinctive and inquisitive prerequisites for movement and learning, capturing the very essence of part of a child's natural progression. We must have the courage and skills as teachers to embellish physical education's special role in the development of young learners. Let's hope that pupils are allowed to be childlike through the physical education programme they receive. For a more detailed discussion of the concept please visit the physical literacy website at www.physical-literacy.org.uk/.

Curriculum interpretation

Many policy documents may be open to a number of different interpretations depending on a number of factors. This is certainly the case with the message delivered by the 2008 physical education curriculum. Indeed, we think that it is part of its remit and that it has been written to allow teachers to make the considered best choices for their pupils and schools. Our interpretations are set out in Figure 1.2.

Pre-2008 curriculum at Key Stage 3		Post-2008 curriculum at Key Stage 3
Teacher-led instruction	⟶	Child-centred learning
Rigid timetabling	⟶	Flexible approach to learning
Subject-orientated learning	⟶	Problem-solving learning
Activity-centered areas	⟶	Concepts and processes

Figure 1.2 Comparison of pre-2008 and revised physical education national curriculum

Source: www.qca.org.uk/curriculum

For physical education the former activity areas of athletics, dance, games, gymnastics, outdoor and adventurous activities, and swimming are now identified within the range and content area of the curriculum. As mentioned previously this relates to the range and breadth of the subject, in which teachers can highlight and teach the key concepts and processes. It is this area of the 2008 physical education curriculum that is open to much debate and interpretation. In this context, the curriculum detail offers guidance and examples of how, for example, learners might learn to 'outwit an opponent, as in games activities'. There may however, be other activities through which 'outwitting an opponent' may be experienced and it is hoped that practitioners would explore the range of content through numerous relevant, motivating, exciting and enjoyable activity areas. A key message which is alluded to throughout the documentation is a broad and relevant set of learning experiences tailored to the needs of the individual and the school. Chapters 4 to 10 of this book will outline the traditional activities associated with learning in athletics, dance, games, gymnastics, outdoor and adventurous activities and swimming, and also outline areas where teachers can be innovative and challenging with regards to activities that will ensure a broad, balanced, relevant and exciting curriculum. We would like to encourage practitioners at Key Stage 2/3 to interpret the curriculum guidelines in such a way, coupled with considerations of offering experiences that gradually develop the child into 'physically literate' pupils.

Breakdown of the physical education curriculum

Pupils are legally required to attend school for 190 days in an academic school year. This represents 38 weeks in a school year. If pupils are receiving two hours of physical education per week this equates to 76 hours of curriculum physical education per pupil per year. In this respect, physical education constitutes 5 per cent of the total curriculum in schools. Research has shown that the physical education curriculum in primary schools is usually weighted towards the performance aspects of the programme of study, with much time devoted to games activities (Ofsted 2004). For pupils in Key Stage 3, games has typically occupied between 50 and 70 per cent of the available time, and under the requirements of the former NCPE (1999) the other three chosen areas of activity required by the national curriculum were squeezed into the remaining time, leaving too little time to develop them fully (Ofsted 1998).

In this respect secondary schools have typically devoted as much as 70 per cent of the physical education curriculum – 56 hours of curriculum time – to the teaching of games, and in particular sex-stereotyped team games (Ofsted 1998). Consequently, 20 hours of physical education curriculum time has to be divided between gymnastics, dance, athletics, health-related exercise, swimming, and outdoor and adventurous activities. Current research (Ofsted 2009) suggests that in some secondary schools very little has changed since the introduction of the national curriculum for physical education in 1999 and that schemes of work are insufficiently broad and often reflect stereotypes of male and female activities, particularly in Key Stage 3. This has frequently resulted in a programme dominated by traditional team games. At one school, for example, nearly 70 per cent of the programme was dedicated to games, while dance and gymnastics shared just 10 per cent of the programme (Ofsted 2009: 40). In secondary schools where a minimum number of four activity areas are included from the six it is often swimming and outdoor and adventurous activities that are left out. In this respect, Ofsted (2009: 39) reported that although the schools visited met the minimum statutory requirements for the coverage of national curriculum activity areas at Key Stages 3, very few of them offered outdoor and adventurous activities or swimming as part of their curriculum programmes.

Breadth, depth and balance in physical education

The NCPE (2008: 194) provides teachers with guidance on what can potentially be included in the range, content and breadth of physical education. Teachers should draw on this when they teach the key concepts and processes. It is disappointing that, although the formal physical education curriculum at Key Stage 3 covers six areas of physical activity, the minimum entitlement to pupils is set at four, thus allowing the potential exclusion of two areas of physical activity. The explanatory notes to teachers outline what might be included within each of the six areas from the range and content.

Outwitting opponents

This includes activities in which the concept of success is to overcome an opponent or opponents in a face-to-face competition. Opponents can directly affect each other's performance and the key is to outwit the opposition. Ideas include:

- invasion games (for example, water polo, netball, football, rugby, gaelic football, American football, polo and hockey);
- net/wall games (for example, volleyball, tennis, table tennis and squash);
- striking/fielding games (for example, softball, stoolball, cricket and table cricket);
- combat activities (for example fencing, judo and karate).

Accurate replication

This includes activities in which success is judged on the ability to repeat actions, phrases and sequences of movement as perfectly as possible. Examples include: synchronised swimming, diving, rebound tumbling, ballroom dancing, gymnastics and skateboarding.

Exploring and communicating ideas, concepts and emotions

This includes activities in which success is considered in relation to how well a performer or choreographer expresses ideas, feelings, concepts or emotions to communicate artistic or choreographic intentions to an audience. Dance styles could include capoeira, contemporary dance, country dancing, ballet, Indian hand dance and street dance.

Performing at maximum levels

This includes activities in which success is measured by personal best scores or times, and in competition by direct comparison with others' scores or times. Examples include racing in the swimming pool or on a skateboard, or having a low score in golf or a high score in archery.

Identifying and solving problems

This includes activities in which success is judged on how efficiently and safely challenges are overcome. Examples include orienteering, personal survival, life saving and expeditions involving walking or using transport such as boats and canoes.

Exercising safely and effectively

This includes activities such as aqua aerobics, weight training, jogging and power walking, in which success is related to improving feelings of health, fitness and wellbeing. Goals might include emotional wellbeing, healthy weight management, toned muscles, healthy skin and a healthy heart.

Whilst changes to the physical education curriculum have been limited since 1999, there is some evidence emerging from Ofsted (2009) which suggests that some schools are offering pupils a wider experience of physical education. Golf, skateboarding, mountain biking and cycling, yoga, archery, cheerleading, martial arts and problem-solving challenges were being taught alongside more traditional activities, often at pupils' request. This not only enriched the provision but provided creative solutions when facilities were limited or the programme of traditional team activities was proving unpopular. This had reduced disaffection and improved engagement, particularly among vulnerable groups (Ofsted 2009: 38).

We believe that the NCPE (2008) provides opportunities for local interpretation of physical education to create a curriculum that reflects a school's locality whilst also offering broad, balanced and engaging learning opportunities. In this respect, we believe that there is a case for teachers to think critically and creatively about what they provide and how it is managed and organised. The physical education curriculum is only limited by the teacher's own imagination and should be based on the voice of the pupils.

In Figure 1.3 we present some ideas in terms of a starting point for curriculum design. Whilst the pie chart is divided up into sections we have not attached specific percentages of time to each area, since numerous school-related factors will ultimately determine any school curriculum.

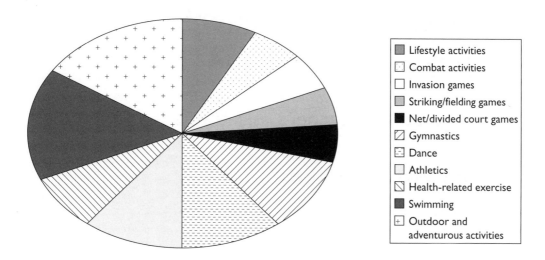

Figure 1.3 A broad and balanced physical education curriculum

References

Gallahue, O.J. (2002) *Understanding Motor Development: Infants, pupils, adolescents, adults,* 5th edition. New York: McGraw-Hill.

Ofsted (1998) *Secondary Education 1993–97: A review of secondary schools in England.* London: The Stationery Office.

Ofsted (2004) *Ofsted Subject Reports 2002/03: Physical education in primary schools.* London: Ofsted.

Ofsted (2009) *Physical Education in Schools 2005/08: Working towards 2012 and beyond.* London: Ofsted. Reference number 080249.

QCA (2007) http://www.qca.org.uk/ Accessed 8 April 2009.

Rose, J. (2009) *Independent Review of the Primary Curriculum: Final Report.* London: Department for Children, Schools and Families. Available at http://www.dcsf.gov.uk/primary curriculumreview/

Websites

http://www.everychildmatters.gov.uk/ Accessed 8 April 2009.
http://www.physical-literacy.org.uk/ Accessed 8 April 2009.

2 Learning and teaching in physical education

A guide for teachers and trainees

Gary Stidder and Sid Hayes

Introduction

In this chapter we provide some general advice on learning and teaching in physical education. The suggestions we have made are designed to help teachers and trainees establish a purposeful working environment for pupils where the learning opportunities can be maximised and participation is inclusive. To this end, we have sub-divided each of the important points and provided a catchphrase that will help you to remember the particular point. Overall, we have attempted to cover what we consider to be some of the most important aspects of learning and teaching through physical education associated with professional attributes, knowledge and skills which include the following:

- your role as a teacher of physical education
- how pupils should learn
- range and content of activities
- progression in teaching
- promoting learning for all pupils
- assessment
- organisation and safety.

We have also highlighted other important issues involved in teaching physical education effectively. For example, we suggest that you consider carefully pupil groupings giving full considerations to any gender implications that may arise from both coeducational and single-sex classes in physical education. Whenever possible, modify rules, use adapted equipment, reduce the numbers of pupils on a team, adjust the size of playing areas and explain your learning outcomes. Attention to these issues will help pupils to understand the purpose of the lesson and enable maximum involvement. Equally, we suggest that you encourage pupils to share, help each other and work together; to be aware of particular disabilities; and to be sensitive to cultural influences. Likewise, teachers should not involve pupils in physical contact if it makes them vulnerable, or include pupils in large groups unless they can be fully involved; they should not involve pupils in too much technique-focused work or make pupils' problems public.

Teaching physical education

Appearance

You must work very hard to look the part. This is the first step to convincing your audience (the pupils) that you know what you are doing. It is advisable that you have both indoor and outdoor clothing. Remember that you are setting an example of the standards you expect the pupils to live up to.

Voice

Make sure that your diction is clear and that you do not speak too quickly. On the field you will need to project your voice to a greater extent. Indoors, speaking quietly will make the pupils listen more and will decrease the level of background noise. Keep your instructions brief and to the point. Make it short, sharp and punchy. Do not make more than one point at a time

- Don't blind them with science

Pupil activity

Pupils should be constantly active unless you are giving instructions or teaching points, demonstrating, or exchanging questions and answers. Pupils should also be given opportunities to evaluate their own and other performance. Think very carefully about the use of relay type games, because there will be much inactivity and non-participation and a greater opportunity for pupils to disrupt the lesson.

- Give them an inch and they'll take a mile

Type of activity

Depending on your learning objectives in your physical education lessons there should be a balance between individual, co-operative and competitive activity. For example, in a one-hour lesson related to games activities there must be time for pupils to work and practise on their own; work with a partner or group; and play or perform against opponents or competitors in a realistic situation. Wherever possible pupils should be working with a ball each particularly at an early age. Small-sided conditioned games are essential for pupils to implement the skills and techniques they have learned and ensure maximum activity, involvement, participation, ball contact, and decision-making experiences.

- Tell a child and they will forget, show a child and they will remember, involve a child and they will understand

Positioning and mobility

Do not teach from the middle of the class. Maintain a peripheral position so that you can see everything that is going on and your pupils can see you. Try to ensure that you see every pupil or group during the lesson as much as possible.

Questions and answers

It is important as teachers that you use questions and answers as much as possible as a means of developing an understanding of what you are teaching and aiding cognitive development. Using a range of questioning techniques, such as open-ended questions or hierarchical questioning, will help pupils understand the what, where, when, how and why in relation to their learning. Table 2.1 describes a net/divided court games lesson and the types of questions that can be used by teachers.

Rewards and sanctions

When you are teaching it is important that you provide competition and incentives, as they generally increase effort. Always check scores and identify those pupils who have achieved a good score otherwise the activity becomes pointless to them. If you need to reprimand a pupil be consistent and follow school/department policy and procedure. Don't be over-generous with praise, or it will eventually become worthless. On your first

Table 2.1 *Examples of questions and answers in a net/divided court games lesson*

Problems	Tactical solutions	Requirements of players
Where shall I play the ball?	Into space on open court To the edges of the court	Look where an opponent is on court.
Why play into open spaces?	To exploit an opponent's weakness	Hit accurately.
When do I play into open spaces?	As early and quickly as possible	Ready, prepare, hit, recover.
How do I force an error from an opponent?	Force opponent to the back and side of the court Limit time available to prepare by hitting at your opponent Use disguise	Take ball as early as possible. Keep ball out of mid-court area.
How do I play a winning shot?	Select the right time Exploit weaknesses Hit ball out of reach Reduce opponent's time Adopt the ready position early	Be aware of opponent's position and weaknesses. Move opponent as much as possible. Dictate the play.
What stroke do I play?	Select appropriate stroke depending on the position of opponent on court	Pin opponent to the back of the court.
What do I do when I'm under pressure?	Create time Regain initiative Recover to optimal position	Use speed and mobility on the court. Anticipate the next shot.

meeting with your pupils it is advisable to talk to them and make them aware of your expectations (they will certainly have high expectations of you).

- Give credit where credit is due

Teacher/pupil demonstrations (visual guidance)

Demonstrations are an essential part of any lesson and should be used at all stages of learning and teaching. Demonstrations are particularly good for introducing a task and setting the scene. They are efficient, 'on the spot' and interesting to the pupils, but must be accurate and relate to age, gender and experience. Don't worry if you are not confident in this respect as you can always use the more accomplished performers to do this for you. Never repeat a good demonstration. Quit while you're ahead and remember:

- A picture paints a thousand words

Differentiated tasks

Each pupil should be allowed to work at their own level and pace and should never feel afraid to make mistakes. Each task or skill should be broken down into bite-sized pieces and follow a logical progressive sequence. Some pupils will learn faster than others, so tasks should be relative according to ability and challenge each pupil. Don't be afraid to try new ideas:

- Nothing ventured is nothing gained

Organisation

Poor organisation will affect your ability to teach effectively. Make sure that you pay particular importance to this. Keep three or four steps ahead of yourself in order to ensure a smooth transition from task to task and maintain order and control of the environment in which you are teaching.

Preparation

This is of vital performance. You must be working to clearly defined aims and objectives within the schemes of work. Think very carefully about what you want the pupils to learn and how you want them to learn it. Make sure that your evaluations are up to date, as these will help you to improve in the long run. Always make sure that you have a wet weather lesson plan, sports quizzes, etc. in your file in case of poor weather; find out if you have the use of a television or video. Be prepared to show initiative and adapt to circumstances as things constantly change in schools. Find out which indoor spaces are available should you need them and be aware of certain events such as CAT tests, mock exams, choir rehearsals, etc., since it is usually the gym and hall that are used.

- Failure to prepare is preparation for failure

Planning

Long-term, medium-term and short-term planning are vital for effective teaching and learning in physical education.

Long-term curriculum planning

Scheme of work – overall provision of physical education at Key Stages 2 or 3. Made up of units of work/sequence of lessons.

Medium-term planning

Sequence of lessons (formerly units) – medium-term plans for one term or less. Sets out the learning objectives that reflect the range and content of activities as well as possible teaching activities and learning outcomes.

Short-term planning

Lesson plan – to match individual class requirements such as different abilities with resources available.

Learning and teaching strategies

- direct teaching through whole-class and small group sessions;
- opportunities for pupils to demonstrate, practise and apply their learning on their own or with another with varying degrees of support;
- opportunities for pupils to solve problems, use their imagination and be creative;
- opportunities for pupils to reflect on their own learning;
- opportunities for pupils to lead others in a variety of situations.

Box 2.1   Example of lesson planning for identifying and solving problems and overcoming challenges of an adventurous nature (short-term planning)

Pupils will complete a course appropriate to the outdoor activity: here, taking part in an established orienteering course which ensures that all safety aspects are covered.

Category: orienteering (map work)

Learning objectives
What do you want your pupils to know, do and understand by the time they leave your classroom?

- Be able to *make and apply navigational decisions and techniques* with and without the aid of a map and understand the distinctive features of a compass.

- *Develop skills* when moving from familiar activities/ground to unfamiliar situations and adapt their approaches to different challenges.
- *Develop mental and physical capacity* when using navigational skills, successfully use a compass and map, in groups and alone, and adapt skills to meet the needs of specific activities.
- *Make informed choices about healthy active lifestyles* through understanding the principles used to prepare for outdoor activities and recognise that different types of activity require different types of fitness.
- Observe others and learn from their own experience to understand the nature of the challenge and make effective *evaluations and improvements* of strengths and weaknesses in performance.

Learning outcomes
After completing this lesson, most pupils will be able to . . .

Develop skills to enable them to navigate with accuracy in environments they are familiar with and identify the main features of a compass.

The learning objectives and outcomes are key to the whole lesson plan. First you need to ensure that they are clear and observable. It is also important that they state the context of the learning. For example, if we are looking at developing the technique of compass work, what is the context: playground, classroom, school field?

1. Does the lesson content allow the learning objectives to be achieved?
2. Check the learning outcomes to see if they are inclusive of the learning objectives. Are the learning objectives achievable and progressive?
3. Does the organisation allow the learning objectives to be achieved?
4. Does the organisation ensure a safe learning environment?

You need to mentally transfer the lesson content into a practical lesson situation and analyse whether it will work with pupils. Will they be bored? Will they be challenged? The content of the lesson plan may reflect the different approaches to teaching and delivery. You need to be familiar with these approaches. For example, a problem-solving lesson plan will probably include a number of relevant questions for the pupils; you will have to decide if these questions are relevant to the learning objectives. Remember that the answers should also appear on the lesson plan when using this approach.

The basic premise remains: will the lesson plan allow the learning objectives to be achieved. Will it work in the practical situation? Does the lesson progress appropriately? Are the teaching points accurate?

Timing

Think about how much time it is going to take the pupils to get to the changing rooms, how long it is going to take them to change, how long it will take to get to and back from the teaching area, how long to change again. This will take up some of the time allocated for the lesson. Younger students may have particular difficulties when changing with zips, button, ties, etc. Make sure that the class is ready to leave just before the bell goes as you may have another lesson to get to and you owe it to your colleagues to get your pupils to their next lesson on time.

Progression

Each pupil should be allowed to learn at their own level and pace and should never feel afraid of making mistakes. Every skill should be broken down into bite-sized pieces and follow a logical progressive sequence. Some pupils will learn faster than others, so tasks should be set relative to ability.

Figures 2.1 and 2.2 illustrate the breakdown of the time you may spend in a games lesson on each activity or activities in a physical education lesson. This is based on one hour of teaching time. Figures 2.1 and 2.2 demonstrate the importance of progression as it relates

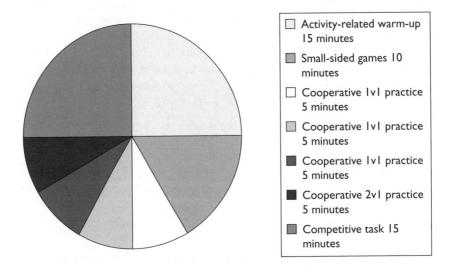

Figure 2.1 Lesson structure of a one-hour lesson, showing the importance of progression

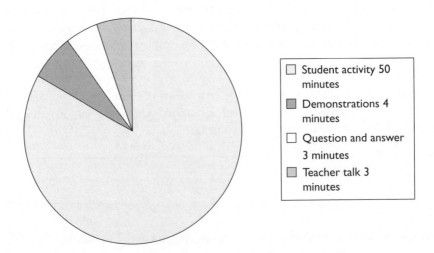

Figure 2.2 Teaching process in a one-hour lesson

to pupil-centred learning. The pupils are on task for most the time and are involved in the learning throughout, which promotes their understanding. This is not a definitive model and should only be used as a guideline and a framework within which to work.

Lesson plans

These are only a guideline or framework within which to work. Don't be tempted to rush through everything you have planned and don't be afraid to change something if necessary.

Observation

Watch experienced staff as much as possible in your specialised subject as well as other curriculum areas. You will notice a variety of different teaching styles, ranging from command, guided discovery to reciprocal, which can be used in your own teaching. If you see something that works for one teacher try it in your own lessons.

Self-evaluation

Be prepared to identify any strengths and weaknesses that you have and how you can improve on them. Be prepared to accept advice and act upon it accordingly.

In general

Pay attention to department policy on kit, jewellery, parental notes, non-participation, security, registers, etc., and always leave equipment the way that you would expect to find it. At the end of the lesson ask yourself 'If I was a member of that class would I have enjoyed it and what would I have learnt?'

Learning strategies for teaching physical education

- Motor learning theorists recommend that at the beginning of the lesson a skill be visually demonstrated as a *whole*.
- In some cases it may be necessary for the skill to be broken down into constituent parts (*sub-routines*).
- *Sub-routines* are taught as separate actions and then put together.
- *Part methods* of teaching can be used for complex, difficult or potentially dangerous skills.
- *Whole-part-whole* method allows the learner to try out the whole skill and to identify easy or difficult elements. The teacher can identify difficult elements and teach them as parts, finally integrating them into the whole again.
- The teacher can break down skills into parts and use *part-progressive* practice. In games teaching *unopposed* practice, *passive* and *active* opposition and decision-making problems will gradually enable the skill to be performed in the whole-game situation.
- *Simplified tasks* played with *modified rules* and equipment can be used to help to develop skills.

- *Open skills* will require *variable* practice to allow a general scheme of work to be developed.
- *Closed skills* will require *fixed* practice to allow for repetition of movements to be over-learned.
- *Massed practice* can be used with highly skilled, motivated and fit performers who work continuously at an activity without a break until the skill is mastered or time runs out.
- *Distributed* or *spaced practice* allows for practice to be split into shorter periods with intervals in between and allows for *mental rehearsal.*

Assessment and monitoring of learning

Assessment is an integral part of good teaching and enables you to find out how much your pupils have learnt. Effective physical education teachers identify clear learning objectives and gather evidence to see if those learning objectives are achieved. This evidence provides the basis for feedback to pupils so that good practice is replicated and weaknesses corrected. It also enables you to check the level of difficulty of the learning objectives and adjust them according to age. Assessment and monitoring informs future planning of lessons

Assessment of learning (AOL)

AOL takes place at a set time. In physical education this is usually at the end of a unit and is separated from teaching. Teachers must be clear about what is being assessed and time must be set aside for assessment.

Assessment for learning (AFL)

AFL takes place during learning, for example during a lesson or unit and helps to determine a pupil's needs. It is used to inform planning and enables the teacher to assess more (key processes) over a period of time.

Summary

The teaching of physical education requires more than just a few practices up your sleeve. It requires careful thought, planning, organisation and management of pupil learning. For this to happen it requires you, as the teacher, to be able to teach effectively through a range of styles and strategies to enable each pupil to progress and achieve their full potential across Key Stages 2 and 3.

3 Health and safety issues in physical education

Gary Stidder and Sid Hayes

Introduction

The old adage that 'prevention is better than cure' is a phrase that every physical education teacher should be familiar with in terms of managing risk within lessons. Many of the activities included within the physical education curriculum have some element of risk associated with them; often it is the element of risk in certain circumstances that appeals to pupils, particularly when there is uncertainty in the outcome of the task. It is important, however, that lessons are planned thoroughly with risk management and risk assessment procedures in place, since a safe and purposeful working environment is critical for pupil learning to take place. The national curriculum for physical education (NCPE 2008) has provided a less prescriptive range of content than before, which has provided teachers with the opportunity to consider a more diverse and wider range of activities. Consequently, there will be times when teachers have to assess the element of risk against the educational benefits that new and exciting activities have to offer. Beaumont (2008: 11) suggests that introducing young people to challenging activities requires teachers to be competent and knowledgeable in the activities they are teaching, and to be able to manage risk through appropriate organisation, progression and emphasis on important safety factors. Moreover, effective health and safety practice in physical education is primarily about using common-sense principles in keeping children and adults from unnecessary harm.

Within schools, teachers have a professional obligation to implement the five outcomes of *Every Child Matters* (2004), one of which is keeping children safe. The Association for Physical Education has produced a very thorough resource for teachers that addresses the need to undertake safe working practices within schools and provides guidance on ensuring good practice (AfPE 2008). The purpose of this chapter is to highlight some of the pertinent issues associated with health and safety issues in physical education and consider the most effective means of ensuring a safe and purposeful working environment at Key Stages 2 and 3.

Learning and teaching on-site

Within the school environment there are several factors that you will need to consider with regard to safe practice in physical education. Within the classroom context you must ensure that pupils are aware of the consequences of poor behaviour and the risks they present to themselves and others when participating in physical education lessons.

Establishing very clear codes of conduct and ground rules is an essential aspect of your teaching and you should refer to your school's behaviour management policy in this respect. You will also need to pay particular attention to the facilities in which you are expecting the pupils to work in terms of size, space, and quality of the playing surface. AfPE (2008) recommends that teachers display safety posters in strategic areas within the physical education department and that teachers undertake pre-activity checks prior to the start of the lesson. Likewise, you should ensure that the equipment you are expecting pupils to use is appropriate for their ages, for example the correct size and weight of a ball or throwing implement. It is also good practice to encourage the pupils to be involved in aspects of risk assessment and risk management, as ultimately this should be part of their own physical education so that they can make informed safe choices about activities they may wish to pursue outside of school hours.

Learning and teaching off-site

When you are organising school journeys, trips, etc., you should always discuss *all* arrangements with your head teacher prior to any planning taking place. You should also inform the Educational Visits Co-ordinator (EVC) and Local Education Authority advisor for physical education and outdoor education. Ideally, a preliminary visit should have already taken place and there should be adequate numbers of staff and other adults to accompany the party of children. If the group is mixed-sex there must be an adequate male and female staff ratio. Parents must be informed in writing of the nature of the trip and should return a signed consent form. Parents should also provide you with a personal details form, which should list emergency phone numbers and the name of the child's doctor and should contain written permission for you to consent to any medical treatment deemed necessary. You must also ensure that the necessary insurance has been taken out prior to the trip taking place. This can usually be done through the school bursar. The duty of care exists for teachers in all situations and it is essential that they know what is expected of them. The Local Education Authority should provide clear guidance on this.

School fixtures

If you are taking pupils to away fixtures you will not be able to transport them in a school minibus without the LEA minibus driving licence. Usually teachers must be at least 25 years old, but in the case of physical education teachers the minimum age is 23. You should inform all parents about the game and the expected time of arrival back to school. Remember always to carry the school's mobile phone and to be aware of how students will be making their way home from school. Administrative and senior staff should also be informed in advance and kept up to date with any changes in arrangements. If your journey is more than one hour it is advisable to have an additional driver.

Accidents and injuries

Every school should have procedures for dealing with accidents and injuries involving either teachers or pupils. As a teacher you should be aware of them. As a physical education teacher it is advisable to have a first aid qualification and you must have the necessary qualification to teach activities that have particular risks (for example, rock climbing, canoeing, trampolining). All accidents and injuries must be reported in the school's accident book and be recorded on the Local Education Authority's accident report form.

School and physical education department policy

Your department should have a risk assessment policy in their handbook which will have identified potential hazards such as sliced tin cans on the playing field, unanchored goal posts, exposed radiators, and dangerous storage of equipment. There should also be procedures for ensuring preventative measures such as the use of a buddy system in the swimming pool, the wearing of correct footwear and protective equipment, and removal of jewellery.

Teacher involvement

As the teacher you must also be careful about your practical involvement in the lesson. Demonstrating a particular skill or technique is a good strategy to enhance the learning for many pupils. However, you should avoid participating in lessons which involve physical contact and competition because there would be a considerable mismatch in terms of strength, competence, skill and knowledge. Obvious examples would include invasion games such as rugby, hockey, football, as well as combat activities. Any physical involvement in the lesson should be there solely to facilitate learning. (See AfPE 2008: 13–21, 'Physical Education and the Law', for more details.)

The National Curriculum for Physical Education

The general teaching requirement for health and safety within the National Curriculum for England applies to the teaching of science, information and communications technology, craft design and technology, art and design and physical education across Key Stages 1 to 4. The National Curriculum for physical education (DfEE and QCA 1999: 39) states that teachers should consider the following advice:

> When working with tools, equipment and materials, in practical activities and in different environments, including those that are unfamiliar, pupils should be taught:

- About hazards, risk, and risk control.
- To recognise hazards, assess consequent risks and take steps to control the risks to themselves and others.
- To use information to assess the immediate and cumulative risks.
- To manage their environment to ensure the health and safety of themselves and others.
- To explain the steps they take to control tasks.

(DfEE and QCA 1999: 39)

As a teacher of physical education you should refer to *Five Steps to Risk Assessment* published by the Health and Safety Executive (HSE 2006) and avoid compromising both yourself and the pupils you teach.

Common causes of accidents and injuries in physical education lessons

This is a list of likely causes of accidents or injuries that can happen when insufficient attention has been paid to assessing the risks involved. It is not a definitive or exhaustive list, but these are situations that in our experience can potentially contribute to accidents and injuries occurring in physical education lessons:

- inadequate use of mats in the gym;
- pupils wearing inappropriate footwear on the school field;
- teaching area not checked before the lesson begins and dangerous items such as glass or cans on the school playing field not picked up;
- pupils not wearing protective equipment such as shin pads, box, helmets, life jackets;
- staff not sufficiently qualified or familiar with a particular activity;
- insufficient time spent on warm-ups;
- pupils not working on task;
- insufficient time or no time spent on procedures for getting out and putting away of equipment;
- pupils allowed to wear jewellery, particularly rings such as nose, tongue, nipple, belly button and ear rings;
- sand pit not raked prior to a long/triple jump lesson;
- pupils not fully briefed in advance about health and safety issues specific to the activity;
- inadequate safety measures and precautions taken in the swimming pool;
- no first aid equipment readily available during school games;
- pupils carrying equipment such as athletic throwing equipment (shot, discus, javelin) unsatisfactorily;
- rules of the game not been properly explained;
- goal posts not fixed or adequately secured;
- incorrect size of equipment related to the age range, such as size four or five footballs;
- incorrect decisions related to participation in poor weather conditions such as rain, ice, snow;
- poor explanation and demonstration of supporting procedures in gymnastics;
- pupils inappropriately positioned within the context of games activities, for example fielding too close to a batter within striking and fielding games;
- inadequate training in how to support a pupil within, for example, gymnastics or trampolining;
- pupils not correctly briefed about safety procedures and precautions in athletics (particularly throwing events), or outdoor and adventurous activities (expeditions, water-based activity) or swimming pools (running on poolside, for example);
- a member of staff not sufficiently competent to referee (particularly rugby) or lead a party group (particularly outdoor and adventurous activities);
- no set procedures for entering and leaving the changing or teaching area;
- no attention paid to physical matching of pupils in particular tasks;
- pupils unsupervised for certain periods of time such as the beginning and end of the lesson.

Health and safety scenarios in physical education

In this section we highlight seven scenarios for you to consider with regard to safe practice in physical education. Ask yourself what action you would take. We provide guidance at the end of the section and recommended action to take, which includes updating your risk assessment using the five-step system (HSE 2006).

SCENARIO 1

You arrive at an AstroTurf pitch for a 9 a.m. invasion games lesson and find half of the pitch is waterlogged due to heavy rain during the night and early morning. The water has collected along one side of the pitch but also impedes the main access onto the pitch. You decide to access the pitch from the other side and carry out a half-hour warm-up. By now, the water has drained away from the pitch but has left a muddy sticky residue, although only on the non-playing part of the surface.

What action should you take?

SCENARIO 2

A pupil attends a physical education lesson wearing a pair of training shoes that appear to be suitable for the pitch surface, but when she runs in the warm-up and tries to change direction she has no control, can only slide to a stop, and falls over.

What action should you take?

SCENARIO 3

For a tennis class you need to use the four full courts to meet the learning objectives. You arrive to check the courts fifteen minutes before the lesson and notice the following situation: leaves are covering most of one court and some of another. There are no brooms to sweep the court and even if there were it would take longer than fifteen minutes to clear the court.

What action should you take?

SCENARIO 4

In athletics, you arrive to teach a jumping session at a local authority athletics centre. A heavy cover in two sections needs to be moved off the long jump pit before you can use it. It normally requires six adults to move each section.

What action should you take?

SCENARIO 5

For a tennis class you need to use the four full courts to meet the learning objectives. You arrive to check the courts fifteen minutes before the lecture, and notice the following situation: heavy rain over the past two days has left a muddy residue on some small sections of three of the courts. These sections of the court can't be avoided once pupils are performing drills or playing a game. There are no implements for removing this residue.

What action should you take?

SCENARIO 6

In Year 7's first lesson at the start of the summer term, you ask them to perform to their maximum level in some athletic events, such as a sprint, high jump and javelin throw. For some reason, perhaps because of lack of fitness or their body shape or weight, pupils pull muscles, go over on their ankles, or develop back strain.

What action should you take?

SCENARIO 7

For your 9 a.m. physical education lesson in athletics, especially at certain times of the year, the track is usually still damp and slippery. Very few pupils have spikes and so may slip if asked to do more than jog around. The pupils themselves often comment on this, and also that the track sometimes has mud left by football players from the evening before. You are aware that it is difficult to use the facilities safely in the way you would like.

What action should you take?

Recommended action

Scenario 1

Access the dry area by taking precautionary measures. Do not use the muddy surface. Use cones to mark the dangerous area ensuring an adequate run-off space between the teaching area and the muddy surface.

Scenario 2

Check the general environment. Check the individual's footwear. Withdraw the pupil from the lesson and find an alternative role for the pupil.

Scenario 3

Report this to the site manager. Clear the leaves with the assistance of the pupils. Only use the courts that are free from leaves.

Scenario 4

Moving heavy equipment without appropriate training should be avoided. The site manager should be informed and measures taken to ensure that the equipment is moved by competent adults not pupils. Ask the site manager about future teaching arrangements and see if the equipment can be organised prior to your arrival.

Scenario 5

Report this to the site manager. Use only the one court free from residue for the drills and adapt the lesson accordingly.

Scenario 6

Avoid this type of practice as a commencement to a lesson or series of lessons. Pupils should be taught progressively and gradually move towards performing at levels that they are comfortable with.

Scenario 7

Report this to the site manager. Do not use this teaching area. Find an alternative safe teaching space.

Summary

As a teacher you have a duty in criminal law, not to mention a liability to be prosecuted under civil law in the event of an accident or injury to a pupil. In this respect you must ensure that you have risk assessments which are up to date and subject to review every year. To a certain extent, you should view your risk assessments in the same way as an annual MOT test on a car. All the checks for health and safety should be carried out and repairs made where necessary. In most cases common-sense approaches to teaching physical education will ensure a safe, secure and purposeful learning environment for pupils. It is advisable, however, that teachers are adequately trained in health and safety issues, including risk assessment in-service training.

Key points to remember:

- teacher's duty of care;
- the management of health and safety at work regulations (1999);
- school trips and journeys;
- driving and transporting pupils;
- accident and injury reporting procedures;
- school and PE department policy on health and safety;
- common causes of accidents and injuries;
- risk assessment and preventative measures.

Exemplar risk assessments

As part of this chapter we have included two fictional risk assessments for activities in badminton (Figure 3.1) and football (Figure 3.2) to help you to clarify your thinking about completion of risk assessments. These exemplar documents are generic in nature and we need to remind you that any risk assessments you complete must be specific to situation and activity and must take into account the pupils' safety. Any such risk assessments should be completed on the in-house / authority risk assessment form.

References

Association for Physical Education (AfPE) (2008) *Safe Practice in Physical Education and School Sport*, Leeds, Coachwise Publications.

Beaumont, G. (2008) 'Cotton wool kids: risk and children', *Physical Education Matters* 3 (3): 10–11.

DfEE and QCA (1999) *Physical Education: The National Curriculum for England,* London, Department for Education and Employment (DfEE) and Qualifications and Curriculum Authority (QCA): 39.

HSE (2006) http://www.hse.gov.uk/pubns/indg163.pdf (accessed on 7 April 2009).

Spencer, K. (2008) 'Safeguarding children and young people', *Physical Education Matters* 3 (3): 12–14.

General Risk Assessment Form

School/Department: Physical Education **Date of assessment: November 2009**

Activity/area: Badminton – Sports hall. **Next review date: November 2010**

Assessed by:

No.	What are the hazards?	Who might be harmed and how?	What controls do you already have in place?	Risk (high, medium, low)
	Physical injury (inherent)	Pupils/teacher: poor balance and overbalancing; strained ligaments, muscles, sprained ankle, injury to the shoulder/neck	All precautions as taken listed below, but even so, these things may occur. Appropriate warm-up	Low
	Wearing jewellery	Pupils: injury to the body caused by impact of balls/shuttlecocks, or by rackets on jewellery	Ask all participants to remove jewellery before the activity starts. STOP play if a student is wearing jewellery and ask them to remove it or leave the area of play.	Low
	Obstacles on or around the playing area	Pupils: tripping, slipping, falling	Instruct all students that any obstacles must be removed from the courts or around the courts prior to starting play. Stop play if there is an obstacle or obstacles in the way. Any protrusion from walls or equipment not being used should be well clear of the playing area boundary.	Low
	Equipment on the courts	Pupils: tripping, slipping, falling	Must be removed before play starts (e.g. shuttlecocks, rackets). Nets should be in good condition, pulled tight, and secured flush with the posts so that there are no holes or gaps through which a shuttlecock can pass. Students must be alerted to potential hazards (e.g. permanent columns, radiators).	Low
	Defective equipment	Pupils: sprains and strains	Equipment checked at the start of every session	Low
	Unsuitable playing surface	Pupils: tripping, slipping, falling	The playing surface should be even, dry, clean, and non-slip.	Low
	Suitable equipment for the participants	Pupils: sprains and strains	Appropriate rackets, shuttlecocks, posts and nets.	Low
	Appropriate footwear	Pupils: tripping, slipping, falling	Dress code including regulations on suitable footwear	Low
	Other participants	Pupils	Students should be told to avoid crossing a court which is in use. Students should be told not to pass too close to someone who is playing. Students should be told NOT to hit the shuttlecock if their drilling partner or opponent is not looking. Students must be told not to hit shuttlecocks from one fence to the next, but to collect balls on their rackets and bring them in.	Low

Figure 3.1 Badminton risk assessment form

General Risk Assessment Form

School/Department: **Physical Education** Date of assessment: **November 2010**

Activity/area: **AstroTurf pitch** Next review date: **November 2011**

Assessed by:

No.	What are the hazards?	Who might be harmed and how?	What controls do you already have in place?	Risk (high, medium, low)
	Playing area (AstroTurf pitch) will sometimes be altered to assist the completion of smaller games across the normal playing area.	Pupils: collisions, slips, trips and falls	Teachers will ensure that any goalposts etc. that are not being used will be removed from any playing area.	Low
	The games covered during this activity involve the risk of injury if the techniques are not correctly applied.	Pupils: sprains and strains	The teaching will adhere specifically to the following recommendations within the *Safe Practice in Physical Education* documentation.* (a) General guidance pp. 165–170 (b) Football Specific Information p. 171. Students will be advised to wear appropriate protection e.g. shin pads.	Low
	Foreign objects on the pitch	Pupils: collisions, slips, trips and falls	This is an unlikely possibility as the pitch is a secured and monitored. Checks of the surface area will be made prior to engagement in practical activities to ensure it is clear from unsuitable objects.	Low
	Goalposts can be a hazard if they are not in good condition or are not secured when being used if they are portable.	Pupils: collisions, slips, trips and falls	Periodically the condition of the posts should be checked. Any portable goals that are used should be secured and/or anchored down to avoid injury.	Low
	Inappropriate kit especially footwear can lead to injury	Pupils: collisions, slips, trips and falls	Any inappropriate footwear will be pointed out. Guidance will be given as to the most appropriate footwear to use.	Low
	Inclement weather conditions may cause surface playing conditions to be dangerous	Pupils: collisions, slips, trips and falls	Playing conditions will be monitored and significant changes to weather that may lead to injury will result in the cessation of the activity.	Low
	Conduct of players and dangerous play	Pupils: sprains and strains and other injuries	Play should follow the rules of the game and play within the 'spirit' of these rules Any players not doing so will be removed from the learning and teaching activity.	Low
	Jewellery: causing injury to others or the wearer	Pupils: cuts and grazes	Insist on the removal of jewellery.	Low

*AfPE (2008) *Safe Practice in Physical Education*, Leeds, Coachwise.

Figure 3.2 Football risk assessment form

4 Learning and teaching through games activities

John Lambert

Introduction

> A game is a system in which players engage in an artificial conflict, defined by
> rules, that results in a quantifiable outcome.
>
> (Salen and Zimmerman 2003)

When we read such a simple definition of games it is difficult to conceive of all the time that is spent on analysing and teaching the numerous activities that we class as games activities. Research has shown that games activities have tended to dominate the physical education curriculum in schools. This situation can be partially explained by the popularity of games in terms of participation and spectator levels. It is also apparent that teachers tend to favour activities that they have been familiar with as a performer when making a judgement about which activities to include in their physical education curriculum. Their subject knowledge is often more secure when teaching games, having played them at school and at university. Therefore the prospect of teaching traditional games activities such as netball and football has an obvious appeal to many. The statutory orders of the Physical Education National Curriculum 1999 stated that at least five of the six activity areas must be taught at Key Stage 2 and at least four at Key Stage 3. Although games activities were compulsory in both Key Stages, this legislation had the potential to create a broad and balanced physical education programme in schools, with games activities occupying less curriculum time than in previous years.

The revised national curriculum for physical education (NCPE 2008) offers no prescribed structure regarding the activity areas through which the range and content should be taught. There is less dependence on strict activity areas in relation to the teaching of key concepts and processes. It will be interesting to observe whether, with this autonomy, physical education departments continue to widen their curriculum when there is no compulsion to do so. It is to be hoped that the range and content, as specified in the NCPE 2008, is taught through a curriculum that has depth, breadth and balance which includes, where possible, health-related exercise, swimming, athletics, dance, outdoor and adventurous activities, gymnastics and games activities.

In recognising the desirability of pupils experiencing all six activity areas, we should not forget that games is an important part of the physical education curriculum in primary and secondary schools. It is the aim of this chapter to offer some effective strategies for teaching games activities that cover key concepts and processes through selected aspects of the range and content of the NCPE 2008 at Key Stage 3. Whilst it is not until September 2011 that the new primary curriculum is taught in schools, it might be assumed with some degree of certainty that the physical education statutory orders will include a similar structure and progressive content to the Key Stage 3 guidelines. This chapter, therefore, explains the pedagogy that surrounds the teaching of games activities and presents some teaching models that you might use to shape your delivery of games in your particular environment. This chapter will also attempt to address some issues pertaining to assessment of learning through games. The linking of theory with practice is a priority throughout.

Games activities are typically classified into five discrete categories: invasion, striking and fielding, divided court, wall, and target. All five categories are taught in schools, although wall and target games, such as squash and golf, are not as commonplace on the curriculum as the first three. Each category of games has generic principles which can be related to all examples within that category. For example, all invasion games require a team to manoeuvre an object through a defended territory to an agreed target by creating space when attacking and using the width and length of the playing area. The laws or rules of a game are specific to it and determine its particular skills, tactics and shape. The facilities available at a school and staff expertise will have an effect on which games activities are taught, especially at primary level. However, with the flexibility to adapt games to different situations there should be scope to provide opportunities to learn and play games from each category. This chapter will offer some ideas for teaching approaches to all five categories of games.

If presented in an engaging, inclusive way, all types of games activities have the potential to offer a range of physical skills and opportunities for problem-solving, decision-making and personal and social development. Playing games can be a source of great fun and enjoyment. Games also have the potential to create feelings of anxiety, isolation, fear, cold and low self-esteem. The success of any unit of games can be measured in terms of the physical, cognitive, affective and social domains. However, the first consideration for any teacher who is planning and teaching that unit is to create a learning environment that will inspire every pupil in the class to regard games as both fun and rewarding.

Teaching games at Key Stage 3 within the National Curriculum for Physical Education (2008)

In order to ensure breadth, the range and content in the NCPE (2008) requires a physical education curriculum to cover at least four out of a list of six competences. One of these is 'outwitting opponents', as described in QCA (2008). Games activities, inevitably, will be regarded as a suitable medium through which to teach pupils how to outwit opponents. The key processes such as developing skills, making and applying decisions, evaluating and improving, and developing physical and mental capacity can all be readily learned through games activities. The key concept of competence, defined as the relationship between a skill and its selection and application to produce effective performance in different contexts, will underpin any games teaching. Likewise, the concept of performance, which can be described as understanding how the components of competence combine and applying them to produce effective outcomes, will feature prominently in education through games activities.

Teaching games for understanding

The example of a Year 7 football lesson in Box 4.1 uses outwitting an opponent through an invasion game to bring out aspects of the key concepts and processes. The instructional model used is 'teaching games for understanding' (TGFU). The TGFU approach typically involves teaching a particular games principle, and its related skills, through conditioned games that present a problem or highlight a principle within that game (for example playing in a narrow area will highlight the need for width in attack) that the pupils need to find solutions to. Through a hierarchical series of planned questions the pupils can, if necessary, be guided towards strategies that will help them understand the decisions and actions required to answer the challenge set. Whether defending (in possession) or attacking (out of possession), striking or fielding, hitting or receiving, players need to outwit their opponents. The TGFU approach will develop their understanding of games principles and, therefore, improve the decision-making ability necessary to gain ascendancy over an opponent and win the game. Skill development takes place in the context of the game.

When we are looking at the ways in which the key processes within the revised NCPE could be developed through learning in games, we need to analyse some of the pedagogy related to games teaching.

The traditional approach to teaching games has been one based around pupils learning a skill or group of skills and transferring these techniques into a game situation. However, as early as 1986 David Bunker and Rod Thorpe, along with various academics since, notably Butler and McCahan (2005) and Mitchell *et al.* (1997), advocated an alternative pedagogic model, teaching games for understanding, which places an emphasis on understanding the principles and tactics of a particular game whilst teaching skills within the context of a game situation rather than in isolation. The advantages to this approach can be identified as:

- Understanding and problem-solving: the TGFU model produces performers who possess sound decision-making skills that can be demonstrated independently of the teacher (Butler and McCahan 2005).
- Skill acquisition: research around constructivist learning theories (Richard and Wallian 2005) support the notion that skills are most effectively learned in context rather than in isolation. The transfer of skill to a variety of situations is more likely if the skill is taught in a game situation.
- Motivational: pupils are more engaged by playing games than performing isolated skill practices.

There is more than one way to teach games activities and, in reality, most teachers use a variety of teaching models. However, the TGFU approach has certain strengths that are conducive to a school games lesson. Allowing pupils to take some responsibility for their learning and giving them access to inclusive games rather than skill drills are two eminent features that have proven successful with learners.

The exemplar Year 7 lesson set out in Box 4.1 demonstrates how a TGFU model can be used to cover key processes such as:

2.1 Developing skills in physical activity
    1. develop the range of skills they use
2.2 Making and applying decisions
    1. select and use tactics and strategies effectively in different competitive contexts
    2. refine and adapt ideas and plans in response to changing circumstances
    3. plan and implement what needs practising to be more effective in performance
2.4 Evaluating and improving
    1. analyse performances, identifying strengths and weaknesses
    2. make decisions about what to do to improve their performance and the performance of others
    3. act on these decisions in future performances

The key concepts of competence (1.1a. selecting and using skills and tactics) and performance (1.2b. knowing and understanding what needs to be achieved, critically evaluating how well it has been achieved and finding ways to improve) are included within the lesson.

NCPE (2008)

Box 4.1   Exemplar Year 7 football lesson (can be adapted for a range of invasion games)

Duration

One hour

Learning objectives

1. To show understanding of the basic principles of movement off the ball in attack. (KP 2.2, 1–3; KC 1.1a)
2. To be able to evaluate and adapt performance in respect to team and individual attacking play. (KP 2.4, 1–3; KC 1.2b)

Learning outcomes

1. To demonstrate when, where and how to move when their team gain possession. (KP 2.2, 1–3, 2.1, 1; KC 1.1a)
2. To demonstrate understanding of how to create and exploit space as an individual and as a team. (KP 2.4, 1–3; KC 1.2b)

Activity 1

Introduction to the learning objectives (2 minutes)
WALT. What are we learning today? Ways in which we can help our team to keep possession and advance towards our opponents' goal.

WILF. What am I looking for? Players who move into areas where they are supporting the player who is in possession.

Activity 2

Warm-up (7 minutes) *Keep ball*
Three versus one in each 10x10 yard grid (see Figure 4.1). The ball is passed through the hands. The one defender (Y) aims to intercept a pass or pressurise the three attackers (X) into passing the ball out of the square. The three attackers aim to keep possession for a specified number of passes (depending on the ability of the group).

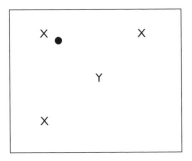

Figure 4.1 Warm-up activity: Keep ball

Change the defender accordingly. No moving whilst in possession or physical contact is allowed. Progression: move the most able groups on to only throwing below head height, then throw–volley/head–catch.

Key questions: for the attackers:

- What do you need to think about when your team mate is in possession? Answer: Whether I can receive a pass or not.
- Do you always need to move? If you do move, where do you move? Answer: No, not when I am at an angle to receive a pass. I might need to move to improve that angle and offer a passing option.

Activity 3

Targetball (14 minutes)

Two versus two in a 20x10 yard area (see Figure 4.2). A feeder has 4 balls at one end and a target player can move along the line at the opposite end. Team X must get as many of the 4 balls from the feeder to the target using their hands. A scoring pass may only be made from beyond the half way line. When the 4 balls are used up then Xs become feeder and target, Ys are attackers and Zs become defenders. No physical contact or moving with the ball is allowed. Add a 'floating player' who is not allowed to score to a low ability group when attacking if necessary.

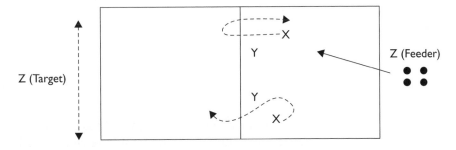

Figure 4.2 Targetball

Key questions:

- How can you create space for yourself and lose your marker? Answer: move away from the ball then back towards it or move towards the ball and then away from it.
- Can you show me those movements?
- How fast should you move? Answer: move the defender and slow her/him down, then accelerate into space.

Activity 4

Two-way football (14 minutes)

Two versus two football with a floating player who cannot be tackled in a 30x20 yard area (see Figure 4.3). A target player moves along a line at each end and returns the ball to the team in possession. A team that scores keeps possession and attacks in the opposite direction until they lose possession. Change the floater and target players over every 3 minutes. Differentiation: remove the floating player or add a two-touch condition for the most able.

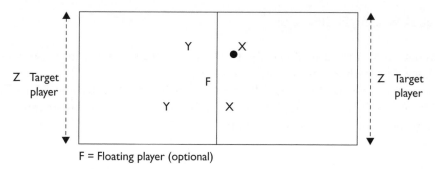

F = Floating player (optional)

Figure 4.3 Two-way football

Key questions:

*   Where do you need to move when you support the player on the ball if there is pressure on the ball? Answer: Support behind at an angle.
*   Where do you need to move when you support the player on the ball if there is no pressure on the ball? Make a forward run into space.

It is more effective if the pupils show where they would run and the teacher can then adjust this if necessary. Encourage the players in possession to take a gentle first touch and be aware of options by looking up.

Activity 5

Two-touch games (20 minutes)

Four versus four, played in 40x30 yard areas with a small unguarded goal at each end (see Figure 4.4). Add a two-touch condition to highlight the need for early

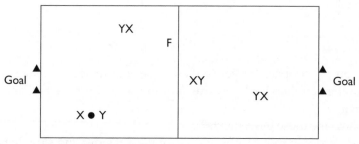

F = Floating player (optional)

Figure 4.4 Two-touch game

supporting runs. No offside rules. Differentiation: low-ability players may have up to three touches and the most able should be restricted to two touches. Add a floating player if necessary in order to make it easier to retain possession as a team.

Remove the limited touch conditions for all in the final five minutes. Allow three minutes in the middle of the games for each team to get together, evaluate their performance and agree strategies to improve it.

Key question for the pupils to consider:

* How can we best create and exploit space as a team? Answer: by using the length and width of the pitch to make ourselves difficult to defend against and then move into that space created in order to receive the ball away from the defenders.

Activity 6

Plenary (3 minutes)
Ask each team to offer a key point which will help their team keep possession and attack effectively. Allow them time to discuss and agree their key point.

The tactical complexity is gradually progressive with each of the modified games introduced. The four small-sided games differ in rules and shape but are all designed to emphasise a specific tactical problem (see lesson learning objective 1). This sampling of different modified games covering similar themes will assist transfer of learning across a variety of game situations (Thorpe and Bunker 1989). Thorpe (2005) draws on skill acquisition research that highlights integration, variable practice and memory as important features of learning technical skills that can be transferred to different situations. He argues that learned skills that are transferable, robust and adaptable are best achieved in game-like situations rather than isolated skill practices.

There are some important points to be made in relation to the TGFU approach that can be related to the above lesson and are worth consideration when planning any games lesson.

Developing skills in physical activity: technical constraints

The lesson begins with two catch–throw games and not with football. The rationale for this is based around the need for the pupils to grasp the basic understanding of movement off the ball. Replacing the technical challenge of controlling and passing using the feet with the easier skills of throwing and catching enables the pupils to get their head up and focus on the cognitive problem of when, where and how to support the player on the ball.

A possible obstacle to using the TGFU approach when teaching technically demanding games can be the skill constraint, which can limit a player's ability to develop cognitive, decision-making skills. In simple terms, the basic technical skills in, for example, football or hockey are so difficult for the majority of players that it is all they can do to control and pass the ball, let alone think about attacking and defending strategies.

Technically proficient players can be asked to solve difficult tactical problems on the field based around attacking and defending principles. In contrast, players with a low level of physical skill must be either given very simple tactical challenges or be placed into games that present a low level of technical difficulty. It is crucial for the teacher to be skilled at maintaining the balance between success and challenge (Light 2006).

The lesson progressed on to football but pitched the level of challenge appropriate to the physical skill level of the players. For example, the relationship between space available and numbers of players is increased when the group is asked to play with their feet. Both the two-way football and two-touch game are to be played in relatively wide areas that are appropriate to a Year 7 group. To offer differentiation, these areas can be adjusted by the teacher or by the pupils, according to the technical proficiency of the players in that game.

This principle would also apply to divided court and striking and fielding games where the technical demands of hitting a tennis ball or striking a rounders ball are very difficult for some pupils to master. In order that pupils can learn the tactics of a game the teacher might need to reduce the technical constraint by using modified equipment or changing the rules. An example from striking and fielding games would be to initially allow pupils to use a tennis racket to hit the ball within a rounders lesson in order to teach shot placement and base running principles. The ball could in this way be placed through gaps in the field far more easily than with a rounders bat, thus allowing the learning objectives to be covered.

One important skill that a physical education teacher needs to develop is to know when to move children forward in their skill learning and how far to progress at each stage. Rink (2003) observed that the decision of what to do is often constrained by the ability to execute a response. Pupils who want to learn football are going to want to develop their passing, dribbling and shooting as well as their tactical knowledge, as they go hand in hand. Likewise, pupils learning cricket are going to want and need to be able to bowl and youngsters following a unit of tennis are going to want to be taught how to serve. They are, understandably, going to want to progress from catch–throw tennis and underarm cricket bowling fairly quickly. Proponents of TGFU will argue for the teaching of physical skills within a modified game situation; however, some skills are so complex and demanding for pupils that they need to be initially learned outside of the competitive environment of a game.

TGFU has its roots in constructivist learning theories where the learner is being actively engaged in learning and drawing on existing knowledge to make sense of learning situations and construct understandings. This applies just as much to skill learning as it does to tactical appreciation. Simply put, learning is an interaction of past learning experiences with present learning experiences. According to Light (2006), the focus is on the pupils and not the teacher; the encouragement of pupil autonomy and interaction and the central role that questioning plays are what sets it apart from directive, teacher-centred approaches. The assertion is that to remove skill learning from the context of the game is to diminish the capacity to apply it to game situations that may have already been experienced or might be experienced in the future.

Whilst the constructivist conceptual framework is a persuasive one, it could, however, be argued that complex techniques such as the volleyball spike, tennis serve or cricket cover drive need to be broken down and taught in stages outside of a competitive games situation. Some practitioners might argue that, based on behaviourist theory, there is room for the technical approach in some games lessons, where content is divided into small steps and modelled for pupils who practise them in progressive drills with the teacher offering corrective feedback. Rink (2003) warns against the polarisation of TGFU versus the technique-focused approach. She argues that all good teachers have worked with both approaches in their sessions. An important skill for the teacher to develop is to recognise when the players have the technical prowess to be given the next stage of games understanding challenge. A game–practice–game format where both understanding and skill-based teaching styles are adopted in different phases of the same lesson is explained later in this chapter.

Conditioned games

Conditioned or modified games are a useful tool for the teaching of games principles or the application of skills. The game form will need to be carefully selected to accent the particular tactical problem that you want to introduce. In badminton, if the learning objective was to understand the need to manoeuvre an opponent forward and backward in order to create space to hit a winning shot, you might select a half-court singles game with rules where (a) a point is scored when any player grounds the shuttle in their opponent's back tramlines or between the net and the service line and (b) any shot landing anywhere else is deemed void. The conditions of this game would bring out the desirability of clearing deep or dropping close over the net rather than playing to mid-court.

Once the appropriate conditioned games are chosen, you will need to plan a hierarchical series of questions to put to the players that most effectively bring out the themes of the session. Sound subject knowledge is required as you will need not only to choose the appropriate modified games but also plan for a suitable sequence of questions in an appropriate order (that is not to say that other appropriate questions may not crop up in the course of the lesson).

If the conditioned games are well designed, learning will take place for some of the pupils without teacher intervention, since the more able pupils can solve problems for themselves. For example, when playing the two-touch football game most pupils will figure out that intelligent movement of the ball to create passing angles will reap dividends in terms of retaining possession. Some pupils will find out for themselves that if there is pressure on the player in possession from a defender then they will need support behind. However, there will usually be pupils who need prompting with relevant questions.

Teaching styles and instructional models

Pill (2007) refers to a game–question–reflect–practice–game process that encourages teachers to move their thinking from the skills of the game to thinking about the nature of the game and the understanding of the game (see Figure 4.5). The choice of these questions and the handling of the questioning are crucial to the success of the lesson. The questions should be planned prior to the session with possible model answers identified. The questions need to be closed enough to focus the pupils in the correct areas of tactical knowledge but open enough to challenge their understanding. For example, in hockey, if you wish the pupils to grasp the concept of being aware of space before the ball arrives with them, the teacher might ask: (a) When do you look around you to be aware of space on your first touch? or (b) How do you know where the space is for your first touch? The question (a) is more closed than question (b) because it alludes to the answer. When responding to question (b) the pupil must think about how he/she can be aware of the space around them (open shape, 'swivel neck') and the timing of that look (as the ball is rolling toward them). It is, therefore, a more effective question in this instance since it allows for a wider answer. Past research (Williams and Hodges 2005) has drawn strong

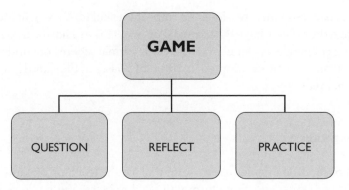

Figure 4.5 Cognitive game processing

links between the use of an open questioning approach with specific feedback and the self-initiated and flexible application of learning behaviours. In other words, teaching styles that allow participants to solve problems with a degree of autonomy create independent players who can transfer learning.

A questioning style, favoured by some teachers, involves asking the pupil(s) to 'show' them what they might do in a given situation. That way, the pupils not only demonstrate their level of understanding of the situation but also offer a visual picture to the teacher and their peers. This pupil demonstration will then be evaluated by the teacher and, after possible adjustments, can be rehearsed by the pupil. This kinaesthetic and visual learning style is likely to consolidate understanding to a greater degree than mere auditory interaction. An example of this approach would be as follows: the teacher is working on defending skills in basketball and asks a pupil to show how they might position themselves in relation to the proximity of the ball and the position of attackers. The teacher will set up different situations and have an image of what they are expecting to see from the pupil in each scenario.

Giving more autonomy to players in problem-solving scenarios can help develop the 'thinking player' that is less dependent on the teacher. An open question – for example 'how might you as a team improve your number of attempts on goal in this game?' – might be posed to each team. The teacher must allow adequate time for group discussion and consensus on a tactical way forward. Adequate time for game play will then be required to carry out the agreed strategies, followed by a period of group evaluation supervised by the teacher. This more divergent teaching method, although time-consuming, can be very rewarding for pupils and teacher alike in that it involves collaboration amongst all involved. This process of situated learning (Kirk 2005) is at its most empowering for performers when, according to Richard and Wallian (2005), it involves both observation of game play by the players and critical thinking through an exchange of ideas. As a result of reflection in action (evaluating one's own game play whilst in action) and reflection on action (evaluating the play of others) performers will be better equipped to engage with other learners, articulate their learning and, consequently, modify performance.

Differentiation

The range of pupil ability in a typical class can be very wide. You need to guard against setting tasks that are not challenging enough or are so difficult that some pupils experience very little success. The most effective way to facilitate learning at the correct level on the same theme for each pupil in a lesson is to differentiate by task. The STEP principle can be a useful guide here. Games and practices can be modified in terms of the **S**pace used, the nature of the **T**ask, the **E**quipment used and the number of **P**layers involved. An invasion game can be made easier by increasing the area, simplifying the rules, using a different ball and having fewer players on each team. A net game can be modified by changing the court areas, the size of the racket or the ball, or by changing the scoring system. By using the STEP principle teachers can construct differentiated learning activities which allow pupils to meet the same learning objectives at different levels.

Developing physical and mental capacity

The manner in which this key process is going to be taught in physical education is the subject of some conjecture. The combination of the physical attributes of strength, stamina, speed and flexibility with mental determination are desirable qualities for a successful games player. The development of mental determination, defined as 'confidence to have a go, determination to face up to challenges, dealing with emotions and the desire to achieve success for oneself and others' (QCA 2008), is an interesting aspect of the revised curriculum. To advance these mental qualities in games activities pupils will need to be placed into situations that test their resolve, motivated to come through them and their behaviours reinforced with praise. For example, teams can be put through a battery of demanding tasks that test physical endurance and skill, as in a games circuit. Each member of the team must play their part and contribute to the team score. A basketball circuit that requires teams of four to successfully complete a designated number of skills, such as lay-ups, dribbling, pass/follow and quick-fire shots, against the clock at each station will test pupils under pressure. Credit should be given for participation, giving maximum effort, taking responsibility and encouraging others.

Curriculum planning

Every school is unique in terms of its location, facilities, pupil intake, staff expertise and philosophy. The NCPE 2008 offers considerable flexibility to choose activities that are engaging and motivating for your pupils and through which each child can progress in their understanding of key concepts and their application of key processes.

Some physical education curriculum leaders will design their school's programme around the national curriculum range and content: outwitting opponents, accurate replication, performing at maximum levels, identifying and solving problems and exercising safely and effectively. They will use a range of activities, including some games, in order to develop the concepts and processes with their pupils whilst covering the recommended range and content. For example, identifying and solving problems may be delivered through aspects of gymnastics, games, OAA and dance. This approach will require teachers to think through which activities are suitable to cover aspects of the range and content whilst making links between these activities. As part of the outwitting opponents units there may be invasion, striking and fielding and divided court games used to show different ways of achieving that aim. The principles are transferable within each games category. However, whilst some of the skills are transferable across the categories, the tactical principles of invasion, striking and fielding and divided court games are quite different and, therefore not transferable. The principle of compactness in defence, for instance, is common to all invasion games but not relevant to fielding in cricket or receiving service in volleyball. Another issue to consider is that technical skill development may be limited if there is no sustained teaching of specific games over several weeks. This may have a limiting effect on the range of responses when trying to outwit an opponent. For example, it is unlikely that many of a typical Year 9 class would be able to master a repertoire of skills in badminton that would equip them to produce a set of responses that will enable them to outwit anybody without being taught that activity for a whole unit. This may have implications for the choice of activity (selecting games with less demanding skills) or blocking of activities (how much time is devoted to each activity within the outwitting opponents units).

An alternative structure would be to develop the key concepts and processes within a structure that retains the six discrete activity areas. The physical education staff would identify across the activities where best to teach each concept and process, highlighting where skills and knowledge are transferable across activities. When teaching each of the striking and fielding games, for instance, the balance between risk and run-scoring (defence and attack) when batting will be presented as ways of developing 'making and applying decisions' as well as elements of competence and performance (QCA 2008) within each game. Where they exist, the links between the principles in each category of game and the skills across all games can be made. In divided court games, for instance, players will use a range of shots to manoeuvre their opponent(s) around the court in order to create space to hit a 'winner'. Catching and throwing skills are fundamental to and transferable across several invasion games and all striking and fielding activities.

How schools deliver the new curriculum is a matter of interpretation and no prescribed curriculum design is presented in the document. However, it is apparent that the emphasis is away from adherence to activity areas and towards a process-led curriculum where the transfer of learning across activity and subject boundaries is a priority. The choice of activities and pedagogical models is very much open and will depend on the situational circumstances of each school.

Units of work

Before you plan games units of work and lesson plans you must have sound knowledge of the games principles and the associated skills relating to that activity. For example, it is possible to identify a list of principles for attacking and defending in invasion games that apply to all games in that category. All invasion games, for example, will require a team to use the width of the playing area in attack and to deny space by being compact when defending. The game principles are the starting point for planning units of work and should be taught, alongside the related skills, in logical progression in terms of their complexity.

Table 4.1 (opposite) sets out a framework for a unit of work for Year 9 badminton which demonstrates the links between principles and skills. Within this framework teachers will have a degree of autonomy as to which learning activities are included in their lesson plans. Learning objectives and teaching points/key questions will be related to the weekly breakdown in the unit of work.

Assessing pupil learning through games

Ofsted has identified the characteristics of schools that exhibited good practice in assessment of physical education:

> The majority of the teachers seen in these schools were able to observe and analyse students' work successfully, leading to timely interventions during activities. In

Table 4.1 *Framework for a unit of work: the link between principles and skills*

Badminton (outwitting an opponent)

Lesson	Tactical problem	Solution: skill or movement
1	Setting up to attack	Overhead forehand clear in the opponent's court – creating space in the front court
2	Setting up to attack	Overhead backhand clear for achieving depth in the opponent's court
3	Setting up to attack	Initiating play with an underhand clear (service) to push the opponent back
4	Setting up to attack	Using a drop shot to bring the opponent forward to use the space in the front court
5	Winning the point	Using a smash into the front court to exploit a weak clear or poor drop shot
6	Defending space	Recovering to centre court following shot attempts
7	Round-robin singles tournament: application of skills assessment	Full range of skills

most cases, feedback during lessons was regular, comprehensive and constructive. Consequently, the vast majority of the students seen in Key Stage 3 knew how well they were doing and what they needed to do to improve further. Most of them also knew their level of attainment and their targets for improvement.

(Ofsted 2009: 35)

The assessment of learning in games activities can be a challenging task for teachers because the skills involved tend to be 'open' and subject to numerous external influences; notably the level of opposition, the weather and the proficiency of the team. Subject knowledge and experience will inevitably improve the validity and reliability of your assessments.

It is important that pupils understand what they need to achieve in order to be assessed at each level and that these competencies are described in relation to their performance in their words. An example of good practice in this regard is to use wall charts that translate the attainment target into tangible actions that each pupil can relate to and identify with. Sharing learning objectives with pupils at the beginning of lessons may focus pupil learning. Assessment for learning strategies will contribute to helping to close the gap between actual achievement and an individual's potential by providing corrective feedback and setting goals.

Opportunities must be provided for pupils to demonstrate these competencies. For example, to gain Level 6, pupils must

plan their own and others' work, and carrying out their own work, . . . draw on what they know about strategy, tactics and composition in response to changing circumstances, and what they know about their own and others' strengths and weaknesses.

(QCA 2008: 10)

In order that these skills are assessed in games activities you will need to design pupil learning experiences that involve group tactical planning, changing competitive situations and evaluation of self and others. The responses to these tasks must be observed and pupils questioned in order to elicit their understanding.

The main advantages of continuity and a smooth transition across from the primary to the secondary phase are that time is not lost at the start of Year 7 and that gifted and talented children, pupils with learning difficulties and those with disabilities are identified early. Sharing of staff expertise, resources and facilities will assist in this respect. The sharing of information covering common assessment criteria is particularly important when teaching games as the range of pupil ability and experience tends to be wide.

Guidance and teaching ideas for Key Stage 2 and Key Stage 3

The game–practice–game approach

A case has already been made for the desirability of being able to vary and adapt teaching styles when teaching games in order that both understanding of games principles and skilled responses can be learned. The game–practice–game lesson format involves the introduction of a 'tactical problem' through a modified or conditioned game. This is followed by progressive practice of skills relevant to that particular tactical theme and then a move back to another game which further highlights the tactical challenge that is the focus of the lesson. An example is given in Box 4.2.

Box 4.2   Year 6 soft ball short tennis lesson

In this Year 6 soft ball short tennis lesson the focus is on when to attack at the net.

Game condition

Points can only be scored from a volley or if you hit a ground shot inside a one metre target zone at the back of the court. All other 'winners' are deemed void. This will set the problem of when to come to the net and when to stay back. The scoring is rally point with the first player to 11 points called the winner.

The skill practice phase

The lesson may then include some progressive volleying practices under varying levels of pressure differentiated according to ability. The lob will be a relevant shot to practice to introduce if time permits.

Game condition

Normal short tennis rules but 2 points will be gained for rallies won with a volley or won after an opponent plays a volley. This will encourage pupils to try to get to the net but recognize that it is a risky move and should be when the opponent is in a 'vulnerable' situation. There will be ample opportunities to apply previously practised volleying skills in the game.

The above format for teaching games is likely to increase pupil motivation as they typically enjoy playing competitive games; their skill learning will be contextualised and, therefore, more relevant. Time is allocated for learning the relatively complex skill of the volley outside of a competitive game situation with an opportunity to later apply that skill in a game.

Creating games

One of the key concepts in the NCPE is creativity. Creativity in its purest form will be characterised by originality. There are few instances in games where pupils are truly original (except possibly those with the exceptional talent to invent their own techniques at top level). However, the process of creating games could be one of benefit to pupils, especially in the later primary years. A short unit on Creating Games with a group of Year 6 pupils will help them to understand why rules, and pupils' behaviour in relation to them, are important. Offering opportunities for children to think creatively with little or no teacher intervention in divergent tasks will give them a feeling of empowerment. Group work will develop the key skills of problem-solving, co-operation and communication.

Additionally, pupils will develop their understanding of games principles, realise how skills and tactics are transferable across games, recognise issues of safety and how the relationship of rules, equipment, players and area will shape a game. Games-making cards have proved to be a useful resource, but have been neglected in recent years. A typical double-sided task card is illustrated in Figure 4.6 (p. 46).

The class, individually or in small groups, can be given access to equipment and space in order to make their games, try them out and then explain their creations to their peers and the teacher. An alternative may be skill-led game cards where their game is devised using two specific games techniques or tactical-led where the game must take an invasion, striking and fielding or divided court format (Lavin 2007).

Alternative games

The inclusion of non-traditional games into the curriculum is becoming increasingly popular at both primary and secondary level. Ofsted states that:

> This not only enriched the provision but provided creative solutions when facilities were limited or the programme of traditional team activities was proving unpopular. This had reduced disaffection and improved engagement, particularly among vulnerable groups.
>
> (Ofsted 2009: 38)

Games such as kabbadi, tri golf, tchoukball, ultimate frisbee and pop lacrosse, to name but a few, are capturing the imagination of pupils who may be disenchanted by football, rugby and hockey. There has always been licence to teach these games in schools. In recent years, a perceived drop in pupil interest in traditional games at some schools has led to their increased use.

Kabbadi is an invasion game, originating from south east Asia, that requires no equipment and, if taught in a progressive way, can be an effective medium through which to teach the outwitting of opponents. It involves entering the opposing team's zone and tagging one of their players whilst avoiding taking a breath or being tagged/captured yourself before returning.

MAKE UP A GAME

For teams of 7v7 or 9v9

> Use a playing area shaped like a triangle

> Use a bat or racket

> Choose a ball to suit the bat or racket

GAMES MAKING

RULES OF THE GAME

You will need
somewhere to play (area)
someone or some people to play with (players)
something to play with (equipment)

your game
how does it start?
how do you score?
how do you start again after a score?
what are the rules of play?
what happens if a player breaks a rule?
when does your game finish?

What is your game called?

Figure 4.6 Games-making cards

Summary

The message that emerges from the revised NCPE is that scope has been created to tailor a physical education curriculum that will motivate pupils to take part and enjoy physical activity within and beyond that curriculum. The nature of games activities within that curriculum will be largely for each school to decide, by taking into account their pupils' needs and interests. Some schools will retain a syllabus dominated by traditional games; others may take a more radical approach and teach the processes through alternative games. A curriculum that puts process and concepts at its heart is one that demands that teachers, and subsequently pupils, look across activity areas for transferable knowledge and skills. Whichever way a school physical education programme is designed, it is the quality of teaching that will make the difference.

Whilst good teachers of games activities do not have to have been top-class games players, it helps to have had experiential knowledge of the game concept so that the principles underpinning teaching sessions are not only understood but have been experienced. The relationship of time and space, as well as cue reception and its relationship to decision-making and technique selection are not concepts that can be learned solely from a book. A teaching model such as TGFU that recognises the development of cognitive processes like thinking strategically and decision-making is equally as important to becoming a good games player as physical dexterity (Kirk 2005). It is actually more demanding of teachers' pedagogical content knowledge and subject matter knowledge than is the traditional approach. As Kirk states, 'TGFU requires teachers to step outside of their comfort zone and design learning experiences that give learners some responsibility for their learning' (2005: 214).

Although it should always be recognised that there is more than one way to teach games, there is a great body of research that supports the TGFU pedagogy. For example, Slade (2007) offers research evidence to suggest that a TGFU teaching approach with young learners increases motivation, enjoyment and self-esteem.

With an open mind, some teacher education and plenty of practice, you can become adept at the teaching strategies highlighted in this chapter. The benefits in terms of your teaching effectiveness and pupils' tactical understanding and skill development will only be apparent if you are prepared to try it. The learners will enjoy their sessions and, consequently, work harder.

According to Nicholls, the eminent educational psychologist, 'we will never have equality of ability; therefore, we can only hope for equivalence in motivation' (2001: 66). Ultimately, if we as teachers are able to create compelling learning experiences that motivate our pupils to want to play games then we are taking a big step toward them sustaining that interest in later life. The manner in which games activities are presented to young people is fundamental in this respect. It is hoped that some of the ideas presented in this chapter assist in contributing towards realising such an aim.

References

Butler, J. and McCahan, B. (2005) Teaching games for understanding as a curriculum model. In Griffin, L. and Butler, J. *Teaching Games for Understanding: Theory, research and practice.* Windsor: Human Kinetics.

Hubball, H., Hayes, S. and Lambert, J. (2007) 'Theory to practice: using the games for understanding approach in the teaching of invasion games'. *Canadian Journal of Physical and Health Education.* Vol. 73, No. 3, pp. 14–20.

Kirk, D. (2005) Future prospects for teaching games for understanding. In L. Griffin and J. Butler (eds), *Teaching Games for Understanding: Theory, research and practice.* Windsor: Human Kinetic. pp. 213–226.

Lavin, J. (2007) 'The creative approach to teaching games in key stage three and four: the forgotten aspect of physical education'. *PE Matters.* Winter edition.

Light, R. (2005) Making sense of chaos: Australian coaches talking about games sense. In L .Griffin, and J. Butler (eds), *Teaching Games for Understanding: Theory, research and practice.* Windsor: Human Kinetics, pp. 213–226.

Light, R. (2006) 'Game sense: innovation or just good coaching?' *Journal of Physical Education New Zealand.* Vol. 39, Issue 1, pp. 8–19.

Mitchell, S., Oslin, J. and Griffin, L. (1997) *Teaching Sport Concepts and Skills: A tactical games approach.* Champaign, IL: Human Kinetics.

Ofsted (2009) *Physical Education in Schools 2005/8: Working towards 2012 and beyond.* April 2005. www.ofsted.gov.uk

O'Leary, N. (2008) 'Teaching games for understanding in learning to "outwit opponents"'. *Physical Education Matters.* Winter edition.

Pill, S. (2007) 'Teaching games for understanding'. *Sports Coach*. Vol. 29, Issue 2, pp. 27–29.

QCA (Qualifications and Curriculum Authority) (2008) *Physical Education Programmes of Study Key Stage 3*. www.qca.uk/curriculum

Richard, J.-F. and Wallian, N. (2005) Emphasizing student engagement in the construction of game performance. In L. Griffin and J. Butler (eds), *Teaching Games for Understanding: Theory, research and practice*. Windsor: Human Kinetics, pp. 213–226.

Rink, J. (2003) Motor learning. In B. Mohnsen (ed.), *Concepts of Physical Education: What every student needs to know*. Reston, VA: NASPE.

Salen, K. and Zimmerman, E. (2003) *Rules of Play*. Cambridge, MA: MIT Press.

Slade, D. (2007) Making first coaching impressions count. *Sports Coach*. Vol. 29, Issue 4, pp. 28–29.

Thorkildsen,T. and Nicholls, J.G. (2001) *Motivation and the Struggle to Learn: Responding to a fractured experience*. Boston, MA: Allyn and Bacon.

Thorpe, R. (2005) Rod Thorpe on Teaching Games for Understanding: how skills develop using TGFU. In L. Kidman, *Athlete-Centred Coaching: Developing inspired and inspiring people*. Christchurch, NZ: Innovative Print Communications, pp. 239–243.

Thorpe, R. and Bunker, D. (1989) A changing focus in games teaching. In L. Almond (ed.), *The Place of Physical Education in Schools*. London: Kogan Page, pp. 42–71.

Williams, A.M. and Hodges, N.J. (2005) 'Practice, instruction and skill acquisition in soccer: challenging tradition'. *Journal of Sports Sciences*. 23, pp. 637–650.

5 Learning and teaching through gymnastics

Jon Binney and Debra Barrett

Gymnastics – the foundation for every activity

Cooper and Trnka defined gymnastics as 'physical activity of any kind' (1994: 1). Gymnastics is one of the foremost activities for developing physical literacy. To become physically literate, pupils need to master fundamental movement skills. Some activities only focus on a limited number of dominant movements, but gymnastics develops a wide variety, all of which can transfer to other activities. Agility, balance, co-ordination and speed (the ABCs of athleticism) are the fundamental movement skills that are the cornerstones of all physical activity. They are key to every activity that is undertaken. Gymnastics assists with the development of correct posture and can contribute to a pupil's general strength and core stability whilst increasing flexibility, enhancing their range of movement, therefore enhancing the movement potential. Gymnastics teaches the body to react to constant changes in direction and speeds, through jumping, falling and flying, all actions perfectly natural to the inquisitive and explorative mind of a pupil. If these fundamental movement patterns are acquired at an early age, natural physical literacy will allow for the growth of pupils who are eager to engage in physical activity, who are confident to perform with control and fluency, and who continue to seek enjoyment and fun in sport long after their education has finished.

Developing creativity

A key concept highlighted within the National Curriculum for Physical Education 2008, states how creativity can be used to 'explore' and 'experiment' with 'techniques' and 'compositional ideas to produce efficient and effective outcomes' (QCA 2008).

Alongside the physical development that gymnastics affords comes the augmentation of cognitive skills, developing unity and co-operation between with the logical, analytical left-hand side of the brain and the creative and imaginative right-hand side of the brain. Gymnastics is the perfect medium to allow pupils' imagination to explore new movements and new shapes whilst discovering inventive and original methods of travelling over, under and around various obstacles and apparatus.

Some traditional concerns

The thought of having to teach gymnastics often arouses feelings of anxiety and insecurity in teachers with limited personal experience of gymnastics. Many may feel unable to appear convincing when demonstrating in front of pupils, and insecure in the need to differentiate skills whilst also ensuring pupils remain safe. Although it is true that many gymnastic skills do require technical subject knowledge, this is no different to any physical skill in physical education, where teachers can research correct teaching points from a wide variety of published texts and resources. But, for many, the challenge remains how to effectively differentiate gymnastic skills and how best to structure individual lessons and sequences of lessons.

Effective gymnastic teaching requires knowledge of how to introduce, differentiate and progress gymnastic activities in order to make lessons enjoyable, challenging and exciting. The following principles aim to explain the many different methods and structures that can be used in order to meet these objectives. These principles are also cyclical in that many will be revisited from one week to the next and from year to year, but via a different learning context and/or a more sophisticated, deeper level of understanding. In this way learning is progressed and pupils are continually challenged, both physically and mentally. A little bit of gymnastic knowledge therefore goes a long way.

We hope that you will feel confident that you can provide exciting gymnastic activities, allowing for differentiation in single lessons. But also that you can suitably differentiate content from Key Stages 2 and 3 without necessarily having to master more and more advanced gymnastic skills in order to deliver gymnastic activities successfully.

Purpose and structure of the chapter

The purpose of this chapter is *not* to give a classification of gymnastic actions and compositional skills suitable to teach at each key stage. This is unlikely to help those struggling with structuring and differentiating lesson content. To be an effective teacher of gymnastics, you do *not* need to be an advanced gymnast yourself or need to have all the answers in terms of what the body can do. Indeed much of the joy of teaching and physically taking part in gymnastics is the discovery of one's own physical capabilities whilst encouraging diversity in response to tasks set. But educators do need to have subject knowledge and physical ability at a *foundation level*, which pupils' future gymnastic knowledge, skills and understanding can then be built upon.

This chapter aims to help you deliver a suitably challenging and exciting gymnastics programme, providing numerous ideas and practical examples that any teacher of physical education will be able to access. At the centre of the chapter will be a consideration of how gymnastics contributes to developing the range and content of 'Accurate replication of actions, phrases and sequences', which has been highlighted by the QCA as being pertinent to the teaching and learning of gymnastics-based activities, and integral to the successful delivery of gymnastics within schools.

Key statistics and facts concerning gymnastics

According to the *Schools Sports Survey* (SSP) 2007–2008, conducted by the Department for Children, Schools and Families (DCSF), gymnastics is one of the most widely available activities within primary and secondary education, with over 95 per cent of schools offering it during an academic year. Such notable figures might suggest that gymnastics, both inside and outside of education, is flourishing and that the sport is set for a pre-Olympic renaissance. However, within the current educational climate, there is much to consider. The gymnastics being taught in today's physical education curriculum faces numerous challenges. Does every physical educator have the necessary confidence, skills or understanding of how to teach developmentally appropriate gymnastics? It is suggested that having a high level of subject knowledge and confidence to demonstrate is key to the delivery of gymnastics – two areas where the physical education profession is lacking in expertise (Werner 2004). Another factor might be that gymnastics remains largely underdeveloped in physical education programmes. The gymnastics curriculum of today is reminiscent of the gymnastics curriculum taught 20 years ago (Lathrop and Drake 1998).

Trainee physical education teachers who had limited exposure to gymnastics in their own physical education come to their initial teacher training with anxiety and fear and with a lack of appreciation of the educational value of what gymnastics has to offer, not to mention with limited physical skills and compositional knowledge of gymnastics itself. When one compares this with the amount of exposure trainee teachers have so far had to activities such as games, it is no wonder students often graduate still feeling anxious and concerned about their ability to effectively teach gymnastics within schools. The result is often that teachers go on to avoid teaching gymnastics altogether, thereby perpetuating their own school physical education experiences, or they teach it at a very fundamental level due to their lack of confidence, limited range of skills and fear of looking incompetent in front of pupils.

Another factor is the 'health and safety' issues that deter teachers from fully exploring the creative and physical boundaries of the sport for fear of litigation (see Chapter 3). These include concern that pupils may be injured and also how teachers physically support pupils without fear of any insidious backlash. The potential consequence of this is that pupils rarely move beyond working on mats repeating foundation skills taught in previous years, which ultimately results in both pupils and teachers experiencing feelings of boredom and apathy towards the activity.

Using gymnastics-based activities to explore and communicate ideas, concepts and emotions (NCPE 2008)

Gymnastics (and indeed all performance-based activities) can play an important role in addressing some of the issues of how best to help pupils effectively manage feelings of anxiety and stress. It is integral to any gymnastic lesson or sequence of lessons that opportunities are provided to enable the pupils to experience a wealth of emotions, from nervousness, anxiety, stress and pressure to relief, satisfaction and, it is hoped, self-fulfilment and enjoyment.

Anxiety towards a performance can potentially be used to the pupil's advantage. Anxiety can increase motivation towards a specified outcome and can increase levels of arousal which can aid performance, but most importantly it allows the pupil to experience the feelings and emotions that are associated with pressure and nervousness. With careful handling and sensitivity, strategies and systems can be shared between teacher and pupil on how best to overcome these fears to perform at their best.

Improving pupils' perceptions of their own ability can play a vital role in the successful teaching of gymnastics. Therefore breaking down the perceived barriers to success is vital for any teacher wishing to observe progress. Pupils' perceived motor competence will be based largely around two factors: intrinsic factors, such as the desire to master new skills, but also extrinsic factors, most notably comparison with their peers. Pupils will fear ridicule from their friends if they are exposed to a performance that may show them in a negative light. Therefore creating the correct environment and structure within a gymnastics lesson is imperative.

Developing the correct motivational climate

- Positive perceptions and imagery from the teacher, about the activity or the task, actively encourage pupils to try new tasks and to push themselves past their normal limits.
- Pupils' perceived ability and their actual ability are often very different. Having an accurate knowledge of a pupil's ability is critical in ensuring that both the teacher and the pupil set realistic and reachable goals.
- Create a 'mastery' environment which focuses on individual standards and performance rather than a 'competition' environment.
- Ensure all feedback is based upon the progress that the pupil has made and not in comparison to other pupils.
- Formal performances are still recommended, but ensure that not every pupil is judged against the same criteria. The 'one size fits all' approach does very little for developing pupils' self-perceptions.

Accurate replication of actions, phrases and sequences (NCPE 2008)

Gymnastics contributes considerably to developing the range and content of 'Accurate replication of actions, phrases and sequences', as outlined in the NCPE 2008. In particular it provides numerous opportunities for 3b – 'accurately replicate gymnastic actions'. Teachers need to have knowledge of a range of 'foundation skills' which they can teach within Key Stages 2 and 3. Pupils are therefore being encouraged to accurately replicate a wide range of actions, agilities and sequences which continually widen their movement vocabulary. In simple terms, gymnastics can be divided into rotation, balance and flight actions, which all have a part to play in developing pupils' physical literacy. It is therefore important that teachers continually vary the physical demands placed on pupils within gymnastic lessons so that they acquire a wide range of taught gymnastic skills. But of equal importance is that pupils learn about their own strengths and limitations whilst responding imaginatively to tasks set, regardless of their individual ability.

Individual foundation skills

Table 5.1 lists the foundations skills under the headings of balance, flight and rotation. This list is not intended to be all-encompassing, but simply to give examples of suitable foundation skills which should be taught within Key Stages 2 and 3. We will refer to these examples again when we discuss different principles of progression.

Progressive lesson planning

The structure of individual lessons should give a logical progression from the beginning to the end of the lesson. In order to provide a context, Box 5.1 shows an example of how teachers could structure a lesson based on one of the rotational tasks: the cartwheel. Every lesson should include an aspect or aspects of 3b – 'accurately replicate gymnastic actions' (NCPE 2008).

Table 5.1 *Individual foundation skills in gymnastics*

Balance	Flight	Rotation
These skills focus on balancing on different body parts, making a variety of body shapes, and being upside down, horizontal and upright	These skills focus on differing body shapes, transferring weight from hand to feet and changing the foot patterns.	These skills focus on rotating through three planes of rotation: vertical (e.g. spinning), horizontal (e.g. forward roll), sagittal (e.g. cartwheel).
Handstand	Star jump	Forward roll
V sit	Tuck jump	Side roll
Shoulder stand	Pin jump	Log roll
Long sit	Half/full twist	Backward roll
One knee balance (resting on two hands)	Jumping one–two feet	Circle roll ('teddy bear' roll)
	Jumping two–one foot	Half/full twist
Hip balance (front support)	Bunny jump	Cartwheel
Headstand	Hopping	Shoulder roll
Arabesque	Leaping	
	Squat on/through vault	
	Straddle on/over vault	

Box 5.1   Structure of a lesson based on a rotational task: cartwheel

Pulse-raiser activity

The warm-up should physiologically and psychologically prepare pupils for the activities to follow. The warm-up should therefore be vigorous and involve whole-body actions which relate to the main activity, including jogging, leaping, galloping and so on. As the lesson is to focus on rotation, in this case the cartwheel, then the pulse-raising activity should also involve aspects of rotation such as log-rolling across mats and spinning on one foot, and also moments of weight on hands such as bunny jumps. The skills must be accessible to *all* pupils, with reasonable effort.

Stretching and conditioning phase

This should focus on body tension and extension, whilst passing through a range of basic gymnastic skills. For example: stretch up on to toes – squat on to haunches – walk hands out to press up – lower hips and swing feet to front – long sit in a straddle leg position – rock back to shoulder stand – rock up to feet into arabesque – repeat.

Teaching the main skill or activity

Finally you can introduce a number of tasks which progressively lead into the main activity. In the example of the cartwheel, this may involve pupils:
- bunny jumping over a bench landing one foot after the other;
- with a supporter who stands astride the bench holding the performer's hips, cartwheeling over the bench;
- then performing the cartwheel (with support initially) away from the bench;
- focusing on the foot–hand–hand–foot pattern.

Progressive tasks

You can then explore any number of different progressions (outlined below), depending on the learning focus and abilities of the pupils. Each of the methods described can be adapted according to the gymnastic context and desired learning outcomes.

Progressive teaching styles

The focus of the lesson and the desired learner objectives will dictate which teaching styles you engage with. Tasks will ultimately range in the amount of choice pupils are given:

> closed tasks (no choice) → moderately open-ended tasks (some choice) → very open-ended tasks (lots of choice).

Closed tasks

As a general guide, the warm-up should be taught via a closed/authoritative style to ensure all pupils are adequately warmed up. This also applies when teaching new skills to ensue correct technical execution and iron out common errors.

Moderately open-ended tasks

Tasks can then be modified by small degrees to give pupils more autonomy and freedom of choice in how to respond. In this way, pupils can begin to explore 3c – 'Identifying and solving problems' (NCPE 2008). This not only encourages diversity and individuality but allows for differentiation. For example, within the cartwheel example in Box 5.1, you could ask the pupils to explore different ways of adapting and performing the cartwheel whilst still involving the bench, for which there are numerous responses. (However, you still need to have thought through some answers to prompt pupils, should they struggle to come up with responses.) This method is also particularly useful in helping pupils to resolve common technical problems themselves, as opposed to the teacher being the 'fount of all knowledge'. For example, you could ask pupils to explore the best place to land the second foot in relation to the second hand (knowing yourself that the optimum place would be as close to the hand as possible).

Very open-ended tasks

Now that pupils have some practical experience of adapting the cartwheel on to the bench, you could open up the task further by asking pupils to explore other ways of rotating on/over/around/off the bench. A note of caution! Some guidance is still needed in order to prompt pupils' creative responses. For example, remind pupils of some of the rotation skills they performed during the warm-up conditioning phase, and the three planes of rotation around which the body can move. Again, you need to have some examples up your sleeve to prompt and guide their explorations. Tasks can be narrowed back down again to ensure pupils stay on task and to keep widening their movement vocabulary. For example, if a pupil performs the forward roll using the bench as an obstacle, the teacher may ask him or her to show this to the whole class, before teaching it to them all. By continually changing the teaching style from open to closed throughout a lesson, pupils continue to be challenged and motivated by acquiring and developing new skills, as well as exploring their own responses, depending on their individual ability.

Progressing single actions into longer sequences

Once pupils have mastered a skill, for example the cartwheel, challenge can be increased by performing the skill as part of a longer phrase. Typically, control is lost when moving from one skill to another, because pupils tend to focus on the actions happening immediately before and after. Good composition needs to be taught. Ultimately the aim is for pupils to create their own sequences, but it would be a mistake to simply expect this to happen without input from you. Pupils should be encouraged to move in harmony with the natural momentum and directional impetus of actions. This is especially true when one movement is resolved by another, for example: half cartwheel into a handstand; cartwheel exiting down onto one knee; cartwheel into arabesque; cartwheel moving straight after into a forward roll, or a tuck jump; and so on. Pupils need to be made aware of where to place their hands and feet to produce an economical and harmonious flow, thereby removing any unnecessary and additional stepping or adjusting actions which detract from the aesthetic quality and fluidity of the sequence.

Begin by teaching one or two examples of exiting the cartwheel, before allowing pupils to explore their own responses. This not only builds pupil confidence, but establishes teacher expectations of good composition work. You would repeat this with one or two teacher examples of entering the cartwheel, before pupils are ultimately set free to explore their own ways into and out of the cartwheel. In this way, pupils move continuously from 'accurately replicating actions' to 'identifying and solving problems'. You would need to repeat this method when you introduce sequence work on apparatus, to ensure a high quality response and to provide appropriate challenge, depending on pupils' age range and general ability. Ultimately, sequences should look logical and aesthetically pleasing as well as feel good to perform.

Progressing skills from simple to advanced execution

The complex range of skills witnessed at the Olympics can all ultimately be sourced back to the foundation skills previously mentioned. Therefore, in order to continue to challenge pupils once they have mastered skills at a foundation level, it is important to recognise how skills can be progressed in order to increase the physical challenge. Typically, this might involve changing the leg shapes, performing actions on the other side of the body, involving smaller body surfaces (for example on one hand or foot), increasing the height or degree of rotation, involving apparatus and or other persons. (Pupils are typically working on 3d – 'Performing at maximum levels', NCPE 2008).

The pupil already able to successfully perform the cartwheel could therefore be asked to perform:

- two cartwheels immediately one after the other;
- on the other side of the body;

- on one hand;
- on/off/partially supported by apparatus or another pupil;
- in co-ordination with another pupil or pupils as part of a sequence;
- altering the exit of the skill by bringing feet together in a round off.

Some of these progressions will now be explored in further detail.

Progressing skills from floor to apparatus

Apparatus can be progressed by performing skills on smaller surfaces, by increasing the number of pieces used and by increasing the height of apparatus. Many of the foundation skills previously mentioned can therefore be progressed in this way. Typically pupils will progress skills from mats to:

- benches and box tops;
- low Swedish beams or three-tier boxes;
- platforms such as: table, pummel horse, five-tier box, higher Swedish beams and ropes.

Ropes typically provide the most challenge due to their instability and small surface area. This is especially true when pupils try to balance using the ropes, because they need strong core strength to maintain a balance position. Less challenging skills should not however be overlooked, and they may include swinging, spiralling, rotating, and so on. *Never* presume that pupils can simply transfer vocabulary learnt on the floor onto apparatus. As discussed in the Progressive teaching styles section on p. 54, activities should start with direct teaching by transferring previously taught skills.

Ways to adapt and extend skills acquired on the floor onto apparatus

1. Initial pupil exploration of apparatus, ideally during the warm-up.
2. Teach set tasks or skills to ensure purposeful, high quality work on the selected apparatus.
3. Allow pupils more choice in slightly more open-ended tasks. This is to encourage creativity and individuality amongst pupils of differing abilities.
4. Encourage simple entries and exits into and out of basic skills in order to combine actions into longer sequences.
5. Join pupils into pairs: revise simple compositional skills of matching, mirroring, complement and contrast, unison and canon, leading and following, same/different direction, crossing, meeting and parting, and so on.
6. Introduce combined apparatus: you initially select one or two pieces but progress to allowing pupils to individually select and design their own apparatus lay out.
7. Teach pair support work incorporating apparatus: counterbalance/tension, partial weight bearing, full weight bearing and tempo work.
8. In Year 9, further progression can be achieved by joining pupils together to make trios, quartets, etc. Skills might include sports acrobatic trio, group balances and tempo work, all of which involve greater degrees of trust, skill, agility, strength and co-operation.

Progressing from solo to pairs or trios using apparatus

Within Key Stage 2, pupils will typically work in solo or pair groupings. Decision-making is often a key feature of group work, and includes the ability to empathise, co-operate, select and discard ideas and so on, which is typically beyond the social development of primary-aged pupils. However, pupils do very much enjoy working with others and there is much to be gained from their doing so. Pair or group work provides numerous opportunities for pupils to engage with 3b – 'Exploring and communicating ideas, concepts and emotions' (NCPE 2008). As already discussed, this could easily involve very simple, low-level apparatus such as a bench, in order to increase challenge and provide a more stimulating environment. This sort of work also provides many learning opportunities for pupils to engage in 3e – 'identifying and solving problems' (NCPE 2008).

Pair-work using the bench

This work would follow introductory work on mats where specific teaching of pair-work skills would have been included, as well as exploratory work by pupils. This example could easily be covered in a single lesson or built upon from week to week, culminating in a final performance piece.

1. Find three ways of passing along the bench with your partner. You can pass each other, go side by side, move away from each other or be one in front of the other. Think about the different surfaces you can travel on. For example, knees, hands and feet, bottom, hips, and so on.
2. Create a sequence from these ideas using three different actions, performed one after the other.
3. Teach pupils how to do a front support on the bench with their hands on the floor (optional), an arabesque on the bench and a one-knee balance on the bench.
4. Now explore other balancing actions with your partner. Explore the different surfaces you can balance on, e.g. knees, hips, shoulders, bottom, shins, back, and so on.
5. Select two balances where you are both copying each other. Your balances must involve the bench in some of the following ways: completely supported/partially supported, under, over across the bench, part on/off the bench. Add these two balances at the beginning and the end of your original sequence.
6. Teach pupils how to safely jump off the end of the bench in a variety of shapes, for example, tuck, star, pin. Pupils now explore other jumping actions involving the bench. For example, bunny jumps from side to side, jumping over the bench completely, jumping on, and so on.
7. With a partner join three different jumping actions together and perform somewhere in the routine. Practise the routine from the very beginning ensuring you and your partner are in time, and know the sequence well.

Clearly there are many different variations of how one might structure similar tasks, and include different gymnastic actions, depending on the age and ability of pupils. But the principles discussed so far are still relevant. For example, frequently changing from open to closed teaching styles ensures pupils remain focused and suitably challenged. Teach high quality and safe examples first to ensure pupils understand how to progress their physical movements from floor to apparatus, before allowing them to explore their own variations. But ultimately the aim should be for pupils to have the opportunity to experience as many ideas as possible.

Trio work using combined apparatus suitable for Key Stage 3

Following floor work and work on benches, this is an example of a logical progression of material to span a block of work, for example six to eight lessons.

1. Teach pupils how to take their weight on their hands, where their lower body is partially supported by the apparatus. Depending on their individual skill level, pupils will take more or less of their own weight on their hands (inversion).
2. Further teach one of the following: the front support, one-knee balance, press up position (horizontal). Then: arabesque, V sit, long sit (vertical).
3. Teach pupils how to move from one balance to the next, changing their relationship with the apparatus each time. For example, pupils kick up to bear weight on their hands, leaning legs or feet against the apparatus. Then they come down and roll back to a shoulder stand with one foot pushing against apparatus, push away over one shoulder and stand, then jump into front support (for example, resting hips on a box or Swedish beam), forward roll down and away.
4. Pupils further explore other ways of balancing on apparatus where they are inverted, horizontal or vertical.
5. Pupils in their trios now explore joining two actions together that embrace the natural impetus and flow with economy and fluency.
6. Repeat the above cycle with rotation and flight actions. In this way the sequence can gradually lengthen and the teacher can include non-contact skills such as matching, mirroring, unison and canon, different levels (low, medium, high), and so on.
7. Teach two contrasting ideas for using or assisting each other to get on or off apparatus through passive or brief contact, e.g. stepping on to thighs, hips, and so on.
8. Teach two contrasting ideas in which pupils actively assist each other, e.g. pulling, lifting, swinging, lifting and lowering each other onto or off apparatus. Allow the class to then explore their own ideas.
9. Teach specific examples of counter balance/counter tension using apparatus: sometimes where all three pupils are completely supported or partially supported or a mixture of both. Allow the class to then explore their own ideas.
10. Using ideas created in (7) and (8), pupils explore getting onto apparatus to form counter balance/tension activities and then assist each other off apparatus.
11. Teach pupils a range of total weight-bearing activities (see next section on sports acrobatic balances). Repeat tasks as for counter balance/tension work.

When you allow pupils to experiment with their own ideas, select good examples from pupils to be demonstrated and then performed by the whole class, thus widening pupils' experiences. Sequences should be constructed after each of the above tasks so that pupils gradually build up longer sequences containing all the categories of pair and trio work, in preparation for an end-of-course assessment.

Using different gymnastic-based activities to cater for the goals and aims of the NCPE (2008)

The previous sections of this chapter have focused specifically on the teaching of educational gymnastics, but with the introduction of the revised curriculum (NCPE 2008) and the greater flexibility that this is now offering, gymnastics could hold an important position in the development of a creative and vibrant physical education curriculum.

Gymnastics, as a metaphorical umbrella, shelters a collection of activities that provides the teacher with a wealth of choice and numerous teaching possibilities. Artistic, rhythmic, compositional/educational, sports acrobatics, cheerleading, trampoline, team gymnastics, aerobics, freestyle gymnastics, modified pupil-friendly Parkour or free running, can all be categorized under the title of gymnastics and can provide for a variety of different and new activities to be taught within schools. This vast assortment can provide learning opportunities for every pupil, allowing for a range of teaching styles to be adopted and an array of learning styles to be catered for. Furthermore, this multiplicity allows for breadth and balance, and the personalisation of the curriculum, a common theme imbedded within the NCPE.

Modified pupil-friendly Parkour, or free running

The sudden growth in activities associated within the discipline known as Parkour has not failed to grasp the imagination and curiosity of today's youth. It has been introduced to us through a variety of different media forms, ranging from the dramatic chase scene at the start of a recent James Bond movie, to documentaries exploring seemingly impossible pathways over numerous architectural landmarks. But there is still much confusion over the differences between the various forms and the key characteristics that separate one from another. There is shared opinion that Parkour and free running offer contrasting philosophies. The former is concerned with creating fluent and efficient pathways, enabling the performer to travel over, on, under or around objects with the minimum of ease. The latter shares similar qualities but offers a more 'free' approach, often including movements that are not essential for the overcoming of obstacles and are associated with more acrobatic movements. However, both were founded in the exploration of travel, movement, balance, flight and rotation and so inevitably the association with gymnastics has occurred. Therefore, the question of whether schools should choose to embrace these activities is one that requires much thought and considerations. (Please consult Association for Physical Education (AfPE) for further guidance.)

A case for the inclusion of modified pupil-friendly Parkour-related activities

The very nature of overcoming obstacles and exploring a variety of possible actions and pathways links Parkour implicitly with the range and content of 'Identifying and solving problems to overcome challenges of an adventurous nature'. Furthermore, embedded within the philosophy of Parkour is the removal of competition and the right to find one's own way. Even though there are recognised basic movements within the discipline, creative improvisation and expression is encouraged. These fewer predefined movements, compared to the often rigid formality of gymnastics, can counteract the fear of failure, a notion that numerous pupils feel when unable to complete complex gymnastic skills. The idea of no set rules or correct technique means that pupils simply cannot fail. The notion of efficiency also has dramatic implications concerning health and safety. Central to Parkour's philosophies is the avoidance of injuries and minimising of risks. If the drop is too big, the gap is too wide or the ledge is too narrow, the right course of action is to find another way. Sharing and respecting the space, recognition of creativity and aesthetic qualities through critical evaluation and even cutting youth crime (Johnson and Wroe 2009) are some of the admirable qualities that Parkour can offer.

There are movements within British gymnastics to respond to the discipline with the introduction of 'freestyle' gymnastics, which offers many similarities to Parkour.

Accredited qualifications in Parkour are becoming available through selected sources, maybe for possible future accreditation, maybe for government approval or maybe for a position within a school curriculum? Such questions remain unanswered. Positioning Parkour within an educational context may not be easy and some significant modifications would have to be made to aspects of lesson content to ensure safe practice, but failing to embrace its numerous qualities and characteristics, when so many of today's youth are already practising the discipline, could mean we are potentially missing a valuable learning opportunity.

So where to now?

It is not suggested that Parkour-related activities replace gymnastics-based activities, in fact, quite the opposite. Parkour and gymnastics share many common themes, and with the introduction of the revised curriculum, a synthesis of approaches may lead to a more personalised and vibrant curriculum. Here are some examples of how to introduce pupil-friendly Parkour-related ideas and movements.

1. *Start* with an introduction to Parkour. Explain what it is all about, highlighting the key aims of the activity and the key safety principles. Simply play some video footage of any Parkour or free running and the pupil's imagination will start to run.
2. *Safe landing* – A key focus must be placed on correct landing and exiting via rolling, continuing the motion forward. Try not to encourage too much 'drop' and 'stop'. This places pressures on the joints. Introduce jumping from varying heights and jumping across varying distances, with correct landing and correct continuation of movement and momentum. Link two jumps together, then three, until a small sequence of varying jumps and landings has been created. Precision jumping can also be explored, jumping from one specific place to another, usually taking off and landing on smaller surface areas.
3. *Balance* – Explore balancing across a number of objects of varying surface areas, e.g. walking along benches, upturned benches, beams and Swedish beams at varying heights.
4. *Explore* how pupils travel when balancing: on two feet, on all fours, alternating feet.
5. *Vaults* – Place obstacles around a gym and encourage pupils to find different methods to overcome them. Key words to explore are: on, off, over, through, around, under. Differentiation is very straightforward: use higher or lower boxes, benches set up normally or upside down, beams high or low, reduced or increased gaps between equipment. You could let the pupils decide these variations to encourage autonomy of learning.
6. *Indoor circuit* – Create varying indoor circuits for pupils to try their newly learnt skills. Pupils can run individually or in pairs, having their own space or sharing it with others.
7. Plan a possible *outdoor* Parkour session, using the schools grounds or the local community. (It is essential to discuss any outdoor Parkour-related activities with the school and the local LEA for their guidelines on such activities.)

Conclusion

In this chapter we have aimed to re-focus thoughts onto the importance of gymnastic-based activities within a vibrant, diverse and balanced physical education curriculum; and to re-address the importance of gymnastics as a major contributor to the development of fundamental movement skills. The importance of developing physically literate pupils cannot be overestimated and the contribution gymnastics can make to this is bettered by no other subject within the curriculum.

We have also shared insights into how aspects of the NCPE (2008) 'range and content' requirements can potentially be delivered through gymnastic activities. The chapter is not intended to be all-inclusive, but more to provide 'food for thought' on the key aims and purposes of gymnastics and how to practically deliver them in schools. We also hope that less experienced teachers of gymnastics will feel more confident and empowered to teach gymnastics and recognise the important contribution gymnastics has to offer to a broad and balanced physical education curriculum.

Finally, with the arrival of the revised curriculum comes increased choice and greater flexibility. Gymnastics offers a whole host of activities that the physical education teacher can use and we hope that this chapter may have just started the ball rolling.

References

AfPE (2008) *Safe Practice in Physical Education and School Sport*, Leeds: Coachwise.

BAALPE (1988) *Gymnastics in the Secondary Schools Curriculum*, Leeds: White Line Press.

Benn, T. and Benn, B. (2000) 'The debate re-opened: teaching gymnastic skills', *BJPE*, Spring.

Casbon, C. and Spackman, L. (2007) *Assessment for Learning in Physical Education*, BAALPE: Coachwise Solutions, University College, Worcester.

Cooper, P.S. and Trnka, M. (1994) *Teaching Basic Gymnastics: A coeducational approach*, New York: Macmillan.

DCSF (2008) *School Sport Survey 2007/2008*, available from http://www.teachernet.gov.uk/_doc/13010/DCSF-RW063.pdf (accessed 10 January 2009).

Johnson, A. and Wroe, S. (2009) *Free running could be taught in secondary school*, available from http://www.independent.co.uk/news/education/education-news/free-running-could-be-taught-in-secondary-schools-1515326.html (accessed 25 January 2009).

Lathrop, A. and Drake, V. (1998) 'Assessment and evaluation procedures in educational gymnastics', *Canadian Association of Health, Physical Education, and Recreation Journal*, 48(6), 9–12.

Mace, R. and Benn, B. (1982) *Gymnastic Skills*, London: Batsford Educational.

Maude, P. and Whitehead, M. (2006) *Observing and Analysing Learners' Movement*, Worcester: Tacklesport (consultancy) Ltd.

Maude, P., Benn, B. and Benn, T. (2007) *A Practical Guide to Teaching Gymnastics*, Leeds: Coachwise Ltd (AfPE).

Mitchell, D., Lopez, R. and Davie, B. (2007) *Teaching FUNdamental Gymnastics Skills*, Leeds: Human Kinetics.

Mori (2002) Young People in Sport, Trends in Participation, available from http://www.sport england.org/young-people-and-sport-2002-report.pdf (accessed 6 January 2009).

Qualifications and Curriculum Authority (2008) *Physical Education: The National Curriculum for England*, London: QCA.

Sabin, V. (2004) *School Gymnastics Key Stages 3 and 4*, Northampton: Val Sabin Publications.

Werner, P. (2004) *Teaching Pupils Gymnastics* (2nd edn), Champaign, IL: Human Kinetics.

Williams, A. (1997) *Curriculum Gymnastics*, London: Hodder and Stoughton.

6 Learning and teaching through dance

Lucy Pocknell and Fiona Smith

> Even very young children understand the power of dance to express what we think and how we feel. Studies have shown that dance can make a huge difference to a child's overall performance in school, as well as developing skills to help them communicate better, analyse further and imagine more.
>
> (Arts Council *et al.* 2006: 6)

Introduction

In order to gain the greatest value from this chapter we suggest that you read it in conjunction with the National Curriculum guidelines for Key Stage 2 and Key Stage 3 physical education. Our purpose here is to identify the distinct contribution that dance makes to the curriculum, consider how the inclusion of dance plays a central role in meeting the aims of the national curriculum and provide practical examples of dance content for use in the classroom.

We examine and interpret the National Curriculum 2008 Programme of Study for physical education from a dance perspective, offering teachers a way to locate dance within the curriculum framework and to make explicit the links between key concepts and processes and the delivery of dance. We discuss the interrelated strands of performing, composing, and appreciating dance as an art form in order to promote the artistic, physical, social and cultural development of the pupil. Some teachers have expressed concern and anxiety about their ability to plan and deliver dance, so we address issues such as the centrality of the body and the lack of teacher knowledge and expertise.

The chapter concludes with three contrasting practical examples suitable for Key Stages 2 and 3 transition. The examples are intended to both provide content for immediate use, as well as illustrate a manageable process which teachers can use as a 'blueprint' for their own future ideas. Finally, reference is made to a selection of key resources, including links to associations that support continual professional development in dance.

Curriculum aims

What is it that we are trying to achieve when we teach dance? The answer to this, ultimately, has to be to meet the broader aims of the national curriculum, that is to contribute to all young pupils becoming:

- successful learners who enjoy learning, make progress and achieve
- confident individuals who are able to live safe, healthy and fulfilling lives
- responsible citizens who make a positive contribution through society.

(QCA 2008: 189)

Learning within dance is twofold; it provides both intrinsic and extrinsic benefits to pupils. The intrinsic, learning *in* dance, is concerned with the implicit value of learning to dance and about dance. For example, gaining knowledge, skill and understanding of dance techniques, choreographers and different dance styles. The extrinsic, learning *through* dance, is concerned with the transferable knowledge, skills and understanding learnt whilst studying dance. In this sense, dance is the vehicle through which learning takes place. For example, when creating group dances pupils understand how they learn from their mistakes and form good working relationships with others.

The importance of dance within physical education

The importance of physical education is outlined within its Programme of Study. Key features of this statement include reference to developing confidence and competence within a range of physical activities, an awareness of the need for a healthy, active lifestyle, opportunity to experience a variety of roles and responsibilities and the development of personal and social skills. Dance is well placed to make both a shared and distinctive contribution towards achieving these goals. Key to this contribution are the possibilities dance offers for an integrated learning experience.

> Due to its physical nature, dance provides a means of expression and communication distinct from other art forms and because of its expressive and creative nature it stands apart from other physical activities.
>
> (NDTA 2004: 4)

If a subject is to be given time within an already crowded curriculum it must have a significant and distinctive contribution to make. If dance offers the same learning experience as a number of other physical activities, its place is at least questionable and at worst redundant. The claim here is that dance, due to its multi-dimensional nature, is perfectly positioned to take a place at the centre of today's curriculum.

At its heart, dance is by its very nature a diverse and inclusive subject, uniquely positioned within the curriculum. It is situated mostly within physical education, yet contributes to pupils' artistic as well as physical development. Rather than seeing this positioning as problematic, we should embrace and exploit it. The opportunities to make links with other subjects and adopt a cross-curricular/thematic learning approach are endless: concepts increasingly used in many schools. For example, using paintings, poems, historic and cultural events or social issues as a starting point for dance provide an opportunity for deeper learning. As pupils learn they make connections between the concepts studied and their attempt to make physical representations of them.

A high quality dance education provides opportunities for learning across the curriculum and meeting current government initiatives. For example, tackling the increase in childhood obesity, addressing issues of social inclusion and promoting participation in cultural activity. The development of functional skills, such as literacy, is embedded within dance teaching. For example, a typical appreciation task in which a pupil is asked to describe and analyse what they have seen in a dance viewed, requires a rich and varied use of language.

Effective planning in dance provides an exciting range of opportunities to develop Personal Learning and Thinking Skills (PLTS), for example the development of creative thinking and team working. In dance pupils are encouraged to generate their own ideas in response to given stimuli and to experiment confidently with a range of creative approaches in order to communicate the dance idea. Working collaboratively with a group is a common scenario in dance. Creating a small group dance requires considerable skill in listening, communicating ideas, negotiating, and a sense of shared responsibility and effort towards a common goal.

When dancing, pupils develop a sense of physicality and mastery of the body with the intention of communicating ideas, moods and emotions. This artistic use of the body sets dance aside from other physical education activities. Whilst there are shared aspects and links with gymnastics and fitness, the potential of dance to consider aspects of human concern, mood and emotion are its justification for inclusion. Through dance pupils extend their movement vocabulary, build confidence and competence in the management of their body and develop a range of technical and expressive skills in relation to different styles of dancing.

When choreographing, pupils explore, select, develop and structure dance material inspired by particular themes. They use simple choreographic strategies to extend and structure their ideas. Through this process they are encouraged to use their imagination, challenged to take risks and guided to work alone and with others collaboratively.

When appreciating, pupils observe, describe, analyse, interpret and evaluate their own and others' dances, including the work of professional artists on video. They are guided to identify key features of dances using appropriate terminology, encouraged to finds the link between the movement and the choreographic intention and prompted to make objective critical judgements about the quality and effectiveness of work observed. Through this process pupils develop the skill to articulate their own personal responses and develop an awareness of the historic and cultural context of dance.

Key concepts

Competence, performance, creativity, healthy and active lifestyles: these are inherent in the broad knowledge and understanding (the big ideas) that underpin learning in dance throughout the key stage. For example, creativity is held up as a key concept. The ability to make unexpected connections, create original phrases of movement, bring an individual interpretation to an idea and approach tasks in a range of ways are all essential in allowing pupils to progress to higher levels of understanding.

Key processes

Interpreting and understanding the key processes requires recognition of the fact that attention must be paid to the process and product of learning.

Developing skills in physical activity

Pupils must be taught and need to understand what it means to *refine, adapt and develop* a skill. Once acquired, this understanding can be applied to the development of skills within any physical activity. Pupils need to know and understand how they progress and improve, along with how to attempt more challenging and sophisticated skills. Making the learning process explicit, by spending time to identify and reflect on how progress is made or hindered is an investment towards independent learning and continued progress.

The implications of this for teachers are that in addition to providing teaching points about an activity-specific skill, they should provide information and questions designed to focus pupils' attention on the learning of the key process. Pupils cannot, however, attend to process only; this would not make sense or be motivating. It is the activity which engages the pupils.

In practice, in the context of dance, the teacher may simultaneously be working to develop pupils' technical and expressive skills, as well as their understanding of the importance of repetition, perseverance, focused practice, guided observation or reflective discussions of their own or peers' practice, performance, and post-performance opinions.

Technical and expressive skills in dance include:

- correct posture – for example, extended straight spine when standing, sitting or kneeling;
- clarity of body shape – for example, extension of the limbs when making stretched, curled, twisted and arched shapes;
- coordination – for example, using opposite arm and leg when stepping;
- flexibility and mobility – for example, range of movement in the joints and flexibility of the muscles;
- sense of fluency – for example, smooth transitions between movements;
- spatial awareness – for example, precision in directional facing, sensitivity to other dancers in a shared space;
- control and precision in basic body actions – for example, jumping, turning, gesturing, balancing, travelling;
- clarity of dynamics – for example, contrasting qualities of movement such as strong, fast, sharp, or soft, gentle and smooth;
- clear focus – for example, knowing where to look when performing;
- musicality – for example, performing in time with the music, with a sense of rhythm and phrasing;
- expression and characterisation – for example, portrayal of different moods and emotions, appropriate use of facial expressions and dramatic skills;
- control and sensitivity when working with other dancers – for example, safe and precise leaning, lifting and supporting of other dancers;
- movement memory – for example, ability to remember an extended phrase.

These are generic skills which apply to all dance styles. It is important that pupils experience learning these skills through a range of dances which portray various moods, concepts and emotions. Pupils should also have the opportunity to experience a range of dance styles popular in today's culture, such as Contemporary, Street and African- and Asian-based genres. Once pupils have mastered the fundamentals of a skill such as jumping (how to take off and land safely and show clarity of shape during flight), the skill can be adapted and stylised for different dance forms. For example, the quick rhythmic jumping associated with a street dance style is in contrast to the grand leaps in a more classical dance style. These skills will help significantly in the development of a physically literate pupil as identified earlier in Chapter 1.

Making and applying decisions

Pupils must learn what it means to *make and apply decisions*. Once acquired, this understanding can be applied to making and applying decisions in any physical activity.

As a transferable skill the confidence and ability to make and apply decisions is applicable to any learning context. In essence, the learning here is related to the making of correct (most effective or appropriate) choices. This involves the ability to select and reject ideas based on their effectiveness or suitability. This requires the knowledge, information and skills of judgement to make an informed choice and then apply the decision or action in practice.

If dance is to be the context for learning how to make and apply decisions, before deciding what pupils must be taught it is necessary to consider the use of key terminology within this section of the National Curriculum. Some of the language used does not fit comfortably within the dance context. For example, words such as 'strategies' and 'tactics' are rarely heard in the dance studio. Within the context of dance the key process of *making and applying decisions* refers to developing pupils' knowledge and understanding of the choreographic process, that is, the making and applying of decisions associated with creating and developing their own dances.

Reference is made in the National Curriculum to the notion of *effectiveness in performance*; within dance this is closely linked with the notion of appropriateness. For a dance to be effective it must successfully communicate the choreographic intention. Much of this will be dependent on the choice of appropriate movement content and use of choreographic devices that help communicate the dance idea. In the process of creating a dance pupils will continually make choices about action, spatial, dynamic and relationship content. For example, in a duet based on the idea of conflict and resolution, pupils will have to make a series of appropriate choices in relation to:

- Actions – what gestures, jumps and turns would best communicate the idea of an argument in progress?
- Space – where should the dancers stand in relation to one another? Would facing one another have the most powerful impact?
- Dynamic – how should the gestures, jumps and turns be performed? Would a strong, firm and forceful quality of movement best portray the anger and rage of an argument?
- Relationship – should the dancers move together in unison or one at a time? Would taking turns in a question and answer manner best portray the constantly changing interactions of a 'heated discussion'?

Choreographic knowledge and skill in dance includes the ability to:

- create movement that relates to a dance idea in an appropriate style – for example, being able to 'make-up' movement that correlates to a given theme and is in an appropriate style;
- explore and develop motifs – for example, being able to extend, change and adapt the action, spatial, dynamic and relationship features of selected movements;
- use contrasting dynamics relevant to the dance idea – for example, knowing when movements should be fast as opposed to slow, strong as opposed to soft, or fluid as opposed to interrupted;
- make effective use of group designs and numerical variations – for example, knowing that different group formations such as lines, blocks, numbers of dancers, have different expressive connotations;
- evoke mood and emotion – for example, knowing that the appropriate selection of actions, dynamics, group design and development of materials combine to portray a particular 'feel and atmosphere'.

Developing physical and mental capacity

Pupils must learn how to develop their own physical and mental attributes; they need to develop self-awareness with regard to their own level of strength, stamina, speed and flexibility and their own level of mental determination. They also need to be clear about the process of how and why they do this and how these skills are transferable to other areas of learning. For example, that being an individual who is confident enough to tackle new challenges and persevere in order to succeed are valuable, sought after employment skills.

Whilst the significance of physical health is well recognised, less attention is typically paid to the area of developing mental attributes. Learning in this area is sometimes taken for granted. For example, in relation to *determination to face up to challenges and keep going* the quality of perseverance and 'stickability' is rarely discussed, yet there is considerable value in helping pupils realise what it means in practice to persevere. Pupils should be taught the value of perseverance and encouraged to keep trying to find a solution to a problem; to refine a skill, giving attention to detail and quality; to work through periods of doubt; and to value achievement born out of hard work.

A group of pupils who have created a dance together will have learnt something about the process of *expressing and dealing with their emotions*. If time is taken to discuss and reflect upon the process of working together, the value of the learning experience will be greatly enhanced. Pupils could be asked to consider how they felt about the effort and contribution of each dancer in the group. Had everyone in the group tried their best? Were people open-minded and willing to try new ideas? How did dancers feel when they made mistakes?

Open-mindedness in dance often refers to embracing new movements, music and dance styles, for example those which go beyond popular culture. Also, being prepared to accept that there are often numerous interpretations to a stimulus and that experimentation is an essential prerequisite of the arts.

Making informed choices about healthy, active lifestyles

It would seem inappropriate to analyse learning related to this key process as a discrete activity. The notion of making 'good decisions' in relation to one's health and activity level should permeate and underpin the entire philosophy and practice in physical education lessons regardless of activity. As we identified at the start of this chapter, dance makes a unique contribution towards meeting the aims of the National Curriculum. Studying dance also provides the opportunity to reinforce the link between activity levels and health and for pupils to see if dance is an activity they wish to pursue outside school.

Evaluating and improving

Pupils must be taught and need to understand what it means to evaluate and improve their own and others' work. As a process this is relatively self-explanatory. Pupils learn to identify and describe, analyse, interpret, evaluate and give and receive feedback. The generic skills underpinning this process include learning the value of critical evaluation, the significance of subject-specific terminology, how to look and what to look for, and the etiquette of criticism.

Two concepts omitted from the National Curriculum, but essential within the context of dance, are the notions of appreciation and interpretation. Whilst the concept of evaluation implies making a value statement, within dance it is not always about judging or improving. On occasions we want to know how pupils respond emotionally to what they have seen, or what they believe certain movements represent. For example, pupils may be asked to explain how watching a dance made them feel, asked to interpret the emotions that a particular character is portraying, asked to compare two dances on a similar theme, or asked to justify the choice of movements in relation to the choreographic intention.

In addition to the generic skills identified, in order to facilitate the development of pupils' specific skills in relation to evaluating and appreciating dance a certain knowledge base is required. This is essential to help pupils get beyond simply describing what they see and what they like towards a more objective and critical response.

The knowledge and skills required for effective evaluation and appreciation are:

- basic information about dance technique being learned – for example, key stylistic features;
- basic information about dance composition – for example, basic choreographic devices such as canon, unison, group design and motif development;
- dance-specific terminology – for example, dynamics, relationships, stimulus and duet;
- basic information about a professional work/choreographer being viewed – for example, name, theme, key characteristics, historic or cultural context;
- basic information about different dance styles – for example, country of origin, purpose of dance.

Range and content

When considering the overall programme of physical education that a pupil should receive, teachers need to make choices ultimately based on the intention of the activity and how success in the activity is judged. Thought should be given to how a combination of complementary and contrasting activities contribute to a broad and balanced curriculum such as is alluded to in Chapter 1. We feel that dance is an essential part of a broad and balanced curriculum and that the nature of dance means it provides significant opportunities to contribute to the general physical literacy of a pupil along with a number of other educational benefits. For example, when pupils are dancing they naturally explore and communicate ideas, concepts and emotions. The ability to do this is an integral part of the activity. How well a dancer succeeds in expressing the choreographic intention is the measure of success. When they dance pupils learn sequences of movement from their teacher that require them to accurately replicate the given content; how close they get to the 'model' is the measure of success. The concepts of exercising safely and effectively along with notions of health and wellbeing permeate participation in dance. The inclusion of dance in the curriculum therefore is integral to a broad and balanced physical education experience for pupils.

Curriculum opportunities in dance

Integral to learning in dance and to enhance pupil engagement with the key concepts and processes, pupils should be provided with opportunities to:

- get involved in a range of dance styles – for example, experience contemporary, street, latin and bhangra dance styles;

- experience a range of roles – for example, performer, choreographer, audience member;
- specialise in specific activities and roles – for example, take a leading role in performance or choreography;
- follow pathways in and beyond school – for example, join the school dance club, a local youth dance company or a private dance school;
- perform as an individual or as part of a group in formal performance settings beyond the classroom – for example, perform as part of a school assembly, at a school celebration event, or as part of a local arts festival;
- use ICT as an aid to improving performance and tracking progress – for example, use video analysis to critique ongoing performance and choreographic work, or observe and analyse professional dance works on video;
- make links between dance and other areas of the curriculum – for example, learn about a shared topic in Dance and History simultaneously and recognise links between the processes of art making in different artistic disciplines.

Attainment target

It is worth remembering that learning in dance is one of a number of activities that, when combined, will contribute to the overall profile and level awarded to the pupil. When you are planning to assess in dance, it is helpful to extract key verbs from the level descriptions which relate to the processes of performance, composition and appreciation. This will ensure that your lesson objectives make reference to the knowledge, skills and understanding inherent within the attainment target. For example, objectives and lesson content based on key verbs such as 'perform', 'improve', 'lead' and 'refine' will ensure that learning related to performance is well focused. Similarly, objectives and lesson content based on key verbs such as 'select', 'combine' and 'apply' along with 'compare', 'explain' and 'describe', ensure worthwhile learning related to composition and appreciation.

Issues facing non-specialists

One of the main barriers of access to dance for pupils is some teachers' lack of subject knowledge, which lowers their confidence and reduces their desire to teach it. For many primary teachers and secondary teachers, especially those trained through a PGCE route, the opportunity to study dance pedagogy during initial teacher training is restricted to a small proportion of the 6–9 hours allocated to physical education (Ofsted 2009). Access to and availability of continual professional development opportunities in dance are also limited and not seen as a priority amongst competing curriculum demands.

Central to teaching dance is a focus on the body. The body is the instrument of expression and communication and it is this fact that often makes the inexperienced teacher feel exposed, vulnerable and uncomfortable. Many teachers feel they cannot dance, therefore cannot teach dance. There is no denying that being able to model aspects of dance content is a desirable skill; it is not, however, essential for a successful dance lesson. There are many strategies that you can adopt to support learning which do not require you to physically demonstrate. For example, using a video of a professional dance company, photographs or work cards will provide pupils with an image of movement to replicate or use as inspiration to create their own vocabulary. As with all teaching, an engaging manner, enthusiasm and the knowledge of how to structure and facilitate learning is key to a worthwhile experience. The following statements reflect typical comments that we have frequently heard when working alongside inexperienced dance teachers. They also highlight that pupil perceptions and feeling are not necessarily the same as the teacher's.

> I couldn't believe what the pupils came up with.
> I was amazed how receptive the pupils were.
> I could think of hardly any ideas but the pupils came up with loads!
> They just seem to love dancing.

Guidance and teaching ideas for working with cluster schools

Introduction to dance ideas

The three practical examples of dance content which follow illustrate how cross-curricular links can be made and an integrated learning approach adopted to suit work at both Key Stage 2 and Key Stage 3. Teachers can adapt these ideas to match the attainment levels associated with Key Stages 2 and 3. In an ideal scenario, pupils would simultaneously be learning about the same theme in a number of subject areas alongside dance. For example, in relation to dance idea 1 (Box 6.1), which focuses on the work of the painter L.S. Lowry, pupils could be studying his work from a number of perspectives in history, art and dance lessons. In this way, the benefits of an integrated learning approach are fully realised and pupils are provided with a 'deep and joined up' learning experience. For each idea that follows we identify the potential cross-curricular links, suggest resources, give hints for getting started, offer ideas for development and identify key words.

Inherent in the learning experience across the three ideas should be opportunity to talk about the work in progress. At various stages of the process, pupils can be asked to describe what they have done, explain their choices and make suggestions for improvement to their own and others' work. Pupils should also be encouraged to share their thoughts and feelings about aspects of the paintings, professional dance work and its historical context in relation to their own work.

Box 6.1   Dance idea 1: Lowry

The content draws on paintings by L.S. Lowry and *A Simple Man* (1987), a professional dance inspired by the life and works of L.S. Lowry, choreographed by Gillian Lynne.

Cross-curricular links: Art and History

This idea provides numerous opportunities to combine learning in Dance with Art and History. Through the study of Lowry's paintings and analysis of key extracts from the ballet *A Simple Man* and related historical information, pupils will gain knowledge and understanding of working-class life in industrial England during the 1930s and 1940s. By viewing a professional dance work pupils will also gain insight into the technical and choreographic skills of the professional world. They will develop awareness of how art can communicate feelings and experiences and document aspects of history.

Resources

- DVD: *A Simple Man* choreographed by Gillian Lynne. Available from www.dancebooks.co.uk or www.amazon.co.uk or large music stores.
- Music: *A Simple Man* composed by Carl Davis (1990). Available from www.amazon.co.uk and other online retailers.
- A variety of industrial landscape images by Lowry, for example, *Going to Work* 1943, *Coming from the Mill* 1930, *An Industrial Town* 1944. Search Google images: Lowry paintings.
- For additional information to support the learning experience refer to relevant art and history text books.

Getting started

This dance will follow a simple narrative structure. The final dance will be in three sections: going to work, at work and coming home. Ideas are taken from Chapter 8 of the DVD: 'Industrial scene and postlogue'. The intention is for pupils to use extracts from the DVD as the inspiration for their own work.

1. Show a selection of Lowry's industrial landscape pictures, discuss key images and focus on narrative aspects of the painting.
   - Ask pupils to describe the scene that they see, for example, in the painting *An Industrial Town* 1944. Responses might include: *busy, lots of different activities, people look the same.*
   - Compare the size of the people to the buildings; what might this suggest? For example, buildings dominate the picture and make the people look small and insignificant.
2. Show part of the DVD: an extract from the opening of Chapter 8, 'Industrial scene and postlogue'. Discuss how the dance 'brings the painting to life'. For example, dancers become physical representations of the two dimensional images.
3. Share historical information about the artist and his work and any interesting facts about what it was like to live and work in industrial England during the 1930s and 1940s.
4. Teach directly yourself or guide pupils to copy (exactly or a simplified version) a range of basic travelling steps seen on the video. For example, rhythmic walking with hands in pockets and upper body leaning forward or side-stepping, dragging one leg in slowly to close, then rocking from foot to foot. Pupils will need at least four different travelling phrases which they can repeat with confidence.

   Attention should be paid to the detail of the movements, such as the strong arm positions and constant changes of direction. Effort should be made to link the purpose and intention of the movement with the imagery in Lowry's paintings. An example of this would be the intention to show the relentless drudgery of their harsh daily working life.

Ideas for development

1. The whole class re-watches the extract from Chapter 8, 'Industrial scene and postlogue'. The focus of the observation is on group formations, pathways and directions. In small groups, pupils list various pathways taken and formations made by the dancers. For example, they cross over, moving in between each other and travelling in large circular pathways. In order to create their 'going to work section', pupils put their travelling steps together, deciding the order, patterns they will make and directions they will travel. Section one should finish with all dancers travelling in the same direction, filing through an imaginary door (to the factory).

2. The whole class watches and describes the short extract within the section, where the men portray machines. Pupils are encouraged to list action words, describe the qualities of the actions identified and suggest how the men represent the machines. For example, they perform strong, rigid, pressing, pulling, levering actions. In small groups, pupils copy or create similar machine-like actions. To develop the idea further, pupils could explore the concept of action–reaction and basic physical contact, for example, how one action causes another action or how one dancer may initiate another's movement.

3. For the final section, 'going home', pupils will return to the stepping material used in section one, but will focus on slowing the movement down to show a sense of exhaustion. Pupils can also return to the DVD (towards the end of Chapter 8, where men and women travel together) to include additional movements from this extract, for example, moments when all the dancers perform reaching, stretching and arching actions. Pupils will then disperse, giving the suggestion that the workers are going their separate ways.

4. To conclude, pupils can create a still tableau image reconstructing a painting they have chosen.

As an extension task, pupils can study some of the individual characters from various paintings or alternative sections of the DVD. They can build their own short scenes which gives an insight into the character, focusing on how the character would move and interact with other dancers. These can then be integrated as short cameo scenes within the last section of the dance.

Key words
stimuli, inspiration, evoke mood, character, atmosphere, vigorous, dwarfing, dominating, gesture, rhythmic, pattern, spatial awareness, industrial, mechanical, effort, tension, force, chorus, two and three dimensions, unison, technique, choreographer, costume, pathway, formation, direction, action, reaction, tableau

Box 6.2 Dance idea 2: extreme landscapes

This sequence draws on content inspired by the Sahara Desert and Antarctica.

Cross-curricular links: Geography

This idea provides numerous opportunities to combine learning in Dance and Geography. Through the analysis of visual images, pupils can identify and discuss the unique physical characteristics of the contrasting landscapes. For example, they can discuss where it is, what it is like, how it came to be like that, then use their imagination to reflect on what it would feel like to be there. Also, they can consider the relationship between the people and places, for example how the physical landscape dictates their way of life and impacts on their routines. As a result, pupils create and perform symbolic movements which physically represent the mood, key aspects of the landscape and the life of the inhabitants.

Resources

- Pictures of the Sahara Desert and Antarctica. Images of these contrasting landscapes can be found in travel brochures, postcards, photographs, textbooks and calendars. Search Google images for: Sahara Desert, Sahara nomads, desert water carrying, Antarctica, icicles and Antarctic icebergs.
- Music for the desert: 'Nierika', 'Indus', 'The Snake and the Moon', 'Song of the Nile', on *Spiritcatcher* by Dead Can Dance (1987); 'Tokyo Kid' on *Revolutions* by Jean Michel Jarre (1988); 'Nirbandh', 'Tovareg', 'Mantra' on *North Africa and the Middle East: The World of Music* (1997).
- Music for Antarctica: 'Emperors', 'Sharks', 'Frozen Oceans', on *Blue Planet* by George Fenton (2006); 'Stalactite Gallery', 'Discovering Antarctica', on *Planet Earth* by George Fenton 2006.

Getting started

1. Show pictures, discuss main characteristics, and write key words (those that have the greatest potential for movement) on the board. Ask questions, for example: What are the first things you notice in the pictures? *Lots of sand! A line of camels, shadows.*
2. Identify aspects of contrast within the picture.
   - *shapes – undulating, gentle dips and curves of the dunes, straight, vertical trunk of the single palm tree;*
   - *light and shade – how the ripples are like stripes of light and dark, how the sun creates shadows and areas of light on the sand.*
3. If you were walking across the landscape in the picture how would you feel? *Hot, weary, aware of the sun on my back and my feet sinking into the sand.*
4. Teach directly yourself or guide pupils (or a combination of both) to create a phrase of movement based on key words derived from the class discussion of the visual images. For example, rise, fall, curve, zigzag, ripple, roll. The phrase

should include movements on the spot and travelling, use of the whole body and isolated body parts. You should also pay attention to encouraging pupils to evoke the mood and atmosphere suggested by the picture by focusing on the contrasting qualities of movement, such as different speeds and tensions.

Ideas for development

Ask the pupils to select from the following:

- Extend the phrase, perform it once, then repeat it, re-ordering the content.
- With a partner or in a small group, design a pathway to take dancers on a journey across the picture. Use the material from the phrase to take you from A to B. To make this more interesting visually, consider repeating some of the movements, making some of the actions bigger, smaller, faster or slower.
- With a partner or in a small group, explore the idea of shadows as seen in the pictures. Dancers copy one another, position themselves to recreate the shadow and explore how it shifts as the sun moves around throughout the day.
- To reflect the undulation of the landscape, with partners or in small groups dancers explore various time relationships between each other. For example, they perform phrases in succession (in canon like a Mexican wave) to create a rippling effect.

Once pupils have explored aspects of the physical landscape, the focus of development can then shift to the relationship between the landscape and the inhabitants. You can return to the pictures for further analysis and questioning, this time with a focus on aspects such as the daily life of the inhabitants, for example collecting water and preparation for cooking.

- In pairs or small groups, dancers create their own phrases of movement, including a range of working actions. For example, a phrase of movement based on water could include gestures that represent washing hands, wringing clothes, scooping water, carrying pots on heads. In order to make the move-ments less like mime, pupils should be encouraged to exaggerate the detail of actions, establish a sense of rhythm and phrasing.
- In pairs or small groups, dancers extend their phrase of movement by exploring how to perform working actions alone and with others. For example, share gathering of water from the well, carrying water individually, in single file.

The movement material from both sections can now be joined together to create a short dance. Pupils will need to decide a starting and finishing position and where necessary build a transition or link between sections. Time should be given for pupils to practise and refine their dances, paying particular attention to the detail of moving in time with their partner, responding to the music and to the clarity of the actions created.

Key words
Environment, landscape, terrain, panorama, sand dunes, undulating, rippling, treading, carrying, heavy, soft, smooth, snaking, imprint, harsh, jagged, sharp, frozen, rigid, crisp, cascade, slippery, symbolic, working actions, pathways,

dynamics, tension, dramatic, vast, pressing, rise and fall, swirl, inhabitants, tranquil, linear, curving.

Box 6.3   Dance idea 3: action, dynamic words and punctuation

Cross-curricular links: English

This idea provides numerous opportunities to combine learning in Dance and English. A wide range of action and dynamic words is used to create a dance vocabulary. Using the analogy of sentences, paragraphs and rules of punctuation as strategies for choreography, vocabulary is developed and extended. Pupils have the opportunity to revise the rules of punctuation and apply them in an unusual physical and creative way.

Resources

- Action/dynamic alphabet (see Table 6.1)
- Contact duet worksheet (this is available as a downloadable resource at (http://www.routledgeeducation.com/books/The-Really-Useful-Physical-Education-Book-isbn9780415498272).

Table 6.1 *Action and dynamic alphabet*

A   Attack, arch, agitate
B   Bounce, brush, barge
C   Crumple, crash, collide, collapse, calm, catapult, curl
D   Duck, dive, dodge, dash, drop, dart
E   Explode, erupt, elastic, envelop, elongate
F   Fidget, flick, fall, fast, frantic, fragment, flop
G   Gallop, glide, grip, grind
H   Hurry, hop, hover, hang, hustle
I   Invert, implode, impulse
J   Jog, jump, jolt, judder, juggle
K   Kick, knock, knead
L   Lunge, lie, lean, leap, lead
M   March, melt, manipulate
N   Nudge, nod, nip
O   Obstruct, open, oscillate
P   Punch, plant, press, pull, panic, plunge, point, pounce, pop, plummet
Q   Quiver, quickly
R   Run, ripple, rebound, ricochet, reach, rumble, rigid
S   Slide, spiral, slump, sway, shuffle, sink, spin, shake, shift, swing
T   Turn, twist, trip, topple, tug, touch, tip
U   Unwind, uncurl, upturn, undulate
V   Vibrate, vault, vigorously
W   Wave, wobble, walk, wriggle
X   !
Y   Yank, yo-yo, yawn
Z   Zigzag

- Music for action, dynamic words and punctuation: 'Bird Cage Walk', on *A–Z Geographers Guide to the Piano* by Jools Holland (2005); 'Chemical Beats', on *Singles 93–03* by Chemical Brothers (2004); 'An Eye for Optical Theory', on *The Draughtman's Contract* by Michael Nyman (2006); 'Scream machine', on *Human After All* by Daft Punk (2005).

Getting started

This dance will have two sections, following the structure of a short piece of writing with two paragraphs.

1. Using the action/dynamic alphabet provided (Table 6.1), or one that you compile with the pupils, discuss the concept of *action* and *dynamic* words within everyday usage and dance. Teach the meaning of the word *onomatopoeia*, then search for words within the alphabet that illustrate this, or example, 'splat' or 'judder'.
2. In pairs, use the first three letters of each pupil's name as the basis for selecting actions or dynamic words from the alphabet. Use these to create a short phrase of movement that combines the six letters. For example, DEB = dodge, explode, bounce and SAM= spin, arch, melt. There are rules for creating the phrase:
    - create more than one action for each word;
    - wherever the first word ends the next word starts (avoid going back to standing with both feet together in between each word).
4. Explain to the class how this phrase is similar to a sentence, but as it stands it lacks punctuation.

Ideas for development

Explain that the rules of punctuation will be used to further develop the phrase created.

- Capital letters – all sentences should start with a capital letter. Apply this rule to the beginning of the phrase by making the action bigger and bolder. For example, it could move off the spot, be repeated to emphasise it, go in to the air.
- Full stops – all sentences should end with a full stop. Apply this rule to the end of the phrase by making the last action bold, sudden and dramatic: showing a strong and definite ending to the movement. For example, the final turn in the phrase could stop abruptly, drop to the floor and then freeze.
- Commas – break up sentences that have more than one point and allow extra bits to be added. By yourself or with the pupils make a short phrase that will represent the comma, for example swing, drop, roll and reach. Pupils learn the comma phrase and then find two moments within their created phrase to add 'commas'. Each time the comma phrase is performed it should begin with a moment of pause to represent the inhalation of breath before the sentence continues.
- Speech marks – show when someone is speaking. Apply this rule by quoting from another pair. Pupils watch the pair and then select a section they would

like to learn to put in their own dance. Once pupils have decided where to place the quotation within their dance sentence, two identical jumps, added to the beginning and end of the quote will represent the speech marks.

Pupils will now create a second sentence:

1. Select four contrasting photographs to copy (examples of contrast include symmetrical/asymmetrical shapes, dancers' identical or different body shapes, use of small/large points of contact between dancers).
2. Practise and refine replicating the positions, paying attention to points of contact, body shape and focus between dancers.
3. Decide an order.
4. Work, with guidance, through one example transition from this list:
   - A pulls and turns B
   - Both dancers push away from one another, moving immediately into a turning action
   - A moves around, under then over B
   - B helps A to the floor then jumps over the top of A
   - Both dancers travel off the spot whilst staying in contact.
5. Create their own sentence, moving from position to position, building in transitions which are their own interpretation of the instructions.
6. Once pupils have their new sentence the rules of punctuation should be applied, for example, capital letter, full stop, commas, speech marks. The comma phrase will stay the same but may have moments of contact added.
7. Link sentence one and two together.

Key words
action, dynamic, punctuation, comma, full stop, capital letter, onomatopoeia, sudden, bold

References

Arts Council England, Dance UK and National Campaign for the Arts (2006) *Dance Manifesto,* London, Arts Council England. http://.danceuk.org/skins/danceik/downloads/manifesto.pdf (accessed 27 July 2009).

NDTA (2004) Maximising opportunity Policy Paper 2004, Burntwood, NDTA. http://www.ndta.org.uk/about-ndta (accessed 27 July 2009).

Ofsted (2009) 'Physical education in schools 2005/08: working towards 2012 and beyond', April, Reference number: 080249.

Qualifications and Curriculum Authority (QCA) (2008) *Physical Education Programme of Study Key Stage 3*, www.qca.org.uk/curriculum

Useful resources

Downloadable resources

Contact Duet Worksheet available at http://www.routledgeeducation.com/books/The-Really-Useful-Physical-Education-Book-isbn9780415498272

Additional reading

AfPE and NDTA (2007) *A Practical Guide to Teaching Dance*, Leeds, Coachwise.

Specialist supplier of dance books, videos, DVDs and CDs

Dance Books www.dancebooks.co.uk

Sources of information and/or continuing professional development for teachers

Association for Physical Education (AfPE)

AfPE is recognised as the national voice for physical education. It seeks to promote and develop high-quality physical education, inside and outside the curriculum. It provides services and resources to support members and the teaching profession.

Tel: 0118 378 6240 (general enquiries) or 01905 855 584 (CPD)
Email: enquiries@afpe.org.uk
Website: www.afpe.org.uk

National Dance Teachers Association (NDTA)

The NDTA is recognised as the national voice for dance education. It works to ensure that all young people in the UK have access to high-quality dance education in schools. It supports teachers at all key stages of the national curriculum, as well as at GCSE, AS and A Level, GNVQ and in initial teacher training.

Tel: 01543-308 618
Email: office@ndta.org.uk
Website: www.ndta.org.uk

National Resource Centre for Dance (NRCD)

The NRCD is a national archive and resource provider for dance. It aims to preserve the nation's dance heritage and to support and enhance the study and teaching of dance.

Tel: 01483-689 316
Email: nrcd@surrey.ac.uk
Website: www.surrey.ac.uk/NRCD

Youth Dance England (YDE)

YDE is the national agency to connect young people and dance. It seeks to raise the profile of youth dance and increase the number and quality of opportunities for young people, such as the National Youth Dance Festival.

Tel: 020 7924 7167
Email: info@yde.org.uk
Website: www.yde.org.uk

7 Learning and teaching through on-site outdoor and adventurous activities

Gary Stidder and Adrian Haasner

Introduction

The purpose of this chapter is to focus on the provision of on-site outdoor and adventurous activities, an area of physical education often marginalised within the curriculum.[1] Ofsted (2004: 1) have provided a working definition of what constitutes outdoor education and the opportunities that can be provided for pupils in schools, linked to aspects of the National Curriculum for Physical Education (NCPE).

> Outdoor education (OE) is a general term used to embrace different types of activity undertaken by primary and secondary students in a range of contexts: outdoor and residential visits; field work; outdoor and adventurous activities (OAA); outdoor pursuits; and 'outward bound' activities.
>
> (Ofsted 2004: 1)

Outdoor and adventurous activities taught on a school site are primarily associated with developing technical, intellectual and social skills and sharing decisions through direct experience of overcoming challenges, without the need to take pupils away from the school environment. The flexibility within the NCPE and teacher interpretations of it, however, have been shown to limit the experiences and opportunities for pupils to experience a range of outdoor and adventurous activities within physical education lessons (Stidder 2007). Secondary schools are not legally bound to teach outdoor and adventurous activities at Key Stages 3 and 4 and teaching at Key Stages 1 and 2 has been limited (Stidder 2006c). The report of Her Majesty's Chief Inspector of Schools (Ofsted 2005) suggested that over the period 1997–2005 outdoor and adventurous activities had diminished in importance in the physical education curriculum. Few pupils who had failed to meet the requirements at Key Stage 2, were given compensatory courses at Key Stage 3. It has been shown, therefore, that pupils continue to have fewer experiences of outdoor and adventurous activities in Years 6 and 7 compared with other NCPE activity areas (Zwozdiak-Myers 2004). Moreover, latest inspection evidence (Ofsted 2009) re-affirms the marginal position that outdoor and adventurous activities has within the physical education curriculum

> Although the schools visited met the minimum statutory requirements for the coverage of National Curriculum activity areas (at Key Stages 3 and 4), very few of them offered outdoor and adventurous activities or swimming as part of their curriculum programmes.
>
> (Ofsted 2009: 39)

Many of the reasons associated with the limited provision of on-site outdoor and adventurous activities in schools may be symptomatic of the many difficulties that schools have with respect to cost, expertise, facilities, time, and training. These significant factors have contributed to the limited number of schools which are able to include outdoor and adventurous activities, and often prevent school staff offering a broad, deep and balanced curriculum. In this respect, the manifesto for outdoor learning (DfES 2006: 7) has pledged support to improve training and professional development opportunities for schools and the wider workforce. This has been a result of previous recommendations that initial teacher education (ITE) courses should focus on the benefits of education outside of the classroom and enable teachers to develop their skills in this area.

Developing key processes through outdoor and adventurous activities

We want to draw attention to ways in which the key processes within the revised NCPE can be developed through outdoor and adventurous activities on a school site. The revised NCPE range of content states that:

> Teachers should draw upon key *concepts and processes* such as identifying and solving problems to overcome challenges of an adventurous nature, as in outdoor education.

> This includes activities in which success is judged on how efficiently and safely the challenges are overcome, such as orienteering and expeditions involving walking or using transport such as boats and canoes.
>
> (QCA 2007: 194)

This chapter will highlight ways in which outdoor and adventurous activities taught on a school site can be introduced in a safe and enjoyable way through a series of progressive lessons that aim to incorporate each of the key processes: developing skills, challenging pupils' physical and mental capacity, and providing opportunities for pupils to make and apply decisions. Each of these activities can enable pupils to evaluate and improve their own and others' performance and help them to make informed choices about healthy, active lifestyles. Likewise, these on-site outdoor and adventurous activities can help pupils to 'recognise hazards' and enable them to 'make decisions about how to control any risks to themselves and others' (QCA 2007: 191). In this context, we have provided examples of activities that can be based in the sports hall, gym, playground, school field or on a climbing wall which can be adapted and personalised to meet the specific needs of individual pupils.

Whilst we acknowledge that teachers may face a number of constraints in the provision of outdoor and adventurous activities, we believe that many of these can be overcome through the use of existing facilities and the immediate surroundings. The examples that we describe of activities within an outdoor and adventurous activities unit of work can be taught safely on-site and therefore address these concerns and anxieties (see Stidder 2006a; Stidder 2006b).

One of the key processes within the NCPE (2.3: 'Developing physical and mental capacities') states that pupils should be provided the opportunity to:

- develop their physical strength, stamina, speed and flexibility to cope with the demands of different activities;
- develop their mental determination to succeed.

Developing mental determination can include pupils developing essential skills and processes that enable them to learn to make progress:

- The confidence to have a go
- The determination to face up to challenges and keep going
- Expressing and dealing with emotions
- The desire to achieve success for oneself and others.

(QCA 2008: 192)

Listed below are key points which relate to the development of mental determination through outdoor and adventurous activities.

- To develop mental capacity and determination, pupils *must* be exposed to situations outside their comfort zones.
- Activities can be manipulated to mimic various situations that pupils may perceive as too difficult or potentially dangerous.
- By overcoming a problematic set of circumstances, pupils can develop their mental capacity; this in turn can foster pupil attitudes regarding their own physical and mental limits.
- Feelings of success, pride and self-respect all contribute to a pupil's overall learning and achievement.
- It is a physical education teacher's role to plan and put into action situations that can provide maximum mental development but with minimum risk.

A rationale for the inclusion of outdoor and adventurous activities

In terms of meeting the requirements of the NCPE (2008) and the *Every Child Matters* (ECM) agenda, these activities can be used to facilitate the development of both body and mind through providing opportunities for pupils to overcome fear, anxiety and physical stress. Teachers can provide opportunities to anticipate, take and manage risks and facilitate the setting of goals with success criteria for personal and peer development.

All the activities described in this chapter should be underpinned by health-related exercise and the promotion of citizenship and key skills. They can be organised within the confines of school grounds without the need to use off-site facilities. This can potentially be achieved either indoors or outdoors. Teachers can promote the development of cross-curricular teaching whereby pupils can improve their own learning and performance, improve their literacy and numeracy skills, and work with others to solve problems using communication skills. The activities can also develop wider concepts and skills that can be applied in other curriculum subjects such as mathematics, geography and science. In this context pupils can be encouraged to plan their own adventure activities and assess the types of problems they may encounter using numerical skills and map-reading techniques.

In Table 7.1 we outline some of the points you need to consider in respect to learning and teaching through on-site outdoor and adventurous activities and a rationale for the inclusion of particular activities through the use of a range of teaching strategies.

Table 7.1 *Learning and teaching through on-site outdoor and adventurous activities*

Activity	Skill
Navigational exercises	Skills related to map and compass work. Simple table/classroom plans. Using a map/compass in orienteering to complete a pre-determined course. Climbing activities designed to determine the most effective means of completing a pre-selected task.
Adventure challenges	Group problem-solving and decision-making. Personal and social development through team working. Appreciation of the environment.
Trust games	Feeling of co-operation and trust. Enhances ability to work together. Develops sense of responsibility. Respect for others.
Cross-curricular themes	Wider concepts and skills. Mathematics, geography, health-related exercise, science, art, information and communications technology, craft, design and technology. Pupils develop their own variations and develop original ideas. Pupils plan their own adventure activities.
Teaching strategies	Direct teaching through whole-class and small-group sessions. Opportunities for pupils to demonstrate practice and apply their learning on their own or with others with varying degrees of support; for pupils to solve problems using their imagination and be creative; for pupils to reflect on their own learning; for pupils to lead others in a variety of situations.

Curriculum planning for outdoor and adventurous activities at Key Stage 2

We recognise that teachers face a number of constraints when they are planning to provide outdoor and adventurous activities within the physical education curriculum at Key Stage 2. The provision of outdoor and adventurous activities is not necessarily a straightforward task. Shortage of equipment, lack of expertise and training, taking large groups, risk assessment, safety, poor facilities are just a few of the difficulties that may affect a teacher's decision-making (Stidder 2006c). We also acknowledge that one of the reasons why outdoor and adventurous activities are neglected within schools is the relative lack of expertise amongst primary school teachers. Initial teacher education does not give sufficient subject knowledge to trainees, which leads to the fear of litigation in the event of an accident (Ofsted 2004). We believe, therefore, that more must be done within ITE so teachers develop both confidence and competence in teaching outdoor and adventurous activities.

We have therefore provided examples of the types of activities that can be included at Key Stage 2. For example, navigational activities develop pupils' skills related to map and compass work. Simple table-top maps and classroom plans can help pupils to develop a theoretical understanding of how to use a map and compass which can then be applied in a practical setting. This can be achieved through adventure challenges and group problem-solving exercises either in the gym, sports hall, playground or playing field. Alternatively, a focus on personal and social development using basic indoor and outdoor activity-related skills can be achieved through a number of trust games which promote feelings of co-operation and trust, enhance pupils' ability to work together and develop a sense of responsibility. These two approaches underpin the TOP outdoor programme.

The TOP outdoor programme

TOP outdoors is specifically aimed at pupils in Key Stage 2 and includes a range of activities related to team work, co-operation, communication, planning, decision-making and independence. The programme consists of a progression of activities and there are a number of very useful resource cards that are easy to understand. All activities have been designed to take place within the confines of the school grounds and require minimal equipment. The activities focus on three broad areas: trails, physical challenges and orienteering.

Trails

The teacher sets out a simple string trail that begins and ends at a specific point. This can be as long or as short as you wish. Pupils are encouraged to negotiate certain obstacles, work in pairs, attempt to complete the course blindfolded with a sighted partner or complete with a partner connected by a wristband. This can also involve pupils in solving particular problems or answer clues as they complete the course.

Physical challenges

These activities are designed to help pupils work in pairs and groups and to develop trust through physically supporting each other. For example, during the 'Human Alphabet' pupils work together to make a letter using their bodies and then to make a word as a group. In 'All Aboard' pupils must attempt to get as many of their group as possible inside a hoop. In the 'Rope Run' a long rope swings slowly towards the class. Pupils have to run through the rope as it swings. Pupils then have to plan on achieving the task in pairs holding hands, then groups of three, four, five and six.

Orienteering

The orienteering activities have been designed to help pupils understand how to use a map in relation to the ground. The first map exercise helps pupils to orientate a map and can take place in a school hall or gymnasium. Pupils move their bodies around a simple map that has basic features drawn on it such as a bench, table and mat. One particularly good exercise is called 'Netball Numbers'. Teachers use a master map of a netball court that shows fourteen cones placed at strategic points and highlighted on the map. Four cones have a numerical value of one point, four cones are worth two points, four cones are worth three points and two cones are worth four points. Pupils have to complete one of six courses and calculate the total value of the cones they have visited. In 'Clock Relay', pupils complete a course using a map of the school grounds and visit each control point in numerical order (1–12, 12–1 and back to 1, etc.).

Curriculum planning for outdoor and adventurous activities at Key Stage 3

At Key Stage 3 the inclusion of outdoor and adventurous activities is a valuable addition to the existing national curriculum framework whereby core values such as trust, responsibility and respect can be integrated into a series of problem-solving and decision-making tasks. Outdoor and adventurous activities can provide opportunities for personal and social development through physical challenges in the outdoors, and this is particularly valuable when pupils from deeply divided social communities are able to experience a sense of teamwork (Stidder and Haasner 2007).

In the context of the school environment, the educational benefits of outdoor and adventurous activities can be achieved through an integrated approach to learning, decision-making and problem-solving. This can be organised and potentially achieved through trust games, team-building activities, problem-solving and decision-making scenarios, as well as through solo, paired and group orienteering over long and short courses that have permanent controls. Alternatively, maps, diagrams and photographs can be used for navigational purposes. Pupils can plan how to complete the course, hand in a copy to the teacher prior to departure, record the order they visit each control and record the time it has taken. Opportunities for evaluation and self-reflection can then be the focal point for team or group discussion. The British Orienteering Federation (BOF) have a very useful CD Rom resource which includes several orienteering exercises taught within the confines of enclosed, secure and safe areas such as the school grounds (see the resources list at the end of the chapter).

Basic orienteering can also be adapted for pupils with particular special educational needs. For example, Trail Orienteering (Trail O), sometimes called 'control choice' orienteering, is a form of orienteering in which the physically disabled can compete on equal terms with the able-bodied. It does not demand speed, strength or navigation but retains the crucial orienteering skill of relating the map to the ground in complex terrain.

Mountain bike orienteering is the most recent development of the sport, using trails and bridleways. It is important of course that pupils have been well briefed in advance regarding cycle safety. Climbing wall activities can also be used to develop skills and help pupils plan and implement what they need to practise in order to be more effective in their performance.

Assessing pupil learning through outdoor and adventurous activities

Teachers will need to decide whether formative or summative assessment should be used when assessing pupils learning in outdoor and adventurous activities. Assessment for learning or formative assessment would seem to lend itself more easily to outdoor and adventurous activities as it takes place during learning over the course of a sequence of lessons. It therefore helps to determine pupils' needs and can be used to inform future planning. Through formative assessment teachers are able to assess key processes over a period of time and allow for pupil absence.

The expected NCPE (2008) level of attainment for pupils by the end of Key Stages 2 and 3 is between levels 4 and 6. Pupils must be able to achieve certain criteria in order to achieve the expected level of attainment by the end of Key Stages 2 and 3. For example, by the end of Key Stage 2 pupils can achieve a level 4 by linking skills, techniques and ideas and applying them accurately and appropriately across a wide range of the activities highlighted earlier, showing precision, control and fluency. Outdoor and adventurous activities can enable pupils to compare and comment on skills, techniques and ideas used in their own and others' work, and use this understanding to improve their performance. In this context pupils can explain and apply basic safety principles in outdoor and adventurous activities when preparing for exercise. They can describe how exercise affects their bodies during outdoor and adventurous activities and why regular, safe activity is good for their health and wellbeing. Taking part in trails and orienteering exercises allows pupils to work with others, plan, and lead simple courses (QCA 2007: 196).

By the end of Key Stage 3 pupils can achieve a level 6 if they are able to select and combine skills, techniques and ideas and use them in a widening range of familiar and unfamiliar physical activities and contexts, performing with consistent precision, control and fluency. In this respect on-site activities such as orienteering or using a climbing wall can provide opportunities for pupils to use imaginative ways to solve problems and overcome challenges. When planning their own and others' work, and implementing it, pupils can draw on what they know about strategy and tactics in response to changing circumstances, and what they know about their own and others' strengths and weaknesses. In this context, pupils can analyse and comment on how skills, techniques and ideas have been used. Through activities such as orienteering, climbing and problem-solving activities pupils can develop their understanding of how the different components of fitness affect performance. They can explain how different types of exercise contribute to their fitness and health and describe their involvement in regular, safe physical activity for the benefit of their health and wellbeing (QCA 2008: 197).

Theory into practice

In the rest of the chapter we provide examples of activities where pupils can be exposed to situations that allow them to make and apply decisions in respect to identifying and solving problems. The activities will also enable them overcome and deal with their own and others' emotions through progressive paired and group activities. In the first section that follows we have included a series of trust games, team-building exercises and problem-solving activities which might constitute up to five hours of teaching. These individual activities should last between five and fifteen minutes each and can prepare pupils for more adventurous activities such as on-site orienteering and using a climbing wall. We have followed this with a series of activities designed for a low climbing wall which might make up three one-hour lessons. Then we describe the activity known as 'slacklines'. Finally, we have included examples of eight one-hour orienteering lessons for Year 6 pupils and seven one-hour lessons for pupils in Years 7, 8 or 9.

Teachers should decide for themselves which activities are best suited for their pupils and the time of year they are best introduced. Many of the trust games and team-building and problem-solving activities are particularly suited to the beginning of the academic year for pupils making the transition from different feeder infant and junior schools. These activities make up a sequence of lessons that can be used as a broader scheme of work covering Key Stages 2 and 3 and would constitute approximately one-sixth of physical education curriculum time, or 5–8 hours per year group per academic year (see Table 7.2).

Table 7.2 *Scheme of work for Key Stage 2 and Key Stage 3*

Range and content	Time	Activity	Activity	Activity	Activity	Activity
Identifying and solving problems to overcome challenges of an adventurous nature	5–8 hours	Team building; trust games	Problem-solving and decision-making	Orienteering (1)	Orienteering (2)	Climbing
Key concept		1.1, 1.2, 1.3	1.3	1.1, 1.2, 1.4	1.1, 1.2, 1.4	1.1, 1.2, 1.3, 1.4
Key process		2.2, 2.3, 2.4	2.2, 2.3, 2.4	2.1, 2.2, 2.3, 2.4, 2.5	2.1, 2.2, 2.3, 2.4, 2.5	2.1, 2.2, 2.3, 2.4, 2.5
Curriculum opportunities		b, c, e, g	b, c, e, g	a, b, c, d, e, f, g	a, b, c, d, e, f, g	a, b, c, d, e, f, g

Paired warm-up activities suitable for Years 5–7

Catch a partner

The pupils form pairs. One pupil stands up right with arms folded and eyes closed. The partner stands behind them and tells them to fall backwards whilst they stop them with outstretched arms. Repeat and change with another partner. Move to threes with a catcher either side. Each of the progressive activities must take place using either a protective sprung floor or with the pupils standing on standard gymnastic mats. Pupils should be matched according to physical size (Photo 7.1).

Photo 7.1
Catch a partner

Rocking horse

Place the top of a gymnastics box on the floor. Place two benches upside down across the bench to form an 'H' shape. The benches will be tilted up on one end to look like see-saws. Pupils work in pairs and attempt to walk along the thin base of the bench whilst holding hands. At some point the benches will gradually tilt forwards. The aim is to get to the end of the bench without falling off and still holding hands the whole way. On all four sides of the gymnastic box there should gymnastic mats or crash mats. Other pupils may act as 'spotters' who walk alongside participants and only offer support when necessary (Photo 7.2).

Progress to one sighted and one blindfolded partner and then both blindfolded. Then progress to one walking forwards while one walks backwards (Photo 7.3).

Body stretch

Place two benches on the floor in a V shape. Pupils work in pairs and stand on opposite benches touching each other's hands, palms together. The aim is for the pair to move gradually along the bench, assisting each other to get to the end without falling off. Progress to one sighted and one blindfolded and then both blindfolded. Protective mats must be in place surrounding the benches.

 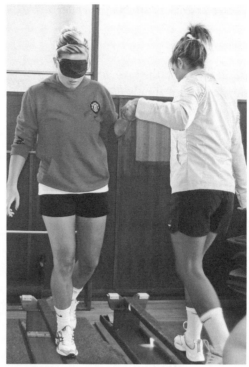

Photo 7.2 Rocking horse   **Photo 7.3** Rocking horse progression

Paired walk

In pairs, pupils walk forwards and backwards across a beam holding both their partner's hands. Repeat with one pupil blindfolded and then progress to both blindfolded.

'Minefield'

One sighted pupil has to guide a blindfolded partner through a 'minefield' as quickly as possible. The minefield could be a tennis or badminton court with marker cones, mats or half-full bottles of water scattered randomly to represent the land mines. Once the blindfolded pupil is in position the sighted pupil cannot speak. The sighted pupil can guide the blindfolded pupil or use forms of non-verbal communication to get their partner through the minefield. If a blindfolded pupil touches a mine they must be returned to their starting position. As a progression the sighted pupil cannot touch the blindfolded pupil, and must stay out of the 'minefield' calling instructions from outside the minefield boundaries.

Paired balance

Pairs of pupils link their left hands to the left forearm of their partner and hold a balance by placing the tips of their toes together whilst leaning back and holding their right arm straight out. Pupils now attempt to squat down to a sitting position and then stand up, still maintaining contact.

Group activities suitable for Years 5–7

Fall of faith

Pupils position themselves in two rows facing each other. One pupil turns their back to the group and stands with feet together and arms crossed. The remaining pupils move into pairs of equal strength and height. A rectangular 'catching' area is formed as pairs move into line facing each other, holding hands by the wrists. The teacher counts down to zero, whereupon the pupil pivots off balance and falls backwards to be caught by their peers.

Pupils could have the option of being blindfolded. Protective mats should be in place.

The Gorebachop!

Pupils stand in two facing lines. They use straight arms to interlink with the pupil in front of them, making a barrier of arms.

In turn, one pupil is asked to run through the arms: pupils must be trusted to bring their arms up to the ceiling so as to not hit the oncoming runner (Photo 7.4).

Photo 7.4
The Gorebachop!

All aboard

In groups of six or eight, pupils try to get as many people as possible inside a hoop. No part of any pupil can touch the ground outside the hoop. The group must be able to hold the balance for at least five seconds.

Human letters and numbers

The teacher calls out a letter or number. Pupils must make the shape of the letter or number as an individual, then must make the shape of a letter or number in pairs and groups of three. Then a group of six makes up a three-letter word or series of numbers including the shape of a plus, minus, multiplication or division. Other groups must try and guess the word or the answer to the sum.

Re-ordering

Line up pupils in groups of five on a bench or on a line. Pupils must re-order themselves without stepping off the bench or line and change places until they are in alphabetical first name order, alphabetical surname order, height order, age order and so forth. Place mats on the floor if you are using benches.

Centipede walk

Pupils in groups of ten line up in single file behind a starting line. Pupils lean forward and hold on to the ankles of the pupil in front of them. Pupils attempt to advance as a team towards a finishing line whilst staying connected. Progress to each team doing a figure-of-eight around two cones.

Dragon tails

In groups of five or six, pupils form a chain by holding the waist of the pupil in front of them. The last pupil has a tail (length of cloth) tucked into their shorts. The front pupil has to try and grab the tail as the group move in a circle.

Hoop circle

A group stands in a circle holding hands. Two hoops are placed between two people (resting on their grasped hands). The group has to move the hoops around the group whilst still holding hands.

Skin the snake

Groups of five or six pupils stand in single file and hold hands by placing one hand between their legs and holding the hand of the pupil behind them. The back pupil begins by crawling through the legs of the pupils in front of him or her whilst still holding hands. This continues with all other group members until the original pupil is at the back.

Blanket fold

Pupils work in groups of five. Place a blanket on the floor. The pupils stand together on top of the blanket and attempt to turn the blanket over without anyone stepping off the blanket. Progress to folding the blanket in half and in quarters (Photo 7.5).

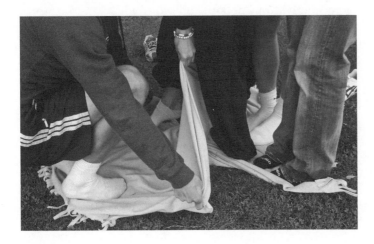

Photo 7.5 Blanket fold

Problem-solving activities suitable for Years 5–7

Human knot

This is an activity for larger groups. Pupils stand in a circle of about ten people. They hold hands with two different pupils in the group thus forming a tight knot of hands. Pupils must untangle themselves without letting go by climbing over, under and through other pairs of hands. Pupils should end up in one complete circle with some facing in and some facing out.

Untying the knot

Eight pupils each have a piece of cord. They stand in a circle and each hold their cord in their right hand. Then with their left hand they connect to another pupil's rope. They may not connect with someone directly next to them and may not let go of the cord or change hands. The aim is for the group to make one connected circle (Photo 7.6).

Photo 7.6 Untying the knot

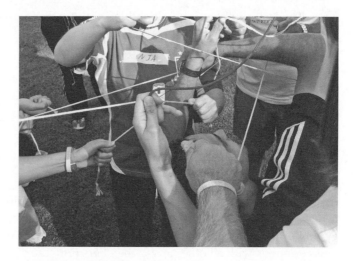

Bomb disposal

You will need eight marker cones, a half-full bottle of water and four short ropes.

Place four cones in a square (A) with the bottle in its centre. Make another square (B) approximately two metres away out of the remaining cones. Without entering either square, the team must use the ropes to get the bottle from A to B without dropping it on the floor. Progress to using ropes at a height to make the squares and not allowing the ropes to be touched by hand or by another rope or bottle (Photo 7.7).

Photo 7.7
Bomb disposal

Blindfold square

You will need blindfolds and a long rope. All but one member of the team are blindfolded. Those blindfolded hold onto the rope with two hands and listen to the instructions of the pupil not blindfolded. The aim is to make a perfect square. Progress to more complex shapes with more pupils.

Reef knot

For this exercise you will need a piece of rope 12m long and one large cone. All members of the team are blindfolded and must hold onto the rope with both hands. They must not let go. The team has to tie a reef knot around the cone.

Floating stick

Pupils form two lines facing each other and touch the opposite pupil's finger tips. A long and light stick such as a bamboo cane is placed on the fingertips. The group must bring the stick to the floor and then back up again without dropping it or releasing finger tips. Progress to each hand touching a different pupil's hand.

Stepping stones

Arrange three blue hoops on the right, a white hoop in the centre and three yellow hoops on the left. These are stepping stones. There are seven stepping stones and six people. The pupils occupy the six outer stepping stones. The centre stone is not occupied but is used when pupils move.

The challenge is for everyone who started on the left-hand (yellow) stepping stones to exchange places with those originally standing on the right-hand (blue) stepping stones, with the centre stone again unoccupied.

The rules:

1. After each move, each pupil must be standing on a stepping stone.
2. If you start on the left, you may only move to the right. If you start on the right, you may only move to the left.
3. You may 'jump' another pupil if there is an empty stone on the other side. You may not jump more than one pupil.
4. Only one pupil can move at a time.

Solitaire

Three pupils stand inside one yellow hoop each; three pupils stand inside one red hoop each. (They can also wear corresponding coloured tops or team bands.) There is one empty white hoop (see Figure 7.1). The three pupils inside the yellow hoops have to change places with the three pupils inside the red hoops. Pupils may move from their spot along a line to an empty space as long as they do not pass over another pupil. If a pupil is in a corner spot they may jump over a pupil of a different colour (red/yellow) providing this is in a straight line into an empty space. A pupil cannot jump over a pupil of the same colour (red/yellow). Only one pupil can move at a time.

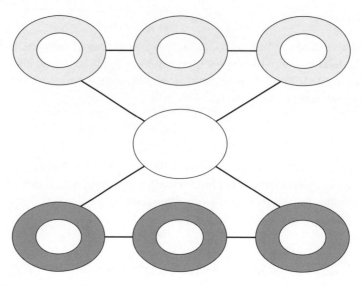

Figure 7.1 Solitaire

All change places

Place ten hoops in a line. Place one green marker cone inside eight of the hoops and one red marker cone in the end hoop to the right. Place a hoop by the second, fourth and sixth green marker cones. There should be one empty hoop to the left.

The object of the exercise is to move the red marker cone from the right end to the left end. Pupils can move the green markers into the hoop spaces, but cannot double them up. Nor can they jump a marker over another.

Developmental activities for the climbing wall suitable for Years 7–9

All of the activities highlighted in this section take pupils out of their comfort zones by requiring them to trust in their peers. They involve heights, which also provide elements of risk and danger and should be thoroughly risk assessed by physical education departments prior to engaging pupils in these activities. Teachers should also check with their Local Education Authority regarding the requirements for the use of climbing walls and slacklines. As an alternative to a climbing wall the climbing activities can be adapted and modified using wall bars in a gymnasium.

Twister

Climbers position themselves at the base of the wall and the teacher (or chosen pupil) shouts out instructions. For example, 'right hand up'. The climber must move the limb in the direction that is instructed and grip a hold (keeping all other limbs stationary). Other instructions are given, such as 'left foot down', 'right', 'up', etc. The instructions depend on what is available to the teacher, such as different colour holds or different types of holds (for example, crimp, jug, side pull), all of which can be adapted to suit ability levels and facilities. The last pupil left on the wall is the winner.

No-eye-dear

The game is played in 'spotting' pairs and involves one pupil (the climber) traversing the wall being guided by the other pupil (spotter). This activity requires pupils to communicate effectively, trust one another, problem solve, make decisions and respect one another and the rules of the game. As an extension to this activity the climber should be blindfolded.

Bungee bouldering

Pupils are joined together with bungee cord in pairs or in teams and are set various tasks. For example 'traverse as far as you can before touching the ground', 'work together to carry an object from point a to point b, fastest time, least number of moves'.

Target practice

In pairs (climber and spotter) participants traverse as far as they can then mark the point that they reached. They can then have a go at beating their own distance or that of their partners. Climbers should be encouraged to set a target to reach and then, in their pairs, evaluate performance in order to improve the next time.

Snakes and ladders

In pairs (climber and spotter). Ladders are represented by holds and features; snakes features only. This can be adapted using different colours and types of holds.

Climb mime

Climbers have to climb in the style of a character set by the teacher (or chosen pupil), for example robot, ballerina, Spiderman, monkey, ninja.

Supreme team

Set the teams some tasks, for example:

- as a team carry this plastic beaker of water from a to b
- as a team only have six feet, eight hands and three knees touching the wall
- as a team decide who will complete which boulder problems.

If there are six in a team then six problems must be completed and every team member must complete at least one (tasks of ranging difficulty present choice).

Copycat

Pupils work in pairs. The first pupil does one move (places a hand or foot on a hold) then climbs off the wall and steps back to observe their partner attempt to copy the move. As more and more moves are added to the sequence it becomes a matter of stamina and mental toughness to carry on.

Conga chain

Pupils do the conga around the wall until the music stops, when it stops or when a chosen word is shouted all pupils must get on the wall as quickly as possible and stay still (freeze). The last pupil to get on the wall is out (free lives can be given at will and pupils that are out can help officiate).

Developmental activities using slacklines

Slacklines or jib lines are essentially heavy duty bands made out of webbing material similar to that in a car seatbelt. They are fixed between two sturdy points such as a tree with a ratchet system to form a tightrope (Photo 7.8). There are many activities that can be introduced to develop group relationships and team work. See the resources section at the end of the chapter for more information on how to obtain the equipment. For beginners, work in groups of three with one pupil performing and supported by the other two. This can be developed into walking backwards, blindfolded, holding two ropes or a pole, and working together on the slacklines in pairs supporting each other.

Photo 7.8
Using a slackline

Orienteering

Boxes 7.1 and 7.2 contain modules on orienteering suitable for Key Stages 2 and 3. Many of the activities require maps of the school grounds and if your school has not been professionally mapped you can approach the British Schools Orienteering Association (BSOA) or the British Orienteering Federation (BOF) for advice. See the resources section at the end of this chapter for more information.

Box 7.1   Orienteering at Key Stage 2 (suitable for Year 6)

Duration: One hour per lesson
Theme: Adventure, technique and review
Activities: Adventure and problem-solving situations based on travel on land
Venue: Safe, secure and enclosed area such as the school grounds
Time of year: Summer term (June/July)

Lesson one

Hold a classroom discussion about orienteering. Ask who, what, when, where, why and how questions. Provide a handout about the key principles of orienteering. Ask the pupils to draw a map of the classroom identifying its key features and then discuss direction (north, east, south and west). Show a DVD about orienteering. The British Orienteering Federation has a number of very useful resources including DVD materials and there are other videos, including one for beginners made by a boy called Alexander and available on YouTube (see the section on resources at the end of the chapter).

Place nine cones in three rows of different colours (for example, red, yellow and green). Pupils must follow a pre-determined course using the cones (Figure 7.2).

Extension activity
Pupils move one cone at a time in a specified direction. For example:

• Start and finish at the centre cone.
• Walk in the direction of North; West; South; South-East, North-East; West.

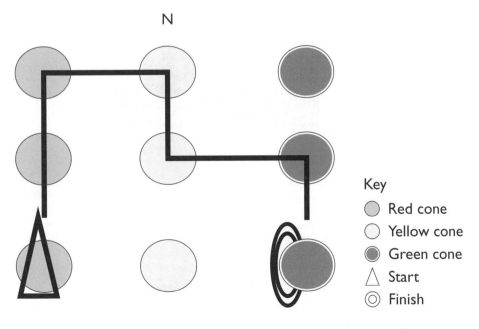

Figure 7.2 Introductory orienteering activity

Give each pupil a different set of directions on a laminated card. As a variation, pupils can collect letters or numbers at each cone and then spell a word or add up the numbers.

Lesson two

Draw a map of the school using different shapes with buildings and trees. Include a north arrow and legend. Pupils now orientate the map, fold it conveniently and pinpoint their position with their thumbs. The teacher would now walk the pupils around the school using the map to identify key features. This could be followed by a treasure hunt with pre-determined clues. Provide a basic map of the school grounds and instructions on how to complete the 'treasure hunt' (for example, walk twenty paces towards the staff car park; turn immediately right and walk twenty paces; now solve the riddle).

Lesson three

Set up an obstacle course using gymnastic equipment and then ask pupils to draw a map of the gym or sport centre to include the position of the various items of equipment. Place an orienteering marker on each item. Ask pupils to set the map and complete the course in pairs as quickly as possible recording the letters at each control point as they go. Record their times and then ask them to work out the quickest possible way to complete the course. Using the legend on a map draw twelve map symbols on small pieces of card and write the word that matches the symbol on separate pieces of card. Place the symbols and words at opposite ends of the gym and in relays ask the pupils to collect one symbol at a time and match with the correct word. See Figures 7.3 and 7.4.

Building

Figure 7.3 Map symbol (1)

Path

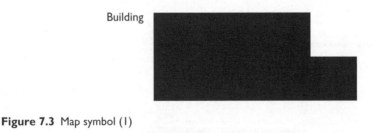

Figure 7.4 Map symbol (2)

This activity can be used to develop pupils' language skills by having the words in another language, for example German:

Tarmac: Asphalt
Building: Gebaude
Pond: Teich
Wall: Mauer
Footpath: Fussweg
Gate: Tor/Gatter
Fence: Zaun
Thicket: Dickicht

As an extension to this activity, map scale can be taught by making a series of laminated cards with map scales (1: 2500; 1: 5000; 1: 10000, for example) and the same number of cards with the definition written on it (for example 1:2500 = one centimetre on the map is equal to 25 metres on the ground; 1:5000 = one centimetre on the map is equal to 50 metres on the ground). The rule of thumb is to take away the last two zeros to reveal the distance.

Lesson four

Ideally, the school should be professionally mapped, but if this is not available a sketch map of the grounds would suffice. If you do not have orienteering markers then empty plastic milk cartons with numbers and coloured pens or crayons can be placed in position.

Pupils work in pairs and complete a course of 12 controls in a different order. They are given a sheet of paper that has 12 boxes which they will colour in as proof they have visited the correct site.

Lesson five

Set up an orienteering course around the grounds using a map of the area. Each control point should be numbered 1–20 and should have two letters. Provide pupils with a map of the campus without the 20 orienteering controls marked on the map. Mark one control point on the map and send pupils off in pairs to one control point at a time, marking the next control point when they return. They must return to the leader each time with the correct letters on each marker until they have visited the allotted amount of controls. The letters could make up a word such as 'Orienteering'.

Lesson six

Use the orienteering map and 30 control points on the grounds. Provide pupils with a map and compass. The nearest 10 control points are worth ten points, the next nearest 10 are twenty, the next nearest 5 are thirty and the furthest 5 are forty points.

Pupils are divided into pairs and given a time limit, for example 30 minutes, to visit as many control points as possible and to score as many points as possible. There is a ten-point penalty for every minute they are late.

Lesson seven

Use the orienteering map and thirty control points on the school grounds. Provide pupils with a map and compass. Pupils work in pairs and must complete a set course of ten control points on the map (for example: 2, 4, 6, 8, 10, 12, 14, 16, 18, and 20). Each pair is sent out at two-minute intervals and must complete as quickly as possible. Record the time out and the time in to give the time completed.

Lesson eight

As an indoor, classroom-based lesson, pupils can draw a map of the classroom and add details such as the furniture, windows and doors. They should indicate north and draw circles at specific locations. They then swap maps with a partner and have to identify specific points on the map.

Other exercises can take place in the playground or school grounds such as a map memory game in which pupils are shown a section of a map with a control point marked on it and then have to visit a control without a map. This can be developed by placing a section of the map at each control point showing the next control point to be visited. Alternatively, a series of photographs of key landmarks of the school grounds can be used to provide clues as to where the controls are located.

Box 7.2   Orienteering at Key Stage 3 (suitable for Years 7–9)

Duration: One hour per lesson
Theme: Navigation
Activities: Identifying and solving problems to overcome challenges of an adventurous nature based on travel on land
Venue: Safe, secure and enclosed area such as the school grounds
Time of year: Autumn term: (September/October)

Lesson one: compass exercises

Provide a handout on the parts of the compass. Explain how to use a compass and take a bearing. Practise taking a bearing of 360 (N); 90 (E); 180 (S); 270 (W). Turn the compass housing to the bearing required; place the compass on the palm of your hand and move your body round until the red magnetic needle lines up with the red arrow. Look at the arrow of direction at the tip of the compass. This should be the desired bearing and the direction in which to travel. Now use the following examples:

- Take the following bearings. What can you see?
  330, 70, 220, 150
- What is the bearing of the gate at the entrance of the school?

Use a map of the school and a compass. Use the edge of the compass to line up two points on the map. Turn the compass housing until it is pointing north. Read the bearing from the arrow of direction. Give pupils a series of bearing in pairs and ask them to run along a bearing of 275, for example, to a particular control and record the letters that they find. Now proceed to a new bearing and repeat the same exercise until at least ten controls have been visited.

Lesson two

Use an orienteering map and 30 control points in the school grounds. Pupils work in pairs with a map and compass. They must complete a set short course (10 control points) within a set time limit. As an alternative exercise indoors, draw a sketch map of a gymnasium or sports hall indicating north and place orienteering markers at strategic points. Pupils complete the set course within a time limit.

Lesson three

Use an orienteering map and 30 control points in the grounds. Provide pupils with a map and compass. Pupils divide into different pairs compared to previous lessons and complete a new set short course of 15 control points.

Lesson four

Use an orienteering map and 30 control points in the grounds. Provide pupils with a map and compass. Pupils must plan a route and consider what is achievable within a set time restriction. Pupils should then evaluate their performance and how they might improve upon this.

Lesson five

In pairs, pupils must complete a pre-prepared orienteering course using the map of the grounds. This should include 10 control points. Pupils should be sent off at two-minute intervals and evaluate their performance upon completion.

Lesson six

In pairs (different pairings from the previous lesson) pupils must complete a pre-prepared orienteering course using the map of the grounds. This should include 10 control points. Send the pupils off at two-minute intervals and evaluate their performance upon completion.

Lesson seven

In groups of four, pupils sub-divide into pairs. Using the map of the school grounds, they must complete a pre-prepared orienteering course which should include 20 control points. As a group pupils must plan how they can complete the course in the quickest time and how they can get to each of the control points in pairs as fast as possible. Groups of pupils should be sent off at two-minute intervals and evaluate their performance upon completion. The same activity could take place using mountain bikes in Key Stage 4.

Summary

In teaching on-site outdoor and adventurous activities we believe that overcoming insecurities in subject knowledge as well as addressing breadth, depth and balance of experience for pupils are important factors to consider. In this respect, physical education teachers and school sports co-ordinators in secondary schools have a major role to play in promoting teaching and learning through the key processes and increasing their own subject knowledge as well as trainee teachers' ability to teach outdoor and adventurous activities. The educational benefits of outdoor and adventurous activities are very convincing and, we believe, by far outweigh any issues related to organisation, time, finance or resources. Teachers, however, require training to teach these types of activities with confidence. Increasing confidence in teaching through experience will enable school staff to provide challenging activities in risk-managed circumstances within school-based settings.

The provision of outdoor and adventurous activities on a school site through the types of activities we have suggested can enable teachers to integrate the key processes through their teaching and at the same time address some of the barriers often cited for the exclusion of outdoor and adventurous activities. That is not to deny that certain challenges will have to be overcome if on-site outdoor and adventurous activities are to be introduced within secondary and junior schools. This includes organising the physical education curriculum to ensure breadth, depth and balance of experience; securing sufficient time within the physical education curriculum for outdoor and adventurous activities; convincing senior managers of the value of activity areas such as outdoor and adventurous activities; personalising the physical education curriculum through outdoor and adventurous activities; developing teaching and learning experiences in outdoor and adventurous activities; promoting progress in outdoor and adventurous activities; and assessment of pupil learning through outdoor and adventurous activities. We hope our ideas and suggestions will help to overcome barriers and enable teachers to provide educational experiences through outdoor and adventurous activities within the physical education curriculum.

Note

1   The term 'outdoor and adventurous activities' is often abbreviated to OAA. We believe that doing so reinforces the marginal status that outdoor and adventurous activities have traditionally occupied within the physical education curriculum. We have, therefore, used the term in its entirety throughout the chapter in order to promote and emphasise the educational value and importance of outdoor and adventurous activities within the physical education curriculum.

Acknowledgements

We would like to thank Graham Spacey, Roger Neuss, Andy Gore, and Sam Carter at the University of Brighton, Chelsea School, and Christine Robinson from the British Orienteering Federation for their assistance in writing this chapter.

References

DfES (Department for Education and Skills) (2006) *Learning Outside the Classroom* (Ref: 04232-2006 DOM-EN), DfES Publications.

Ofsted (2004) *Outdoor Education*, London, HMSO.

Ofsted (2005) The Annual Report of Her Majesty's Chief Inspector of Schools 2004/2005: Ofsted Subject Reports 2004/05: Physical Education in Secondary Schools, October 2005, www.ofsted.gov.uk

Ofsted (2009) *Physical Education in Schools 2005/08: Working towards 2012 and beyond,* April (Ref: 080249), www.ofsted.gov.uk

QCA (Qualifications and Curriculum Authority) (2008) *'Physical Education: Programmes of Study Key Stage 3,* www.qca.org.uk/curriculum

Stidder, G. (2006a) 'Raising the profile of outdoor and adventurous activities in secondary school physical education: a developmental approach', *Physical Education Matters* (formerly *The British Journal of Teaching Physical Education*), (1) Summer, 1, 12–14.

Stidder, G. (2006b) 'A developmental approach to teaching outdoor and adventurous activities in schools', *Physical Education Matters* (formerly *The British Journal of Teaching Physical Education*) (1) Autumn, 2, 13–16.

Stidder, G. (2006c) 'Developing junior and primary school teachers' subject knowledge in outdoor and adventurous activities through TOP outdoors training', *Physical Education Matters* (formerly *The British Journal of Teaching Physical Education*), (1) Winter, 3, v–vii.

Stidder, G. (2007) 'Outdoor and adventurous activities in secondary schools and the development of subject knowledge amongst trainee physical education teachers in south-east England', *Physical Education Matters* (formerly *The British Journal of Teaching Physical Education*), Autumn, (2), 3, 34–40.

Stidder, G. and Haasner, A. (2007) 'Developing outdoor and adventurous activities for co-existence and reconciliation in Israel: an Anglo-German approach', *Journal of Adventure Education and Outdoor Learning*, (7), 2, 131–140.

Stidder, G. and Hayes, S. (2006) 'A longitudinal survey of physical education trainees' experiences on school placements in the south-east of England (2000–2004)', *European Physical Education Review*, Autumn, (12), 3, 317–338.

Zwozdiak-Myers, P. (2004) 'Breadth, balance and relevance! A report of Year 6 and Year 7 curricular and extra-curricular experiences in the east of England', *British Journal of Teaching Physical Education*, (35), 2, 43–49.

Useful contacts and resources

British Orienteering Federation

www.Britishorienteering.org.uk
Telephone 01629 734042
Suppliers of the DVD 'Orienteering: The adventure sport for all' (2008).

British Schools Orienteering Association

www.bsoa.org
Telephone 01562 631561

Supplier of slacklines

www.gibbon-slacklines.com

Video on orienteering for beginners

There is a very useful YouTube video related to orienteering for beginners made by an 11-year-old boy called Alexander. http://www.youtube.com/watch?v=OZOI9kKuA4I

8 Learning and teaching through swimming and water-based activities

James Wallis and Jon Binney

The distinctive nature and importance of swimming and water-based activities

Ensuring that every pupil is taught to swim and learns to be confident and safe in and around water is a vision worthy of the much-lauded Olympic legacy. Swimming and its place within a pupil's education can be a matter of life or death. A school's impact on a pupil's swimming education is critical and can be the foundation for a lifetime of water-based activity. Aside from the positive health benefits it brings, swimming is one of the truly vital life skills in the curriculum, as important to a child's life as numeracy, reading and writing. According to the Royal Society for the Prevention of Accidents (2007), drowning is the third most common accidental death for under-16s. Each tragedy can be considered a failing of systems that any society surrounded by water should treat with paramount importance.

The health benefits are considerable. Swimming provides an excellent cardiovascular workout that elevates the heart and respiratory rates, improving overall health and exercising all of the main muscle groups. Due to the body's density being comparable to that of water, swimming can provide a complete weight-bearing experience, a much needed flotation device in the ever-increasing fight against obesity and a string of hypo-kinetic illnesses.

Learning to swim enables pupils to experience valuable learning opportunities in a wide variety of water-based activities. Surfing, canoeing, kayaking, sailing, water skiing or windsurfing would be unavailable to those who are fearful of water or unable to swim. Furthermore it can provide a learning environment that is fully inclusive, with everyone at some point having specific learning difficulties, as the environment provides physical and sensory challenges to all participants. Everyone was a non-swimmer at some time or other. A child's first experience of swimming may be during their first swim lesson at school, so making these early experiences memorable can develop an interest in swimming and water-based activities that will remain with them throughout their life.

Purpose and process

In this chapter we will draw attention to the current situation of swimming in the United Kingdom, in order to provide a rationale for the inclusion of swimming within an educational context and to highlight how successfully and effectively the revised National Curriculum for Physical Education (NCPE 2008) 'range and content' can be exemplified through the teaching of swimming and water-based activities (SWBA).

To assist teachers to interpret the revised physical education curriculum, we will look closely at how each of the 'range and content' elements can be delivered, providing practical examples that can be easily taught. In a sequence of lessons it would be perfectly feasible to cover 'outwitting an opponent' by teaching aspects of water polo, 'accurate replication' by developing stroke technique, 'performing at maximum levels' whilst swimming in a class gala, 'exploring concepts' by investigating buoyancy in the water, 'identifying problems' through dealing with life-saving situations, and 'improving fitness' through aqua aerobics.

Each section will highlight a number of ways that the 'range of content' can be delivered, considering a selection of:

1.   warm-up or introductory activities
2.   stroke refinement and technique work
3.   life saving and/or personal survival.

We will pay particular attention to the range of content 'identifying and solving problems to overcome challenges', highlighted by the Qualifications and Curriculum Authority (QCA) as being particularly relevant to the teaching of swimming-based activities. A crucial consideration of any discrete activity area within the planning and teaching of physical education is an awareness of the potential impacts of lessons on the long-term activity choices of pupils. In this respect teachers should make constant attempts to present content in ways which are going to continually motivate and encourage voluntary adherence to activity. A later chapter in this book (Chapter 10) discusses the importance of viewing every physical education lesson as a lesson in health and wellbeing, albeit as implicit concepts in the practical activity being delivered. In this way health concepts can be communicated on a regular basis in a multiplicity of ways, reinforcing the value and benefits of increased activity. In relation to swimming and water-based activities this is a vital point to consider, given the distinctive nature of the activity and the long-term, even lifelong, potential of the activity. Our intention for this chapter is to consider careful construction of the environment for swimming teaching and to provide examples which reinforce fundamental principles of lifelong physical activity adherence which do not compromise the safety and wellbeing of pupils.

The key facts about swimming

Swimming is the most participated sport in England.

(DCMS 2007)

According to Sport England's *Active People* survey, which surveyed 363,000 adults in England between October 2005 and October 2006, swimming was the physical activity that had the most people participating (apart from walking). A government survey released in 2007 by the Department for Culture, Media and Sport (DCMS) revealed that swimming is the nation's most popular participation sport. The 'Everyday Swim' findings show that over the past 20 years, swimming participation levels have remained consistently high across the whole country. According to the General Household Survey (GHS) swimming has the highest level of latent demand for any sport or recreational activity. According to the School Sport Survey 2007/08, opportunities to experience swimming were offered by 85 per cent of the schools. Furthermore, swimming is a notable counter to the often perceived male dominance of sports participation, with 17 per cent of women participating in swimming compared to only 10 per cent of men (Active Sports

Survey, 2007). And let us not forget that swimming is spearheading the government's push for a more active nation ready for 2012. As Andy Burnham stated in 2008, when he was Secretary of State for Culture, Media and Sport:

> Since 1997 almost £250 million of public money has been invested in swimming – more than any other sport.
>
> (DCMS 2008)

Ofsted (2004: 9) found that the provision of swimming continues to cause particular problems in primary schools. In this respect, an increasing number of primary school head teachers were solving the problems of access to a pool by carefully planning the use of local secondary school and community facilities to secure swimming lessons for all pupils. Others were working with the local education authority (LEA) to overcome the costs involved in transport or adjusting the curriculum to ensure pupils have access to swimming throughout Key Stage 2. In stark contrast, the 2007/08 School Sport Survey found that 28 per cent of pupils in Year 6 were unable to meet the minimum compulsory elements of the swimming primary National Curriculum. In 2008, the British Market Research Bureau showed the proportion of teenagers who swam regularly had dropped dramatically in the past decade. One in four 11- to 18-year-olds were swimming weekly in 1993; after ten years it was closer to one in ten. According to the Amateur Swimming Association (ASA), school swimming pools are disappearing at a rate of 10 per cent a year and were expected to drop to below 750 nationally in 2008, from 3,000 in the 1980s. As recent reports in the press have shown, large numbers of parents now have to contribute to the cost of their child's swimming education.

The Top Up swimming programme, which was introduced in 2004 by the government to support the weakest swimmers in primary schools, was reviewed by Ofsted in 2007. Ofsted found that:

> In half the schools visited, the impact of the national top-up programme was inadequate so that a significant minority of pupils entered Key Stage 3 unable to swim the expected 25 metres.
>
> (Ofsted 2007: 5)

The School Sports Partnerships have the responsibility for delivering the swimming Top Up programme, but Ofsted found that:

> Very few partnerships had set an explicit target relating to the proportion of pupils who should meet the end of Key Stage 2 expectation for swimming.
>
> (2007: 5)

More worrying still was that:

> too many pupils failed to reach the 25 metre target; this was associated with weak teaching, insufficient curriculum time, poor assessment and ineffective deployment of funding.
>
> (2007: 5)

There are numerous reasons for the Ofsted findings, ranging from transport issues, subject knowledge concerns for members of staff, pupil to staff ratios, distance from the closest swimming pool, pools closing and the cost of hiring facilities. However, it is vitally important that schools understand the responsibility that they have in ensuring that every pupil can achieve basic minimum swimming competences, not just being to able to swim 25 metres. Allowing sufficient curriculum time is vital and so is the development of effective working relationships with local partnership secondary schools and the local authority swimming provider, in order to tackle known pupil weaknesses. Target setting and tracking and monitoring pupils can also provide key information for their transition from Key Stage 2 to Key Stage 3, another area for development identified in the recent Ofsted report. The recent pledge to invest £140 million to make swimming 'free for all' is an indication of the government's awareness of the challenges still facing swimming. Stage two of this process discusses free swimming for all under 16 years of age.

The ASA School Swimming Strategy provides further indications of swimming's national importance, with its four-year 'Vision', outlining its objectives and strategies from 2009 to 2013. Key to the success of the swimming strategy up to 2013 is to ensure that 95 per cent of pupils leaving primary school are able to complete the full programme detailed in the Key Stage 2 NCPE. The ASA have expressed the desire that every school nominate a member of staff who will be responsible for measuring and evaluating the swimming in their school. Questions remain regarding how primary schools will find the time, the resources and the finances to fulfil these visions.

A philosophy of SWBA teaching

One traditional perspective of the teaching of swimming is the recommended use of closed teaching styles because of the perceptions of risk and threat from a dangerous environment. Such knee-jerk reactions are clearly well meaning in their intent and can draw on numerous tragic anecdotes and statistics which support the notion that swimming and water-based activities are a common cause of accidental death. Viewing such negative press from an alternative perspective is to see swimming lessons as the most safe, secure and controlled exposure to this vital life skill that children are ever likely to receive. Given this and the limited time afforded to such a vital aspect of child's development, swimming lessons need to be structured in the most enthusing and motivating format possible in order to provoke high levels of interest and positive future choices. Achieving regular activity habits will lead to elevated swimming proficiency and in turn address the comparatively high numbers of accidental death in and around water.

Accepting swimming as a dangerous, high-risk activity is likely to proliferate teaching which fails to inspire regular activity. Paradoxically, it is more dangerous because the activity does not catch pupil's imagination and therefore proficiency is hampered, leaving pupils exposed to risks. If we followed this line of thought to its logical conclusion, withdrawing swimming from the physical education curriculum entirely solves the problem of risk and threat to pupils but is clearly an unsatisfactory measure in the bigger picture of a child's long-term welfare. It would be preposterous to offer this as a rationale for the exclusion of swimming from the curriculum and is equally preposterous to justify the sole use of command teaching style on the grounds of safety. This section of the chapter aims to provide the swimming teacher with a philosophy of swimming teaching which employs many of the principles of open-ended, autonomous practice whilst not compromising the immediate safety of the pupils and dispels common myths associated with the activity.

Landmark research into the development of intrinsic motivation, which possesses appeal to practitioners in encouraging long-term activity habits, has revealed three central components: autonomy, perceived competence and relatedness. Autonomy is based on pupil choice and pupils are more likely to opt to take part if the activity is within their capabilities. Perceived competence refers to an individual's need to feel success within the subject and environment and feeling that they have sufficient competence to achieve intended outcomes. The route to high perceived competence is to offer a range of tasks from which pupils can choose the ones most suited to their level. In this way success is more likely to be achieved and perceived competence is enhanced. Relatedness refers to pupils' efforts to become accepted by others in the class and to feel a sense of belonging or relation to the activity. Relatedness is likely to be far higher in individuals who gain success in an activity. The dimensions of perceived competence and relatedness are unpinned by the affordance of autonomy. If pupils are given freedom to choose their tasks they are more likely to achieve success and the upward spiral in motivation begins.

Deci and Ryan's self-determination theory (1985) holds a great deal of potential in the attempt to understand pupils' decisions relating to voluntary uptake and maintenance of activity. This research places priority on the creation of learning environments which offer pupils autonomy, perceived competence and relatedness.

Autonomy, or choice, is the construct which we as teachers can most easily influence with our teaching strategies. First and foremost we should consider how we can offer pupils a level of graded decision making and personal control on their actions and decisions, which means moving away from the didactic relationship associated with teaching styles situated on the 'teacher decisions' end of Mosston's spectrum (see Chapter 12). Many examples of autonomy are employed with little conscious thought and come into the 'common-sense' bracket of teaching practice. The following scenarios offer several examples of pupil autonomy and may be introduced, adapted and delivered to suit pupils at either Key Stage 2 or 3 depending on their levels of water confidence and competence.

Example of autonomy 1: target warm-up

- Pupils congregate at poolside prior to further instruction and are told to find a partner of similar swimming ability.
- Pupils are told to find a space along the length of the pool at a depth they are comfortable with.
- The poolside has an ordered 'littering' of buoyancy aids which pupils can employ at any stage of any lesson.
- Pupils are asked to number themselves 1 or 2 and to choose a stroke to swim for two widths.
- Pupil 1 swims two widths of their chosen stroke at their own intensity while pupil 2 times their two-width swim. Then the roles are reversed.
- Pupils are asked to set a target for two minutes of continuous relay swimming where they can choose their stroke and intensity. They are to stay in motion for the full two minutes regularly adjusting their intensity, speed and stroke according to their target number.
- Pupils evaluate their score in relation to their stated target and how they went about the task of hitting their target.
- Pupil praise and reward is based upon closeness of target and actual scores.
- Pupils decide upon two key points which they record for future attempts.

Example of autonomy 2: investigating streamlining

- Pupils are asked to create as many different body shapes as they can whilst pushing and gliding from the side of the pool.

- Pupils are encouraged to use buoyancy aids to assist in their invention of a wide range of creative body shapes.
- Pupils are asked to grade each body shape in terms of how far they managed to propel across the pool.
- Pupils are guided to the correct body shape for the streamlined position by only retaining those which propelled them furthest across the pool.
- Discussion on the outcomes of these divergent and guided discovery tasks enables pupils to find out explicit rules of streamlining in interactive, autonomous modes of teaching.

The number of pupil choices in these two examples provide many opportunities for pupils to construct their own learning from open-ended tasks which, when well managed, do not compromise pupil safety. Critics may question the potential for pupils to select inappropriate tasks for themselves when given too much choice. In the limited number of cases where this happens a fallback position for teachers is to revert back to a more directed style of teaching for pupils who abuse the responsibility afforded to them.

It should also be noted that whilst an approach centring on 'pupil finding out' as opposed to the traditional style of 'teacher information giving' is far more planning-intense and time-consuming, the potential for learning due to cognitive as well as physical engagement in tasks makes the trade-off worthwhile. It is also likely that the robustness and longevity of knowledge obtained will further justify such approaches.

Range and content: identifying and solving problems to overcome challenges

The revised NCPE provides unlimited opportunities to deliver a range of water-based activities, due to the increased flexibility and the removal of the prescribed activity areas. Based on the unique environment of the swimming pool, problem-solving situations and scenarios can be readily and easily delivered, providing pupils with thought-provoking and engaging tasks, using a variety of teaching styles and methods that will not only develop their confidence in the water but will develop their problem, learning and thinking skills (PLTs) (see Chapter 12), a key area highlighted within the revised NCPE. Regurgitating answers to pupils, preventing them from devising their own solutions, and over-using traditional methods of teaching swimming will have a detrimental effect on the perceptions pupils have towards swimming-based activities. It is essential to challenge them, intrigue them, to engage their imagination and, above all, to set them tasks that get them thinking, talking and socialising, all common skills required for the wider world after education. Physical education also has a cross-curricular responsibility to deliver aspects of the Secondary National Strategy (SNS) ensuring that, through physical activity, pupils develop their literacy, numeracy and ICT skills. The following activities highlight how PLTs and SNS cross-curricular ideas can be easily introduced through a variety of warm-up tasks and stroke development.

Warm-up activities

Supermarket sweep

- The problem: to collect objects from the swimming pool, which vary in numerical value depending on their position, in an attempt to gain the highest points total.
- Activity guidance: divide the group up into four equally sized, mixed-ability teams. Allow them time to devise their swimming order. The lowest value objects will either

be floating or sunk at the most shallow end of the pool. The highest value objects will either be furthest away from the shallow end or will be at the bottom of the pool. The pupils must clear the swimming pool of the objects and then, as a team, calculate their total score. Do the pupils take longer to collect the highest scoring points or do they opt for the lowest scoring objects closer to them?

Wave machine

- The problem: in two groups the pupils must devise the best way to create large waves using their bodies' momentum and the side of the pool.
- Activity guidance: divide the class in two, as shown in Figure 8.1. They must be able to stand and should be holding onto the side of the pool and facing the side.
- As a group they must pull their upper body towards the poolside. Then, as a group they push their bodies away from the poolside. If this is successfully coordinated, the groups should start to create waves. The team working together the best will usually create the largest waves. Move the group further up the pool and get them to explore what happens to the wave height. Discuss how the more shallow water helps to create greater wave heights and why. Possibly discuss the effect of a shelving floor on wave length and height.

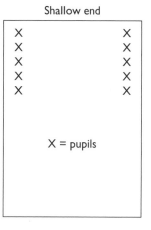

Figure 8.1 Wave machine

Blockbusters (more warm-up activities)

Swimming conundrums

- The problem: knowing the position of letters in key words.
- Activity guidance: sit the class along the width of the pool. Ensure everyone can see you. State a key word from today's learning and then say a letter from that word. The pupils must work out where that letter comes in the word and then swim that answer.
- For example: key word = front crawl. If you say the letter 'N', the pupils must work out where this letter is positioned in the word. 'N' is the fourth letter so the pupils should swim four widths.

Simple sums

- The problem: swimming the answers to numerical equations.
- Activity guidance: sit the class along the width of the pool. Ensure everyone can see you. State a numerical equation and tell the pupils to swim the answer.
- For example: $10 \div 5 + 3 = 5$.
- Variations and progressions: increase the difficulty and complexity of the equations. Get the pupils to work in pairs or groups and get them to devise sums for each other.

Hector, Sylvester and Tweety

- The problem: pupils must transport objects which represent 'Hector the Bulldog', 'Sylvester the Cat' and 'Tweety the Bird', across the pool in the correct order. Only one object can be carried at once. Tweety cannot be left on the side with Sylvester and Sylvester cannot be left on the side with Hector.

- Activity guidance: leave Tweety and Hector at the start and transport Sylvester to the other side. Swim back and collect Hector. Swim across and drop off Hector. Collect Sylvester again and swim back to the start position. Drop off Sylvester and collect Tweety. Swim Tweety across the pool and drop off with Hector. Finally swim back across and collect Sylvester. Swim Sylvester across to the other side.

Stroke development

Backstroke

- The problem: trying to balance a full plastic cup of water on your forehead whilst swimming backstroke without spilling any of the water.
- Activity guidance: the activity encourages pupils to place their head back in the water (a common fault is placing the chin near the chest which encourages the hips to drop lower in the water). It also prevents their head from tipping from side to side.

Front crawl

- The problem: trying to view pictures, letters or numbers whilst swimming front crawl.
- Activity guidance: the activity encourages pupils to breathe only from the side (and not to lift their heads to breathe). Place pictures, letters or numbers along the side of the pool at water level. The pupils have to add up all of the numbers, or remember the pictures or letters that they see.

Butterfly

- The problem: trying to dive over woggles and then continue through underwater hoops.
- Activity guidance: the activity encourages the pupils to develop the correct undulation motion required for butterfly. Working in pairs, one pupil must hold a woggle on the surface of the water and a hoop under the water approximately a metre away. The partner has to leap over the woggle, submerge, change direction through the undulation of the body, and re-emerge through the hoop.

Life saving and personal survival

Raft building

- The problem: design and build a raft, using a variety of floats and ropes that will transport a member of the group from one end of the pool to the other.
- Activity guidance: give pupils 15 minutes to design and build their raft using woggles, kick boards and ropes. They must then swim a member of their team to the other end of the pool.
- Emphasise the winning team will be the team with the *driest* casualty and that it is not about who gets their casualty to the other end first.

Swimming and seeing

- The problem: pupils must swim widths in relay with a partner whilst always keeping the teacher in full view. The teacher is constantly changing their position around the poolside.
- Activity guidance: pupils are told to change their body position to be able to keep the teacher in view. Buoyancy aids are freely available.
- Variation: pupils look for hand signals from the teacher and call out the number or item being held up. Alternatively on a given visual signal pupils must swim back to their partner as quickly as possible still keeping the teacher in view in case of another command.

Range and content

Accurate replication of actions, phrases and sequences

When considering the key processes which can be achieved within a unit of swimming and water-based activities, a process concerning consistent replication of body movements is clearly well suited to the activity. This is so much so that a stereotypical unit of swimming may reflect a disproportionate focus on this process and in so doing restrict the use of teaching styles which are more inclined to motivate and engage pupils. One enduring image of swimming is as an individual pursuit performed in relative solitude providing very few opportunities for pupils to develop many of the personal, social and moral qualities which are central to quality physical education. A common thread to the philosophy presented in this chapter is the avoidance of situations which reduce the likelihood of pupils' continued involvement in swimming and water-based activities. In this respect the objective is to prevent the proliferation of negative, traditional perceptions of such a vital life skill.

The example activities that we have already presented in this chapter are well suited to developing accurate replication of actions but have avoided the traditional forms of teaching which revolve around command and practice teaching. Devising activities which challenge the thinking as well as the action of pupils is central to this philosophy; we maintain that, regardless of the priority focus of a sequence of lessons, the concepts we have discussed should be employed throughout. Moving to a default position of adopting typical technical practices and organisation for stroke development undermines this philosophy. To accentuate this point our focus in this chapter has been to avoid additional reference to practices which have replication of actions as their principal focus and instead have emphasised alternative priorities, with stroke improvement occurring as a by-product of the activities.

Performing at maximum levels in relation to speed, height, distance, strength or accuracy

The teaching of technical proficiency is indisputably integral to the teaching of swimming. Without the ability to freely move in the water and to travel comfortably with a degree of control showing some attention to effective streamlining, swimming can become frustratingly difficult and increasingly hard work. Furthermore, allowing pupils to perform at their fastest or with great accuracy, is an essential ingredient to any successful lesson. However, how the teacher manages 'maximum' performance within the lesson is crucial in creating a suitable learning environment where pupils feel comfortable to perform at their best without fear of persecution from others.

The climate that is created within the swimming lesson can have a huge impact on the learning achievements of the pupils. Get it right, and the pupils will feel intrinsically motivated to improve and progress. Get it wrong and the pupils will start to feel anxious, bored and will undoubtedly start to compare themselves to others within the group. Duda (1989, 1992) discusses how pupils perceive their own ability within a group. They are either 'task' orientated or 'ego' orientated. The task-orientated pupil is concerned with learning new skills, making progress and doing their best. The ego-orientated pupil is concerned with doing better than others, doing as well as others or hiding their incompetence. It is therefore suggested that a 'task' climate is more often encouraged within physical education. A critical factor as to whether this occurs will be the approach taken by the teacher and how much focus they place on the task and not on the individual pupils. Below are a few suggestions that encourage a task climate.

Task design

- novelty, variety, diversity, pleasure, excitement;
- develop lists with a variety of tasks for each class;
- meaningful, easily adapted to child's environment;
- difficulty should fit individual abilities;
- teach students how to change the difficulty of tasks;
- use tasks where progress is easily seen by the pupils;
- use criteria sheets with the task broken down into logical sections;
- design tasks that increase co-operation of pupils from both sexes or of varying abilities.

Autonomy of learning

Allow pupils to:

- choose their activities from a given range;
- choose when and how to use buoyancy aids;
- set up equipment, drills and games;
- monitor and evaluate their own and their partner's performance;
- change the rules of games and create new drills and new games.

Feedback

Direct attention to the task, not the student's ego.

- Reward individual improvement, effort and persistence.
- Encourage students, particularly those with low ability.
- Recognition/feedback should be private.
- When feedback is public it should deal with the performance not the person.
- Never direct criticism to a student's ego.
- Criticism should be accompanied by corrections.
- Remind students that mistakes are part of learning.

The following activities highlight how a task-orientated climate can be created that still allows the pupils to perform at maximum levels. Pupils are encouraged to swim maximally but at their own level, and to focus on setting realistic and achievable targets, irrespective of other pupils in the group. You should emphasise that success for pupils comes from achieving their own goals or by being close to their guesses or estimations.

1. Judgements and pacing

The pupils have to judge how far to swim away from the side, before returning in a given time limit.

Example: Give them 31 seconds to swim as far as they can but they must be back to the start position by the end of the time. Encourage the pupils to swim at an even pace and do not communicate the countdown. This will encourage personal reflection and an ability to understand pacing.

2. Pulse-raising

Get pupils to measure their pulse. State how much you would like their heart rates to increase by. The pupils must now devise how many widths, and at what intensity, they must complete to achieve their new target heart rate.

3. Measuring optimum kick/pull speed during strokes

The pupils have to time themselves swimming two widths kicking, taking as few kicks as possible. Then they have to re-time themselves, but this time using as many kicks cycles as possible. The pupils need to analyse the times for both of these swims and decide the optimum speed of kick and the optimum length of the kick.

4. Diving through hoops

In this activity you are altering the distance away from the side and the angle of hoops. Working in pairs, one pupil will be in the pool with a hoop. The other pupil, the diver, must decide what they consider to be the optimum distance away from the side, and what angle the hoop should face in the water (the more shallow the hoop in the water the flatter the dive angle).

Outwitting an opponent

Along with athletics, swimming and water-based activities are often bracketed as individual pursuits with little opportunity for collaboration between pupils. In much the same way 'outwitting an opponent' may be viewed as an opportunity for pupils to compete against one another in head-to-head activities. In keeping with the drive to create sustained activity many pupils perceive such a climate as threatening and potentially damaging to their self-esteem, given that competition yields a winner and a loser as well as, in many circumstances, a very public display of incompetence. Here, we are not advocating a cessation of competitive activity in physical education. Rather, we recommend employing pupil autonomy in tasks for those who are content to compete and compare against others while others focus on mastery and personal improvement. Similarly, competition used effectively is a very valuable tool for enhancing performance and understanding of concepts when used in groups and teams as opposed to individuals.

Opportunities to outwit opponents may include outwitting using race strategy, in finding solutions to tasks, in devising tactics in water polo or in a plethora of ways through the well-considered use of a sport education curriculum model. Successful outwitting may not only be graded on outcome criteria such as winning or the fastest time. In keeping with the creation of a mastery environment, outwitting may be measured on subjective measures such as process, method or improvement.

The following examples attempt to clarify this position on content relating to outwitting opponents .

Stroke/technique

Pupils swim doggy paddle side by side on the length or the width. Pupil one can suddenly change pace and direction using their choice of stroke to get to the side of their choice before their partner. Variations would include allowing the pupils to fake or select stroke and distance according to their perception of their partner's weaknesses.

Entries

Split pupils into four teams and ask them to enter into the water creating the most and then the least splash possible. Grade them on water displaced on each trial. Ask the pupils to select different methods with each trial. Lead into a discussion on resistance and streamlining. This task may lead into an introduction to diving and straddle entries in personal survival.

Personal survival

Pupils in teams of five, three at one end and two at the other, are all treading water. They are not allowed contact with the side but must be in contact with one another. Give them a selection of buoyancy aids for their use. Pupil one swims out to collect and form a chain with pupil two. The chain must then swim to pick up pupil three. This continues until there is a chain of five pupils. The winning team is the team which congregates in the huddle position with buoyancy aids in the deep end of the pool. Variations may include use of bricks, allocating hypothetical injuries and non-swimmer status to some pupils, or providing an object which must stay dry all through the race.

Summary

We have focused in this chapter on a philosophy and examples of the teaching of SWBA which aim to assist practitioners in creating innovative and pupil-centred practices. Whilst our underlying objective has been to provide ideas for enhancing swimming proficiency, we have also emphasised a teaching practice which can be applied across all activities in order to create well-structured and engaging environments which inspire on-going voluntary physical activity within all pupils. SWBA is a very distinctive element of physical education but its distinctive status should not necessarily limit the scope and diversity of teaching and learning strategies. Whilst there are clear dangers associated with SWBA this should be viewed as a reason to further broaden teaching approaches to employ some of the philosophies and practices in this chapter to nurture intrinsic motivation and to encourage sustained swimming and water-based activity.

References

DCMS (2007) *Taking Part: The National Survey of Culture, Leisure and Sport, Annual Report 2005/2006* (online), available from http://www.culture.gov.uk/images/research/TPMay2007_8_Active Sport.pdf (accessed 6 September 2008).

DCMS (2008) *Massive sport reform to spearhead 2012 legacy plans* (online), available from http://www.culture.gov.uk/reference_library/media_releases/5163.aspx (accessed 14 January 2009).

Deci, E. and Ryan, R. (1985) *Intrinsic Motivation and Self-Determination in Human Behaviour*, New York: Plenum Press.

Duda, J.L. (1989) 'Relationship between task and ego orientation and the perceived purpose of sport among high school athletes', *Journal of Sport and Exercise Psychology*, 11, 318–335.

Duda, J.L. (1992) 'Motivation in sport settings: a goal perspective approach', in Roberts, G.C., *Motivation in Sport and Exercise*, Champaign, IL: Human Kinetics.

Ofsted (2004) *Ofsted Subject Reports 2002/03: Physical education in primary schools*. London: Ofsted.

Ofsted (2007) *Reaching the Key Stage 2 standard in swimming* (online), available from http://www.asaner.sportcentric.com/vsite/vfile/page/fileurl/0,11040,5118-187136-204358-129983-0-file,00.pdf (accessed 16 January 2009).

Royal Society for the Prevention of Accidents (2007) *Child Accidental Drowning 2005* (online), available from http://www.rospa.com/leisuresafety/information/CHILD_DROWNING 2005.pdf (accessed 10 January 2009).

Sport England (2007) 'Active People Survey 2005–06' (online), available from http://www.sport england.org/research/active_people_survey.aspx (accessed 19 January 2009).

9 Learning and teaching through athletic activities

Andy Theodoulides and Sue Keen

Introduction

The teaching of athletics activities has traditionally focused on the teaching of recognised Olympic-style events. As O'Neill (1992: 13) pointed out, 'no other key activity area within physical education has modelled itself so rigidly and so uncompromisingly on the adult sporting format in the way athletics has'. Perhaps this explains why pupils' learning in athletics often focuses on one event each lesson: for example long jump in lesson one followed by javelin in lesson two, high jump in lesson three, etc., until all events have been covered. Ofsted (2002) has pointed out that pupils' learning is inhibited when there are long gaps between activities which are learned over short periods of time, such as those which generally occur in the teaching of athletics activities. The approach to teaching athletics outlined in this chapter offers a different approach; it is one that builds on the development of fundamental skills of running, throwing and jumping at Key Stage 2, before moving on to the teaching of modified athletic activities in Years 7 and 8 of Key Stage 3. These activities might include running over plastic mini hurdles, or using modified equipment, such as foam javelins. This approach will provide pupils with the knowledge, skills and understanding necessary to move on to learning fully recognised events towards the final year of Key Stage 3 and into Key Stage 4.

Developing skills in physical activity

When they are 'developing skills in physical activity' pupils should be able to 'refine and adapt skills into techniques, develop the range of skills they use and develop the precision, control and fluency of their skills' (QCA 2008: 192). In the development of running skills this would include running at maximum speed over short distances, running over obstacles and paced running over a longer distance, gradually moving on to the recognised track events of 100 metres, 200 metres, 70–80 metres hurdles, 800 metres, 1500 metres and 4x100 metres relay. For jumping skills, basic skills of hopping, skipping and bounding can be developed into plyometric exercises and then refined into recognised techniques such as the 'sail', 'hang' and 'hitch kick' in the long jump; the hop, step and jump for the triple jump; the 'Fosbury flop' in the high jump. Similarly, throwing balls, quoits, bean bags and hoops with pushing, pulling, slinging and heaving actions are easily transformed into refined techniques of shot putt, javelin, discus and hammer.

Making and applying decisions

Making and applying decisions in athletic activities requires pupils to take an active part in the planning and development of their work through the selection and use of tactics, refining and adapting ideas, planning their future work and being aware of health and safety issues. For example, when making decisions about the use of tactics and strategies pupils might be asked to decide on the order of a relay team, decide which team member is going to run longer distances or what pace they are going to run when running longer distances. Pupils might make decisions such as which component of fitness they want to improve and work out their own training programme to improve this area. Pupils can set themselves achievable goals in terms of their performance and make decisions about how to work safely alongside others. Finally, pupils ought to be encouraged to take on different roles, such as official, and make decisions about applying the rules of running, throwing and jumping activities.

Developing physical and mental capacity

The NCPE requires that pupils 'develop their strength, stamina, speed and flexibility to cope with the demands of different activities and develop their mental determination to succeed' (QCA 2008 : 192). These are easily addressed through athletic activities. Three main areas of strength – maximum strength, elastic strength and strength endurance – can be developed in practice drills in athletic activities. Drills with appropriately weighted balls such as medicine balls, plyometric drills, harness resistance work, and circuits all contain an element of strength development. It is important to remember, however, that care must be taken to use a pupil's own body weight, low impact exercises with few repetitions and correctly weighted implements when incorporating learning activities of this nature.

Stamina is an area that is often associated with running laps of a track and can lead to negative feelings from pupils about athletic activities. By introducing mini-tracks, sustained running over specific times rather than distances (for example, pupils run for two minutes rather than 800 metres), linking running with equipment and working in groups, a positive approach to running activities can be created.

Speed is essential for all athletic events as well as sprinting. Controlled speed is needed in the approach runs for the jumps and javelin. A shot putter needs speed to glide across the circle and speed endurance is needed in longer races. Quick reaction work, sprint drills, explosive jumping and fast arm actions for throws will enhance pupil's development in this area.

The development of flexibility can be introduced through warming up and cooling down with static and dynamic stretches to highlight the importance of developing a good range of movement to aid performance. Teaching pupils the names of muscles can promote their understanding of anatomical features of the body.

In order to perform to maximum levels pupils need to learn to recognise what their bodies are capable of and how they can develop the determination to succeed. By providing a motivational climate in which pupils are encouraged to work to beat their previous best performances (Morgan 2000) and to identify and develop their strengths and weaker areas, pupils can gain satisfaction and encouragement from improving performance.

Evaluating and improving

Pupils are expected to evaluate and improve performance by identifying strengths and weaknesses and deciding upon what they need to do next to improve. Quantitative measurements of time and distance give pupils opportunities for self-evaluation and goal-setting as they strive to beat their previous performance. Watching a video of top athletes can help pupils understand the skills required for a good performance and in watching other pupils on a video they can learn to pick out faults in performance. Similarly, reciprocal teaching tasks are valuable to develop the skills for analysing performance. Drills to improve their weak areas can be selected by pupils; skills should be isolated through practices before being performed in the context of the whole event. For example, the long jump can be broken down into four phases (approach, take-off, flight, landing) and each phase practised and evaluated: controlled sprinting over a short distance for the approach phase; plyometric drills to aid take-off; assisted flight from boxes to allow time to concentrate on the flight phase; landing can be isolated when working from a short run up; before finally combining all phases together in the complete movement.

Making informed choices about healthy active lifestyles

This requires pupils to 'identify the types of activities they are best suited to, identify the types of roles they would like to take on and make choices about their involvement in healthy physical activity' (QCA 2008 : 193). Athletics provides an opportunity for all pupils to gain confidence. Pupils who struggle in running events may have strength and power to sling the discus or the ability to jump high. Running, throwing and jumping skills transfer to other physical activities or can be continued in later life to maintain a healthy lifestyle. Jogging and visiting the gym, for example, are very popular in adulthood. Whilst some pupils will excel in their performance, others may rise to the role of coach or official and develop their knowledge and gain confidence in the process.

Guidance and teaching ideas for working with cluster schools

Set out below are examples of the types of learning activities which focus on the development of running, throwing and jumping skills whilst at the same time address learning across the NCPE key processes. These examples are broken down into eight lessons. You will need to make decisions about continuity and progression of learning material in order to meet the learning needs of the pupils you teach and the time available for teaching. Decisions about what to teach and when to progress onto new material will be based upon effective assessment of pupils' learning. Developing pupils' knowledge, skills and understanding in order for them to perform effectively will require that learning is reinforced over time in many ways. Consequently, the learning activities put forward here are not exhaustive and you may need to utilise other drills and practices to supplement those outlined below.

Typical athletics challenges for pupils in Years 5 or 6

The following activities can be taught on any area of playing field. Pupils can be introduced to the Aviva Shine Awards when appropriate.

Lesson one (running for speed)

Equipment – cones, whistle, bean bags.

1. Learning activity – warm-up
   - Tag games – partner tag, chain tag (see Chapter 12).
   - Active stretches – pupils working in pairs over a distance of 20 metres.
2. Learning activity – speed reaction work
   - Pupils lie on their back with heels on a line – on the whistle or your command they get up and sprint 20 metres.
   - Pupils start in the press-up position with fingers on a line – on the whistle or your command they get up and sprint 20 metres (see Photo 9.1).

Photo 9.1 Running for speed

3. Learning activity – how far in 4 seconds?
   - Pupils estimate how far they think they can run in 4 seconds.
   - Mark from 20 to 35 metres along the side of running lanes with different coloured cones.
   - From a standing start and command from the teacher, pupils run along track for 4 seconds. On the whistle they look to see which cone they have reached and if they have beaten their estimated mark.
   - Working with a partner, pupils do the same run and this time on the whistle drop a bean bag on the track. Their partner then tries to reach the bean bag in 4 seconds.
4. Learning activity – 40-metre shuttle relays in groups of four
   - Two pupils stand at each end of a 40-metre track.
   - Pupils run to tag next team member.
   - Number one runs and collects number two, who then both run and collect number three and lastly collect number four (teams will need to decide who is the strongest to run number one).

Lesson two (running and jumping for distance)

Equipment – cones, skipping ropes, tape measure, whistle.

1. Learning activity – warm-up: skipping with ropes
   - Skipping on the spot by jumping on two feet to two feet or springing from one foot to the other.
   - Skipping while running along.

2.   Learning activity – acceleration work
     • Pupils run on the spot, pumping arms quickly.
     • On the whistle they sprint forward to a marked cone 30 metres away.
3.   Learning activity – jumping
     • Practise jumping from two feet to two feet.
     • Measure out 8.95 metres, which is the current world record for the long jump held by Mike Powell.
     • With a partner, pupils see how many jumps it takes them to equal the world record.
4.   Learning activity – relays
     • Four runners at one end of 40-metre track.
     • Shuttle runs with jumping activities at one end, e.g. run and then complete five star jumps before running back.
     • Run and perform five speed bounces before running back.

Lesson three (sustained running and pull throw)

Equipment – cones, bean bags, foam javelins.

1.   Learning activity – warm-up
     Mark out a mini oval track 60 metres long by 30 metres wide.
     • Have a chat jog around the track with partner.
     • Upon a whistle pupils change from walk to jog or run (one blow of the whistle = walk; two blows = jog; three blows = run).
     • Pupils take it in turns to chose a dynamic stretch to perform with a partner (dynamic stretches must cover one for the upper body and one for the legs – see Appendix, p. 130).
2.   Learning activity – sustained running
     • Each pair puts a cone as starting point on the track.
     • Pupils take it in turns to complete laps of the track in a combined time of 3 minutes (laps should be completed without walking, therefore pupils must think about pacing themselves).
3.   Learning activity – throwing actions
     Pupils practise throwing a bean bag first then progress to a foam javelin.
     • Seated throw, kneeling throw and standing.
     • Standing sideways transferring weight from back to front.
4.   Learning activity – throwing relay
     • Divide into teams of four with two pupils standing 80 metres apart – use different coloured bean bags, one per team.
     • Number one throws the bean bag towards the next team member (number two), then runs to pick it up and throws again until they reach number two. He/she at the other end does the same until the bean bag reaches number three. This continues until number four has completed their turn back to the starting position. Pupils must not run when holding bean bag.

Lesson four (running and pull throw)

Equipment – javelins, cones, hoops, bean bags.

1.   Learning activity – warm-up: follow the leader
     • In pairs, one pupil leads the other running round a set area.
     • Vary the way of moving so pupils have to hop, skip, jump on two feet, etc.
     • Pupils then follow each other and incorporate active stretches.

2. Learning activity – pull throw for distance
   - Pupils throw a bean bag as far as they can to partner.
3. Learning activity – pull throw for accuracy
   - Place football on a cone in between pairs of pupils.
   - Pupils throw the bean bag to knock the ball off the cone.
   - Pupils take two steps back each time they knock the ball off the cone (see Photo 9.2).

Photo 9.2 Pull throw for accuracy

4. Learning activity – pull throw using a soft javelin (foam or rubber turbo javelins)
   - Combine the skills learnt in previous activities to throwing the soft javelins.
   - All throw in the same direction on command to prepare for safety in throws.
5. Learning activity – tick relay
   - Pupils stand in teams of four forming spokes of a wheel inside a circle of cones with a diameter of 30 metres.
   - Pupils on the outside run clockwise round the outside of circle and when they get back to team tag the next person.
   - Next runner does the same.
   - The aim is to catch the team in front then call out 'TICK' (see Figure 9.1).

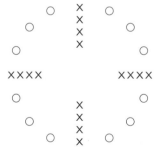

Figure 9.1 Tick relay

Lesson five (running and throwing foam javelin)

Equipment – soft javelins, cones, hoops

1. Learning activity – warm-up: jumping bean game
   Pupils stand in a space and perform the following tasks:
   - Jumping beans – tuck jumps on the spot.
   - Runner beans – run around in the space allocated.

- Baked beans – lie on the floor.
- Broad beans – astride jumps with feet apart and then together.
- Jelly beans – wiggle their body to touch toes and stand up again.

2. Learning activity – pull throw using soft javelin
   - Throw for accuracy – pupils have to throw a javelin into a hoop placed on the ground. Each time the javelin lands in the hoop the pupils should move two paces further back.
   - Throw for distance – pupils throw to reach cones set at 5-metre intervals.

Lesson six (relay with a baton and combination jumps)

Equipment – relay batons, cones, hurdles (or canes across high cones), two ropes, low boxes and other equipment that children can jump over.

1. Learning activity – long course relay in groups of four
   Teacher maps out a running course using four landmarks on school field
   - Each team member starts at a landmark and the aim is to get baton round course as quickly as possible.
2. Learning activity – warm-up: DVD game
   - Play – run round space.
   - Fast forward – run in and out of each other at faster pace.
   - Rewind – run backwards (look over shoulder).
   - Pause – hold good running position.
   - Stop – crouch down and touch ground.
3. Learning activity – jumping combinations
   Set up as much equipment as possible for pupils to jump over either for height or distance.
   - Jump from one foot to the other.
   - One foot to the same foot.
   - One foot to two feet.
   - Two feet to one foot and two feet to two feet.
4. Learning activity – running over obstacles
   Set up mini hurdles equal distance apart (six metres). At least four pupils in each lane.
   - Pupils run over hurdles thinking about rhythm and taking an equal number of strides in between each hurdle – aim for three, four or five.
   - Keep pupils focused on the rhythm of running – not 'jumping' the hurdles.
   - Once this has been mastered move on to hurdle races in one direction.
5. Learning activity – shuttle relays over 40 metres
   In teams of four with all pupils starting at same end.
   - Run to a line 40 metres away and back to give baton to next team member.

Lesson seven (running and throwing with a push action)

Equipment – basketballs, footballs, hoops, cones, and any other equipment for pupils to experiment with throwing.

1. Learning activity – warm-up
   - Run around a set area, chest passing ball in pairs while on the move
2. Learning activity – push throw

- Pupils aim to land a ball into a hoop with a two-handed chest (push) pass – with each successful push pass the pupils take one step back to increase the difficulty of the next throw.
- Chest pass ball while side skipping between two cones.
- If right-handed kneel on right knee and push pass ball from right shoulder to land in a hoop – each successful push pass the pupils take one step back to increase the difficulty of the next throw.
- Standing opposite a partner, pupils aim to push a ball from the shoulder as high as possible for their partner to catch.
- Pupils can then make up their own throwing task using the equipment available.

3. Learning activity – paced running

Mark out a mini track of 200 metres. Pupils work in groups of four.

- One pair runs round track while the others perform a skill such as dribble a ball round cones (keep score of number of turns).
- Change over to try and better the other pair.
- Set several tasks and include pupils' ideas.

Lesson eight (running and push action)

Equipment – batons, cones, basketballs.

1. Learning activity – warm-up: circle name game

Pupils stand in a circle (nine or ten in each group)

- Teacher calls out a letter and if a pupil has that letter in their name they run round the outside of the circle.
- Vary the task by getting pupils to perform other exercises in the centre of circle such as star jumps, press-ups, astride jumps.

2. Learning activity – push throw

- Pupils push throw a football for distance.

3. Learning activity – find a good starting position

- Practise standing starts with left foot on line and right arm forward, leaning slightly forward with body (or the opposite).
- Sprint for 20 metres.
- Use commands: 'On your marks', 'Set', 'GO!'
- Work in groups to practise starting each other and running over short distance.

4. Learning activity – continuous relay

Group the pupils into teams of four and give each member a number, 1 to 4. Mark out three starting points 50 metres apart. Pupils 1 and 4 stand at one point; pupils 2 and 3 each start at the other two points (see Figure 9.2).

- Number 1 starts, runs to pass the baton to number 2 and then stays in that position. Number 2 then runs to pass the baton to number 3, who then passes the baton to number 4 and so on.

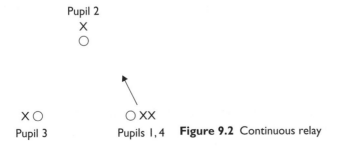

Figure 9.2 Continuous relay

- The relay continues until all runners are back to where they started.
- The distance of each leg of the relay can be extended.
- Take the pupils' time and then see if they can beat it on their next attempt.

Typical athletic challenges for pupils in Years 7 and 8

The following lessons build upon the running, throwing and jumping skills learned at Key Stage 2. Paced running is introduced, along with the slinging action of the discus and the introduction of jumping for height.

These lessons are best taught on a running track with a long jump pit and a high jump landing bed, with a grass area for throws.

Lesson one (sprinting)

Equipment – cones, whistle, stop watches, recording sheets/notebooks.

1. Learning activity – warm-up
   - In groups of four, pupils group jog around the track. Each pupil takes it in turn to lead the group for 100 metres, running at a different speed to the person before.
   - Dynamic stretches.
2. Learning activity – sprinting
   - Run 20 metres with *very* fast arms (take *small*, quick steps).
   - Run 20 metres with *big* arm action (take longer slower strides – over stride).
   - Run 20 metres – find a happy medium between *fast* arm action and *big* arm action.
3. Learning activity – fast finish
   Mark out lanes of 60 metres with cones positioned at the half-way point.
   - Pupils work in pairs at opposite ends to each other.
   - Give starting commands – 'on your marks', 'set', 'GO!'
   - Pupils run towards the centre point in adjacent lanes to see who can get to the middle first.
   - Extend the distance to 80 metres and 100 metres.
4. Learning activity – recording a time
   Carry out as above but with pupils in groups of four.
   - One pupil acts as timekeeper, one as starter, and the other two run
   - Pupils choose 60 or 100 metres and record their times.
   - Introduce pupils to the Aviva Shine Awards scheme so they can check how many points they have scored.

Lesson two (throwing: push, pull, sling and heave)

Equipment – tennis balls, footballs, bean bags, turbo javelins, rubber shot, rubber discus, rubber hammers, medicine balls, quoits, hoops, shuttlecocks, frisbees, cones, tape measures and notebooks.

1. Learning activity – warm-up: ball tag
   - Pupils work in small groups in a coned area.
   - One person is free and runs round the area.
   - The others try and touch the free runner with the ball in their hands.
   - The group cannot run with the ball but must pass quickly to each other.

2. Learning activity – divergent teaching challenge
   - Pupils are given a selection of throwing implements and asked to find 'which implement best matches each distance when thrown as far as possible'.
   - Set up distances of 5, 10, 15, 20, and over 25 metres (pupils can mark with cones).
   - As above but pupils experiment with different throwing actions, i.e. push, pull, sling and heave.
3. Learning activity – slinging action
   - Pupils practise slinging action using quoits, hoops, and footballs.
4. Learning activity – ultimate frisbee
   - Finish with a game of ultimate frisbee. This is an invasion game between two teams in which the aim is to throw a frisbee through a defended territory in order to cross the opponents' goal line.

Lesson three (sprinting and discus)

Equipment – video camcorder, discus, tape measure, CD player and Multi-stage Fitness Test CD.

1. Learning activity – warm-up: bleep test
   - Measure out 20 metres.
   - Both pupils start at same end.
   - On the bleep one pupil moves to the other side then their partner follows on next bleep. Start with power walking, skipping forwards and sideways, other low impact drills or dynamic stretching, and finish off with running.
2. Learning activity – back to backs
   Pupils are divided into groups of three or five. Pupils numbered 1, 3 and 5 start at one end of the course; two and four at the other. They run over a distance of 30 metres (NB this should not be run as a race – the focus should be on technique).
   - Number 1 runs to 2, and so on until all pupils have run four times and are back where they started.
   - After a rest of 5 minutes pupils run again three times each.
   - Pupils can be videoed whilst performing for evaluation and analysis later or in another lesson.
3. Learning activity – discus
   - Pupils practise slinging action using quoits and hoops.
   - Record the distance thrown with quoit.
4. Learning activity – video evaluation and analysis of a pupil's sprinting technique
   - Film a pupil's sprinting performance and ask the pupil to evaluate their own performance.

Lesson four (jumping for distance and paced running)

Equipment – SAQ ladders, mini hurdles, cones, brush, rake, reciprocal sheets.

1. Learning activity – warm-up
   Set up SAQ ladders, mini hurdles and cones radiating from a central point (see Photo 9.3).
   - Pupils run lightly over ladders and over hurdles.
   - Pupils side-step in and out of ladder and jump from two feet to two feet over hurdles.

Photo 9.3 Jumping for distance: warm-up

2. Learning activity – jumping for distance
    *   Pupils practise jumping from two feet to two feet on grass or in the pit.
    *   Mark out the distance of the long jump world record and see how many two-footed jumps it takes pupils to cover that distance.
    *   Move onto the runway. Pupils take six to eight strides to run and take off from one foot at any point so as to land safely in the sand on two feet.
3. Learning activity – 'there and back'
    *   Standing in the middle of the track / field, pupils pick a landmark somewhere on the field. A partner then times how long it takes them to run to the landmark and back. Do this five times, picking a different landmark each time.
    *   Pupils now run to all five landmarks without stopping. The athlete must return to the centre of the field / start position each time before running to the next landmark. Record times as a target for further attempts.

Lesson five (jumping for distance and running)

Equipment – skipping ropes, mini hurdles, rake, tape measures, notebooks.

1. Learning activity – warm-up
    *   Skipping with ropes on the spot or moving.
2. Learning activity – jumping combinations
    *   Pupils perform five strides.
    *   Pupils perform five two-footed jumps.
    *   Three strides followed by three two-footed jumps.
    *   Dynamic stretches.
3. Learning activity – jumping for distance
    *   Using three-stride approach, pupils jump for distance.
    *   As above but with mini-hurdle just after take off point to encourage height.
    *   Using the runway run (ten strides), pupils take off from any point, with a partner recording the distance.
4. Learning activity – 'How far can you run in 30 seconds?'
    *   Pupils start from various positions around the track and have to see how far they can run in 30 seconds.
    *   Pupils record results in notebooks as a target for further attempts.

Lesson six (paced running and turbo javelin)

Equipment – basketballs, turbo javelins, cones, hoops, tape measures, notebooks.

1. Learning activity – warm-up
   - In groups of four or six, pupils make up their own warm-up which involves throwing a basketball or tennis ball.
2. Learning activity – sustained running
   Place a marked cone every 50 metres around a track.
   - Based on their 30-second run, pupils estimate how far they think they can run in a given time such as two minutes or Kelly Holmes's winning time at the Athens Olympics – 1 minute 56.38 seconds.
   - Working in pairs, one athlete one coach, each has a turn to try and reach their predicted distance. By counting how many cones they pass pupils can work out how far they ran.
3. Learning activity – javelin throw with modified equipment
   - In small groups throwing from a central point, pupils throw for accuracy and distance with turbo javelins into a hoop on the field.
   - Pupils devise their own competition for throwing for accuracy and distance.
   - Measured throw (refer to Aviva Shine Awards).

Lesson seven (jumping for height and running over obstacles)

Equipment – hurdles, cones, netballs.

1. Learning activity – warm-up
   - In groups of three, follow the leader – start with walking, then skipping, bounding, jogging. On the whistle change activity and leader.
   - In small groups pupils chose and perform dynamic stretches.
   - In pairs, from standing pupils have to throw a ball and jump and catch it above their head.
2. Learning activity – jumping for height
- Pupils run and catch a netball above their head which is thrown to them by a partner.
   - Using a foam or plastic hurdle, children approach from the front, take-off on one leg and land on two.
   - Using foam or plastic hurdles at approximately knee height, pupils approach from the side to complete a scissor kick over the hurdle. Pupils should approach from both sides, taking off from the foot furthest away from the hurdle.
3. Learning activity – running over obstacles
   Place four mini hurdles in each lane, six strides apart.
   - Pupils practise running in one direction over the hurdles with speed and rhythm.
   - Pupils can change the position of the mini hurdles to suit their stride length and to promote speed and rhythm.
4. Learning activity – hurdle relay
   - Hurdle relays clearing from the side with a scissor kick (Photo 9.4).

Photo 9.4 Hurdle relay

Lesson eight (jumping for height, relay)

Equipment – cones, relay batons, soft hurdles.

1. Learning activity – warm-up
   • Pupils devise their own warm-up for a jumping event. This should include pulse raiser, dynamic stretches and a related jumping activity.
2. Learning activity – jumping onto a high jump bed
   • Pupils approach the landing bed for the high jump from the side and scissor onto the bed. Do not use a bar. To begin with, take approximately six strides.
   • Introduce a foam bar tied to the uprights to encourage pupils to gain height on the jump and swing free knee high.
   • Progress so that pupils land on the bed with a seat drop.
3. Learning activity – passing a baton
   • In groups of four, stand in line with person at the back holding the baton.
   • The person at the front jogs and the others follow.
   • The pupil at the back passes the baton forward then runs to the front of the line.
4. Learning activity – linear relay
   Set out two cones 50 metres apart and position team as in Figure 9.3.
   • Teams practise running and passing the baton at half pace.
   • Run through at a faster pace so that the outgoing runner starts to move when incoming runner is 5 metres away and accelerates quickly.
   • Hurdle relay – as above, but incorporate soft hurdles at various points.
5. Learning activity – relay
   • In groups of four, team relay around one lap of a track (400 metres).
   • Pupils decide how far they are going to run and in which position. Each pupil must run minimum of 50 metres.

Figure 9.3 Linear relay

Assessment in athletics

One way of assessing performance in athletics activities is to use times and distances. This is the method used in competition and provides a measure of achievement. The Aviva Shine Awards scheme is based upon times and distances and these determine the level of award that pupils receive.

Good learning and teaching requires that teachers assess pupils *summatively* against NCPE levels of attainment and *formatively* during lessons. Formative assessment will dictate the speed with which knowledge, skills and understanding are progressed and the direction future learning takes. Teachers should not stick rigidly to the structure of the learning activities given above if, when assessing pupils, they feel more time is warranted upon a particular skill.

Teachers will need to draw upon a variety of methods of assessment to assess pupils' learning. The main method of assessment for making decisions about pupils' attainment in the acquisition of running, jumping and throwing skills is observation. Learning activities in which pupils plan and lead sessions, such as a warm-up or short teaching episode, will enable teachers to assess pupils' ability to make and apply decisions. Where skills are broken down into phases, pupils can observe each other, comment, analyse and evaluate on how skills can be improved. Teachers will need to gather evidence of how effective pupils are in this area through question and answer sessions and assessment of pupils' performance when engaged in reciprocal teaching and self-assessment. Knowledge and understanding of fitness and health can be assessed through observation of a warm-up which pupils plan themselves and perform, through discussions about how exercise affects the body, or through written work such as training programmes designed to improve one or more components of fitness.

At Key Stage 3 assessment is likely to occur in the context of modified recognised athletic events such as running for speed (60 metres or 100 metres, hurdles), paced running (800 metres), jumping for distance (long jump, plyometric drills), jumping for height (high jump), and throwing actions of slinging (discus), pulling (javelin), push (shot putt) and heave (hammer). At Key Stage 3 teachers ought to plan and assess pupils' knowledge, skills and understanding in roles other than performer, for example as time keeper, recorder of results or judge. In addition, assessment should be made of pupils' understanding of health and safety and how to apply rules and conventions of athletics events. In terms of health and fitness pupils should be able to recognise their strengths and weaknesses and show knowledge and understanding of fitness levels and how they can improve. For example, pupils should know that if, when jumping for height, they are unable to drive effectively at take-off that they can develop strength in quadriceps through squat and plyometric exercises. Pupils' ability to plan suitable drills and implement their own training sessions will also indicate their level of knowledge and understanding of health and fitness issues. Pupils will then be able to use this knowledge to find the event or events to which they are best suited.

Summary

Pupils' ability to perform recognised athletics events is an extension of skills in running, throwing and jumping. However, all too often pupils are asked to perform recognised athletic events before they have mastered the basic skills required to perform them successfully. A programme of learning which focuses on the progression of running, throwing and jumping skills into modified events with modified equipment, such as that outlined here, will lead to a more enjoyable, meaningful and successful experience of athletic activities for all pupils of all abilities.

Appendix: examples of dynamic stretches

- Alternate walking on heels and toes, pumping arms at the same time.
- Make side skips, swinging arms out to the sides.
- Swing right leg high in front and try to touch toes with left hand reaching across body – move forward and alternate leg swings.
- Jog forward, flicking feet out in front.
- Whilst standing, hold arms out parallel with the ground and circle the arms. Circles can be big (the size of a beach ball) or small (the size of a tennis ball).
- Jog forward, picking feet up behind.
- Skip, gradually getting knees high in front of body and swinging arms.
- Caterpillar walk – start with both hands and feet on the ground, keep hands still and walk feet forward to meet hands, then keep feet still and walk hands away.
- Walk/jog and move the arms in front-crawl swimming action.
- Walk/jog and move the arms in back-crawl swimming action.
- Hot coals (athletes take as many little steps as they can by lifting their feet off the ground as if they are travelling over hot coals).
- On-the-spot pumping arms.
- Hamstring stretch: sweeping floor with hands while knees are together, one leg straight, one leg bent, push chest towards knees.
- Quadriceps stretch: start with feet together, lift knee high under hips then lunge forward to place the foot so the knee is bent at 90 degrees with back leg straight. Arms should be bent at 90 degrees with right arm forward when the left leg is forward.
- Sumo squats – skip sideways and stop to squat with knees at 90 degrees.

Acknowledgement

Photographs in this chapter are provided courtesy of Martina Ingram.

Bibliography

Aviva Shine Awards (www.avivashineawards.com).
DfEE/QCA (1999) *Physical Education: The National Curriculum for England.* London. HMSO.
Morgan, K. (2000) 'Motivation in athletics', *The British Journal of Teaching Physical Education,* 31 (1), 16–18.
Ofsted (2002) *Physical Education in Secondary Schools: Ofsted subject report series 2001/02.* London, HMSO.
O'Neill, J. (1992) 'Athletics teaching in schools – change at last? An interpretation of "Athletic Activities" in the PE National Curriculum', *The British Journal of Physical Education,* 23 (1), 12–17.
QCA (2008) http://www.qca.org.uk/ (accessed 8 April 2009).

10 Learning and teaching through fitness and health activities

James Wallis and Rob Harley

Introduction

The ambition to teach health, exercise and fitness has too often been thwarted by a one-dimensional view of the processes through which these vital concepts can be learned. In many respects this weakness exists as an extension of misunderstandings about the processes of teaching and learning. Such limitations are usually characterised by an over-emphasis on modes of delivery which are explicit in nature and therefore rely almost exclusively on formal teaching through structured lessons and the presentation of concepts in a traditional format. In this chapter we aim to consider implicit as well as explicit modes of delivery of the pivotal concepts of health and exercise. We will focus on both hidden and formal curricula in schools, as well as on how a physical education department and, in turn, the physical education teacher can begin to construct an inclusive and motivating environment accessible to all pupils.

A traditional view of the relationship between physical education and the numerous concepts bracketed under broad terms such as health-related fitness (HRF) or health-related exercise (HRE) has resulted in physical education lessons adopting a formal role in the explicit delivery of material relating to health and wellbeing. Lessons have been dominated by content on areas such as fitness assessment, training methods and principles, nutrition and other concepts more at home in various forms of accredited physical education. In this chapter we will dedicate only part of the content to the formal delivery of HRE and HRF in pupil-friendly, unthreatening ways. The main body of the chapter will consist of a series of sub-sections that will discuss features of school and department practice, mainly implicit or subliminal in nature, which extend the health and activity messages to pupils.

Health and fitness in the National Curriculum for Physical Education

Under the 1999 version of the National Curriculum 'knowledge and understanding of fitness and health' was included as a stand-alone key strand alongside 'acquiring and developing skills', 'selecting and applying skills' and 'evaluating and improving performance'. It would be premature and misleading, however, to celebrate the formal inclusion of health, exercise and fitness. At first sight it would seem to be a promoted position and to give equality with the traditionally more highly regarded dimensions of physical education. This, however, was not the case. Successive subject inspections considered the teaching of the fitness and health strand to be the weakest of the four.

Despite the 'open door' to teach health and fitness concepts through a permeated approach by embedding content into the six activity areas, the default position for the majority of health and fitness teaching remained in discrete lessons, hampered by the old-fashioned labels of HRE or HRF and conjuring recurrent images of fitness testing and theory-based sessions in classrooms. Ofsted (2009) reported that health and fitness programmes do not feature consistently within the secondary school physical education curriculum and are often marginalised or subsumed into other activities. The report states that 'this is worrying, given the widespread concerns over childhood obesity and the increasingly sedentary lifestyles that many young people lead' (Ofsted 2009: 39). Moreover, the report states that whilst physical education has contributed effectively to the *Every Child Matters* outcomes, particularly to 'being healthy', 'enjoying and achieving' and 'making a positive contribution', 'it has yet to have sufficient impact on tackling the health issue of childhood obesity' (Ofsted 2009: 6).

Moving forward nine years to the 2008 version of the National Curriculum for Physical Education (NCPE) for Key Stage 3, health components feature more heavily than aesthetics, performance, problem-solving, challenge or personal and social dimensions of physical education. Surely more cause for celebration is that health messages are now included as one key concept – 'healthy, active lifestyles'; one key process – 'making informed choices about healthy lifestyles'; and one area of range and content – 'exercising safely and effectively'. A simple way to analyse the Key Stage 3 programme of study in the 2008 curriculum is to count the number of references to the key terms of health and physical activity on the one hand and sport and fitness on the other. The overwhelming majority is with the former, which therefore gives further evidence of physical education's shifting emphasis towards health and away from performance.

Looking at history it is important not to be drawn into the false position of thinking that increasing the emphasis on health and fitness in the NCPE will create the desired outcomes in pupils' long-term physical activity and suitable lifestyle choices. Following this line of thought places an unrealistic expectation on the impact of physical education lessons in moulding the lifestyle choices of children. Health, fitness and physical activity education is less about what is accomplished in the miserly physical education time afforded to most schools but much more about the creation of a multi-faceted health environment which pupils (and staff!) can constantly interact with on a daily basis. Each school, each physical education department and each physical education teacher needs to consider a multiplicity of strategies for achieving functional outcomes to the health and exercise education of pupils.

The health and activity agenda for schools

Taking a multi-faceted approach to the teaching of health and activity in schools requires a consideration of the many factors which combine to construct a school's hidden curriculum. Many features of the hidden curriculum can be easily overlooked, which means that schools miss out on some opportunities to promote health. Examples to take into consideration include:

1. The school canteen and general eating environment. Aside from the obvious consideration of the types of foods provided in the school canteen it is important to observe some factors such as presentation and protocols of the dining area. Seemingly minor issues such as the supervision arrangements, decoration, queuing and payment protocols can all impact upon the quality of the experience for pupils and staff and ultimately lead to an acceptance or rejection of the educative opportunity that lunchtime brings.

2. The availability of clean and well maintained water fountains presents key implicit messages to pupils. Physical education lessons could actively encourage the use of water bottles to re-hydrate during or after practical activity. There are even some compelling arguments for encouraging re-hydration during classroom-based lessons to aid recovery post exercise and to increase concentration.

3. Schools should be taking proactive measures in assisting pupils to achieve the recommended level of physical activity every day. One suggestion is the provision, quality and maintenance of safe, clean cycle storage. Making changing and washing facilities accessible for those who cycle to school can overcome some of the perceived barriers to cycling to school.

4. A very contentious point of implicit health and activity education is the action and behaviour of school staff. Whilst staff can rightly question the extent to which their action and behaviours can be prescribed by the school, they should be made well aware that they are role models whose actions will be mirrored by pupils. The potential to make or break pupils' health and lifestyle choices is often missed when listing the impacts of teachers. To the critical eye this presents a fantastic, untapped opportunity in the presentation of functional health behaviours. The flip side to this is that poor role models have the potential to reduce the likelihood of the adherence to health and activity likely to provide long-term benefits to pupils. Therefore staff are presented with some moral dilemmas surrounding their own lifestyle choices in areas such as food choices, smoking, levels of activity and their general health.

There will be further examples of good practice in creating a proactive health environment which depend upon the individual situational and contextual factors which are distinctive of each school. Some of these features of good practice may contribute towards the Healthy Schools Award given by Department for Children, Schools and Families.

The physical education department's health and activity agenda

Health and activity cannot be regarded as the remit of the physical education department alone. The brief overview and examples cited above begin to create a more coherent and multi-faceted health environment and begin to implicitly 'teach' pupils functional habits, 'delivered' through numerous modes. Given the evolving priorities of physical education, however, it is clearly acknowledged that physical education should take the leading role in further advancing the health agenda. In this section we will discuss both implicit and explicit delivery of health-related concepts through the formal, structured curriculum (such as physical education lessons) and through the creation of the department's hidden curriculum.

Contributory factors to the creation of a function-hidden health curriculum might include:

1. Functional health and lifestyle habits of physical education staff. It is difficult to overstate the impact of the physical education teacher as a role model to pupils in terms of what is communicated through word and action. The formal curriculum is likely to build a series of structured lessons which will highlight and accentuate the value of healthy activity and lifestyle choices. However, the value of even the most well considered and well delivered curriculum is likely to be totally undermined by contradictory messages via teacher behaviours. Lifestyle and activity choices must match the formal messages of curriculum content. Whilst it is a point of debate to what extent any individual's life choices should be expected to be restrained by their

career, the ethical considerations and the moral obligation of a powerful socialising force in the health of children should take precedence. This can be viewed as an extension of the professional values and practice strand of teacher competence.

2. Presentation of the physical education environment. Too often the term 'physical education' is used synonymously with 'sport'. Whilst we do not intend to contribute to this debate here, it should be recognised that confusing the relationship between these two terms can often serve as a demotivating factor to some pupils. Sport is not physical education. Sport can form part of physical education for those who are engaged by competition, performance and structured, codified situations. This chapter is not anti-sport but pro-physical activity, a concept into which sport clearly fits – along with rollerblading, mountain biking, aqua aerobics and latin dancing. We do hold the opinion that everyone should experience sport in many different contexts but be given the opportunity to withdraw from sport to engage in self-paced, semi- or un-structured physical activity which meets the HEA recommendations for health. In reality, sport is less popular than many imagine. Avoiding repeated reference to 'sport' when the term 'physical activity' is more appropriate can be considered an important first step in avoiding emotional and subsequently physical disengagement from the subject.

3. One way in which the physical education department can create an inclusive environment may be to consider the nature of posters which are used to decorate changing rooms and communal areas. The images of sporting icons should reflect equality and diversity, rather than giving the traditional dominance to male team sports. In keeping with this principle, the department could use images of the school's physical education and sport in practice to advertise the quality of lessons and to motivate a wide cross-section of pupils. At the same time this could be a way of encouraging the use of information and communications technology to aid learning.

4. How success is defined and celebrated is an important factor in maintaining pupil engagement. This consideration is heavily linked with the creation of an appropriate motivational climate. Pupils will approach a task with a task/mastery orientation or an ego orientation. Pupils who are task- or mastery-orientated are characterised by high levels of effort, enjoying challenges and solving problems, developing their own level of skill and striving for personal best performances. In contrast an ego-orientated child will be driven by inter-person competition or comparison and will take pride in defeating others whilst showing minimal effort. The way in which a physical education teacher rewards and celebrates positive outcomes can shape the orientation of pupils and ultimately their motivation. The value of a mastery environment is clear, in that every pupil can achieve success and gain tangible or non-tangible rewards. An ego environment, by contrast, merely further confirms the dominance of a select group of talented performers. Some general principles include:

    *   Defining success as self-improvement. Reward 'improvers' as opposed to 'winners'. In this way everyone has the opportunity to experience success.
    *   Including images of physical education in practice as well as sports team representatives in communal physical education areas. Update images on a weekly basis to include a wide cross-section of performers and activities.
    *   Publicly celebrate and reward a range of categories within physical education and sport participation and performance, as opposed to merely reinforcing the celebration of sports team representation.

    Examples of methods which can assist in creating a mastery environment in a range of physical education practical activity areas are given in the section on the formal curriculum below.

Independently conducted research on behalf of the Department for Children, Schools and Families (DCSF) has shown a steady increase in the numbers of schoolchildren participating in at least two hours of physical education and sport per week. This figure has risen from 62 per cent in 2003/04 to 86 per cent in 2006/07 and then up to 90 per cent in 2007/08. This is clearly significant progress in moving towards the ultimate achievement of 100 per cent, but is also significant in surpassing the Public Service Agreement (PSA) of 85 per cent set by the Government for achievement by 2008.

On first sight these figures are encouraging. However, it is important to recall the recommended levels of regular exercise and physical activity as stated by the Department for Culture, Media and Sport (DCMS) in 2003, which suggest that any such activity should be performed three to five times per week for 20 to 60 minutes per session. In addition to this many have supported the recommended advice to take regular exercise for the health benefits it would bring to individuals and the reduced risk of hypokinetic diseases (Bailey, 2005; DfES/DCMS, 2003; Cale, 2000; Parker and Curtner-Smith, 2005; Portman, 2003). Given this vital statistic relating to volume of physical activity, it is not so much a question of the numbers of children being given access to two hours of quality physical education and sport but much more a question of what is happening within the two-hour provision to create intrinsically motivated individuals who are engaged enough to seek continued activity. In this light, the process of careful and well informed curriculum planning is of paramount importance. Achieving a captive audience for two hours per week is only half the challenge.

The achievement of the Government's Public Service Agreement for every pupil to receive at least two hours of high quality physical education and sport per week can, in part, be attributed to extra-curricular provision. A traditional vision of extra-curricular physical education and sport is that of exclusive competition-based activities which are based around school team selection and performance. A common perception for the majority of pupils is that, whilst willing and motivated to engage in additional physical activity, they do not consider themselves good enough to attend. Programming extra-curricular provision for the sole benefit of advancing the performance of the privileged few is an outdated notion which has no place in a school's obligation to provide inclusive physical opportunities for all pupils. In many ways this notion is an historical legacy of previous interpretations of the role and function of physical education. The content of the new NCPE (2008) is loud and clear in its emphasis on health and physical activity rather than more traditional conceptions of the subject which used sport and physical education interchangeably. Creating an environment which is open, inclusive and equitable for all pupils emerges from coherent communication of the opportunities available to pupils as well as a celebration of regular participation of a wide cross-section of pupils.

The formal curriculum – the permeation of health and activity messages

The relationship between health concepts and the formal curriculum has traditionally been dominated by limited interpretations of what constitutes a 'health message'. Health and activity education in physical education has tended to be limited to a block of lessons with a broad title such as HRE, with coverage of explicit health, fitness and exercise concepts. A more appropriate interpretation is the consideration of how every physical education lesson can be presented in a fully inclusive way by considering the motivational climate of the lesson and how tasks are presented to pupils. In this context health and activity may not feature as an explicit element of the lesson but becomes an implicit message as pupils become engaged, enthused and more likely to make favourable future choices concerning activity. It is a common error to bracket the education of health and activity habits as a formal process when, in reality, the education of these vital life skills happens all the time, every day, through a multiplicity of planned and unplanned processes.

Examples of implicit processes in physical education activities which can contribute to the promotion of positive physical activity experiences include:

1. Teaching 800 metres (middle-distance running) – you might need to question the extent to which you need to obtain and record performance data against individual disciplines, for much the same reasons as discussed in the context of fitness assessment below. A more important consideration is the extent to which pupils are able to monitor pace and distance and judge for themselves their own sustainable pace for the duration of the run. On the basis of this information pupils may then place any recorded times into context with previous attempts and reflect upon processes, as opposed to merely outcome and inter-person comparisons.

    Child-centred organisation for such a lesson would feature pupil target times based upon previous attempts, along with rewards and praise for achieving targets as opposed to celebrating the fastest performers. The organisation of the session would utilise pupil autonomy in selecting a start position around the outside of the track as well as the direction of the run (clockwise or anti-clockwise). Such organisational features are less threatening than conventional practices, which are often gross public displays of athletic incompetence.

2. Teaching front foot attacking shots in cricket – key features of teaching the application of skills into games situations are: to raise awareness of personal improvement as well as finding success in appropriate application of skills, correct decision-making, and execution of correct or improved technique. Teaching front foot attacking shots may include feeding a range of different coloured balls to the batter, who must process the colour of ball and play shots according to the colour of the ball. In this practice the focus is on processing information and making the correct decision. Technical execution and outcome can be largely ignored as feedback focuses on correct decisions. An alternative practice may involve the same processes but with alternative length feeds with batters again being required to make decisions based upon the situation they are placed in.

At first glance these examples may not appear to focus on the teaching of health concepts. This is the central principle of this philosophy! Health and activity messages are most effectively conveyed through constant presentation of well considered tasks which are inclusive and un-threatening to pupils' self-esteem. At the core of pupils' acceptance of or disengagement from any activity is the extent to which they feel motivated to adhere to tasks on offer. The importance of perceived competence is central to well respected theories of motivation. These two examples give inclusive opportunities to praise and celebrate success within every pupil.

Chapter 8 provides further elucidation of this philosophy of a suitable motivational climate, along with several examples for the teaching of swimming and water-based activities.

Should fitness assessment be part of the formal curriculum time of health-related exercise?

If the ultimate goal of health-related education is to encourage lifelong health-enhancing physical activity patterns then we must ask what role fitness assessment plays in this process.

For a number of years fitness assessment has often formed part of the formal explicit health-related curriculum. Unfortunately the most common term used to describe the procedure for assessment of fitness is 'fitness test'. This term by its nature implies that, just as in your driving test, you can pass or fail, so it sets the wrong tone before the lesson has even started. For those students who are active, take part in sport and enjoy physical competition the thought of undertaking a fitness test to demonstrate their physical prowess may be appealing. However, for those pupils who do not see themselves as sporty or fit just hearing the term fitness test will undoubtedly demotivate them. Teachers need to think seriously about the pros and cons of using some of the limited valuable time they have with children on assessing fitness levels. Teachers should ask themselves what is the purpose of the session. If it is to aid behaviour change from a sedentary life style to one which involves more physical activity, then teachers must ask where the evidence to support performing fitness assessment in this process is. To date little, if any, evidence has been published to demonstrate how performing fitness assessments lead to an increase in physical activity patterns. You should also bear in mind that regular physical activity has been correlated to lower rates of disease and improved health status, not levels of fitness. A fitness assessment score is influenced by a number of factors, not least hereditary make-up, which means that the scores do not always answer the question which is most important in relation to health-related exercise: how active is this child?

Child-centred fitness assessment

In order for the focus of any fitness assessment session to be child-centred the correct motivational climate must be set. The emphasis should be on investigation and self-improvement and not on comparison with others or normative tables. Teachers need to create a task-orientated climate by placing the emphasis on:

- personal effort and progress
- mastery of the task/skill
- learning from mistakes
- participation for its own sake.

To create the correct climate you need to start with the use of appropriate language. For example, use terms like fitness challenge, fitness assessment and monitoring rather than testing. Pupils should record their own results and therefore take ownership of the process, through to appropriate encouragement and feedback being given. You should avoid the following pitfalls, which will set an ego-orientated climate and will lead to a large number of pupils being de-motivated and disenchanted with the experience.

- interpersonal competition
- public evaluation
- comparison of results to normative data
- mistakes being highlighted and emphasised not to be acceptable
- participation for recognition.

It is fairly obvious that in a class of 30 pupils you can only have one winner (for example, the person who gets the best results) and that the 15 who come in the bottom half of the class in terms of their rank order scores could have their self-esteem and confidence related to undertaking physical activity damaged. With maturation playing such a large role in influencing fitness assessments results for most school-aged children, this ego-orientated environment needs to be avoided. However, for some pupils and for gifted and talented sports performers an ego-orientated climate may be appropriate, since this allows the active and sporty pupils to compete against each other as they would do in a sporting environment. However, caution should still be applied when comparisons are made between individuals based upon the maturation and genetic influences on fitness results as discussed earlier.

Adhering to some simple principles can help create a task-orientated climate and aid the learning experience of the pupils, shifting their mindset away from one of thinking that they are being tested to one of self-evaluation and reflection. This will help in the process of personal improvement and encourage habitually physically active individuals. For example:

- Pupils should record their own scores.
- They should be involved in the designing and selection process of appropriate fitness assessment tools.
- Pupils should understand how these assessment tools relate to different components of fitness and how they in turn relate to health.
- Limit the public nature of assessments where possible. For instance set assessments up as stations around the gym/sports hall. Pupils can rotate round in a small group with friends to perform the assessments.

Health-related practical activities

One positive role fitness assessment can perform in a health-related fitness curriculum is in the process of educating children about the different components of fitness and to get them thinking about what they need to do to improve these areas of fitness.

Figure 10.1 shows different components of fitness (with definitions) and tools which can be used to assess those components of fitness. You can set up a variety of fitness stations in your sports hall and have pupils rotate around them in small groups with their friends, recording their own scores. These activities can be modified and adapted according to facilities and the age range of the pupils.

Using the data recording sheets in Figure 10.2 you can also set the pupils questions to answer which will aid their learning (see examples below).

An alternative to fitness assessment: physical profile

As part of HRE lessons it is more appropriate to find other ways of raising pupils awareness to the importance of fitness, types of fitness (strength, aerobic endurance, etc.) and to help them gauge how fit they are without putting them in a testing environment. If the purpose of your session is to raise pupil awareness of the different components of fitness and to get them to reflect on their current fitness levels then a simple physical profile (see Figure 10.3) can be used. Here, pupils give themselves a rating on a scale of 1 to 10 (1 being a very low level of fitness and 10 being very high and the best that they can be). Pupils fill in the important components of fitness around the outside of the wagon wheel and shade up to the level they rate themselves. The aim is to get them to give themselves a rating based upon how good they think they are in each of the components of fitness they identify. Their rating should be influenced by their current exercise patterns rather than by comparison with their peers, which will be influenced by maturation and genetic factors. This simple tool helps set a task-orientated climate and engages the pupils

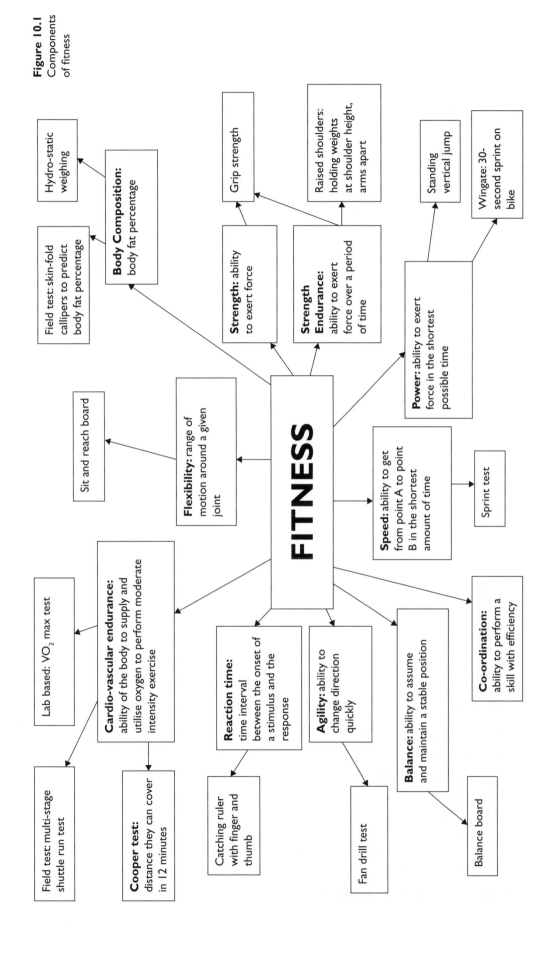

Figure 10.1
Components
of fitness

(i) Fitness assessment tasks

1. Strength endurance (time in seconds)   _____

2. Lower back/hamstring flexibility (cm past toes)   _____

3. Upper body power (Distance thrown in metres)
    a. _____
    b. _____

4. Agility run (time in seconds)
    a. _____
    b. _____
    c. _____

5. Standing broad jump (lower leg power – distance in metres)
    a. _____
    b. _____
    c. _____

6. Speed (20 metre sprint time in seconds)
    a. _____
    b. _____
    c. _____

7. Vertical jump (lower leg power – height jumped in cm)
    a. _____
    b. _____
    c. _____

8. Grip strength (strength in kg)
    Right _____   Left _____

9. Aerobic task (3 minutes of step-ups – record heart rate at end of task)

    _____

(ii) Understanding assessment tools

Instruction	Questions	Answers	Your score	Comment on what you would need to do to improve this area of fitness
Strength assessment using a hand grip dynamo-meter Hold the dynamometer between the palm of your hand and your fingers. Raise your arm straight above your head and then lower the arm (keeping the arm straight) down to your side, squeezing as hard as possible.	1. Is this a measure of static strength, explosive strength, dynamic strength or strength endurance? 2. Define strength 3. What sort of muscle fibres generate force for this action?			

Figure 10.2 Examples of data recording sheets

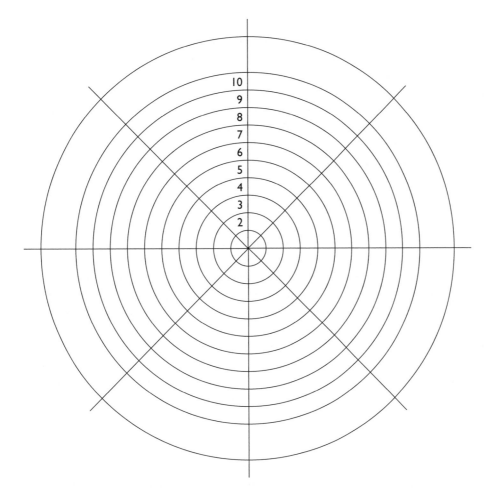

Figure 10.3 The physical profile

in the process of self-reflection related to their activity patterns and the effect those activity patterns have on their levels of fitness.

Other alternatives to fitness assessment

At the National Cricket Centre, strength and conditioning coaches have designed and implemented a physical challenge that players undertake on a regular basis to help assess their overall fitness levels. The fitness challenge involves players undertaking a variety of physical tasks in the weights room with the aim of completing the circuit in as short a period of time as possible. The tasks they perform include things such as running 800 metres on the treadmill at 10 per cent gradient (players self-select the speed), lifting 40 kilograms on the bench press forty times, rowing 400 metres, performing 40 step-ups with 10 kilogram weights in each hand, climbing 200 metres on the versa climber (see the resources section at the end of the chapter for more information), performing 20 seated shoulder raises with 8 kilograms in each hand, etc. These exercises are performed in a specific order and are performed back to back with as little change over time as possible. This type of challenge requires a combination of aerobic fitness and strength endurance. The time to complete the fitness challenge usually ranges from 20 down to 15 minutes.

You can develop your own school fitness challenge, remembering to emphasise personal achievement, personal development and mastery of the task. Incorporate a variety of circuit-type exercises that you can set up around the sports hall with the equipment you have available, such as shuttle runs, step-ups, press-ups, skipping, etc. Specify a set number of repetitions for each exercise. The aim would be to set this up in a way that would allow each individual to work at their own pace related to their levels of fitness. The fitter ones who complete the task the quickest could then encourage the others during the latter stages of the task. They could also answer questions on a handout about the types of fitness involved in the challenge. You can also set circuits up so that everybody works for the same duration on each exercise but they record their own number of repetitions on each of the exercises.

Summary

This chapter began by stating that the ultimate goal of health-related physical education is to encourage lifelong, health-enhancing physical activity patterns. We also alluded to the fact that UK government policy contains many mixed messages, not least is that the term 'sport' is often used within the title of official policy texts. As the editors have suggested in the introduction to this book this is potentially misleading as many pupils will perceive physical education as a substitute for sport, which can de-motivate some pupils from taking part in health-promoting physical activity. The important point to consider is to integrate health-related messages into every physical education lesson and to ensure that health-related issues are core components rather than seen as a bolt-on extra to formal physical education lessons. The bolt-on approach suggests that vital health messages should be added to a daily routine. The sentiment of this chapter is that health messages should permeate the whole physical education curriculum through mainly implicit means and with little explicit teaching of the content, which has traditionally underpinned health-related exercise teaching. Adherence to the health messages in physical education is more likely to be achieved by pupils when such messages are given consideration in every lesson and with the ultimate aim of influencing lifelong physical activity habits. In this context, pupils will be able to exercise safely and effectively and, in the process, improve their health and wellbeing through fitness and health activities.

References

Bailey, R. (2005) 'Evaluating the relationship between physical education, sport and social inclusion', *Educational Review*, 57 (1), 71–90.

Cale, L. (2000) 'Physical activity promotion in secondary schools', *European Physical Education Review*, 6 (1), 71–90.

DfES/DCMS (2003) *Learning through PE and Sport: A guide to the Physical Education, School Sport and Club Links Strategy*. London, DfES.

Ofsted (2009) 'Physical education in schools 2005/08: Working towards 2012 and beyond', April, Reference number: 080249.

Parker, M. and Curtner-Smith, M. (2005) 'Health-related fitness in sport education and multi-activity teaching', *Physical Education and Sport Pedagogy*, 10 (1), 1–18.

Portman, P.A. (2003) 'Are physical education classes encouraging students to be physically active? Experiences of ninth graders in their last semester of required physical education', *Physical Educator*, 60 (3), 150–161.

Useful resources

Versaclimber exercise machine
www.versaclimber.co.uk

11 Learning and teaching citizenship through physical education

John Lambert and Joanna Gardiner

Introduction

The physical component of physical education is what establishes the subject as unique within the school curriculum. It largely justifies its place in the curriculum and is a major reason why physical education is such a popular subject for so many pupils. There is, however, a persuasive case for looking beyond the physical and unlocking the wider potential of the subject. Laker (2001) argued that physical education can contribute to the development of the whole person by developing not only physical capacity but also emotional, social and personal (affective) competence, spiritual awareness and community understanding. He makes the point that each aspect of physical education, including the personal and social components, should be seen to have equal importance, even if the weighting might understandably favour the physical.

The Crick report (DfEE and QCA 1998) identified three strands that form the basis of a balanced citizenship programme: social and moral responsibility, community involvement and political literacy. In this chapter we will highlight the ways in which physical education might have a part to play in delivering some of the citizenship programmes of study: notably those linked to the first two of the above strands. We identify some of the teaching styles that are most effective when facilitating learning in the affective and social domain. We include practical examples of how the key processes and concepts from the citizenship national curriculum are taught through physical education in schools.

There has been much debate over whether physical education brings out the best behaviour in people or the worst. The evidence, empirical and anecdotal, suggests that, depending on the situation, either could be true. However, what does emerge from studies documented in this area is that given a suitable learning environment and teachers adopting 'an eclectic pedagogy that is holistic and philanthropic in nature' (Laker 2001: 2) there is scope for learning in domains outside of the purely physical. Citizenship is taught in schools as either a discrete subject, in a cross-curricular way, or, most commonly, as a combination of both. This chapter offers ideas and strategies for delivering some of the citizenship national curriculum content by putting an alternative emphasis on the teaching of physical education. These activities can be adapted to suit the age range of pupils across Key Stages 2 and 3.

Identifying links between the physical education and citizenship programmes of study

It is important first to establish the status of both subjects and their respective programmes of study. The draft Key Stage 2 National Curriculum guidance (QCA 2009) links physical education with citizenship and with personal, social and health education (PSHE) learning under the heading of 'Understanding physical development, health and wellbeing'. There seems to be recognition that physical education sits neatly alongside the wider development of healthy and responsible lifestyles. Citizenship, physical education and PSHE will no longer be seen as discrete subjects in the primary curriculum but will be integrated as an area of learning. Some elements of citizenship, for instance rights and responsibilities, have been integrated into the historical, geographical and social understanding programme of learning. The Rose report (DCSF 2009) is to undergo a lengthy consultation process before its proposals are due to come to fruition in 2011. Citizenship is a compulsory subject at Key Stage 3 with statutory guidance in the form of programmes of study. Presently, citizenship at Key Stage 2 continues to be a non-statutory subject.

An analysis of the citizenship programmes of study in relation to those for physical education at Key Stage 3 demonstrates that only a limited amount of explicit reference is made to development of personal and social education within physical education. Under 'learning across the curriculum', the 1999 document offers some examples of how spiritual, moral, social and cultural development can be advanced through physical education. The revised Key Stage 3 National Curriculum (2008) states in its rationale for the teaching of physical education that:

> PE helps pupils develop personally and socially. They work as individuals, in groups and in teams, developing concepts of fairness and of personal and social responsibility. They take on different roles and responsibilities, including leadership, coaching and officiating. Through the range of experiences that PE offers, they learn how to be effective in competitive, creative and challenging situations.
>
> (QCA 2008: 2)

There is little in the physical education key processes or concepts at Key Stage 3 that alludes directly to either moral and social responsibility or community involvement. That said, however, on examination of the citizenship programmes of study there are clearly examples of where the processes can be taught through the medium of physical education. Tables 11.1 and 11.2 illustrate how some of these links can be explored at Key Stage 2 and Key Stage 3.

Having presented some examples of the 'what' (content that can be taught through physical education), it is now appropriate to address the 'how' (pedagogical strategies that will facilitate learning) – the importance of which cannot be overemphasised.

Teaching in the affective and social domains

Much of the engagement of physical education with citizenship involves the development of human values which translate into socially and morally responsible behaviour. Values, such as respect, responsibility and trust manifest themselves in certain behaviours. For example, a pupil who shakes hands with their opponent is showing respect. A pupil who collects and puts away the table tennis equipment at the end of the lesson without being told to is showing responsibility. If a pupil takes their spotting role seriously in a trampoline session or is given a timekeeping task in athletics they can be said to be

Table 11.1 *Links between citizenship programmes of study and physical education at Key Stage 2*

Citizenship programme of study	Examples of opportunities to teach citizenship through physical education
Key Stage 2 Programmes of Study*	
Knowledge, skills and understanding:	
2. Preparing to play an active role as citizens (b) Why and how rules and laws are made and enforced; why different rules are needed in different situations and how to take part in making and changing rules.	Applying rules and conventions for different activities. Learning why the rules of each activity are important. Dealing with competition, including disputes over rules and their interpretation, for example, games making, pupils as referees, games without referees.
(f) To resolve differences by looking at alternatives, making decisions and explaining choices.	Learning to play with others and approaches to issues of equity and inclusion that arise. How fairness improves the enjoyment and value of competition. Co-operation and compromise, for example, pupils selecting their own equitable teams.
3. Developing a healthy, safer lifestyle (a) What makes a healthy lifestyle, including the benefits of exercise and healthy eating, what affects mental health, and how to make informed choices.	How exercise affects the body in the short term. How to warm up and prepare appropriately for different activities, for example, pupils devise their own warm-ups. Why physical activity is good for health and wellbeing. Why wearing appropriate clothing, using equipment properly and being hygienic is good for health and safety, for example, using athletics and gymnastics equipment safely.
4. Developing good relationships and respecting the differences between people (a) Understanding that their actions affect themselves and others, to care about other people's feelings and to try to see things from their points of view.	Reciprocal learning: for example, teaching a gymnastic or dance routine to a peer, offering guidance and feedback. Taking on different roles in games: for example, referee, team captain. Highlighting issues of fair play.

Note * The Key Stage 2 Programmes of Study relate to the 1999 Citizenship Curriculum.

Table 11.2 *Links between citizenship programmes of study and physical education at Key Stage 3*

Citizenship programme of study	Examples of opportunities to teach citizenship through physical education
Key Stage 3 Key Processes	
2.1 Critical thinking and enquiry	
(a) Engage with and reflect on different ideas, opinions, beliefs and values when exploring topical and controversial issues and problems.	Games making: why rules and their implementation are so important to creating the shape of a game and ensuring fairness and safety. Explore the attitudes and ethics surrounding different games. For example, what is fair play and unfair play?
2.2 Advocacy and representation	
(b) Communicate an argument, taking account of different viewpoints and drawing on what they have learnt through research, action and debate.	Reflect upon issues of equity and inclusion in physical education: for example, the selection of equitable teams, gender issues. Modelling of good practice by the teacher. Outdoor and adventurous activities problem-solving and team-building tasks.
(d) Represent the views of others, with which they may or may not agree.	Highlighting respect as a value in physical education. For example, respecting opponents, teammates, and officials. Modelling of key values by the teacher.
2.3 Taking informed and responsible action	
(a) Explore creative approaches to taking action on problems and issues to achieve intended purposes.	Developing responsibility: for example, taking leadership roles as captain or coach. Group co-operative work: for example, creating dance or gymnastics routines. Problem-solving in outdoor and adventurous activities as a group: skills of communication, negotiation.
(b) Work individually and with others to negotiate, plan, and take action on citizenship issues to try to bring about change or resist unwanted change, using time and resources appropriately.	Life-saving and personal survival tasks in swimming that involve trust and responsibility. Outdoor and adventurous activities tasks that simulate group survival. Showing responsibility when putting out, using and returning equipment.

trustworthy in that context. The ultimate aim should be the 'internalising' of these positive behaviours, and consequently the attached values, so that they are transferred across a variety of situations. There would be a tangible development in responsible citizenship if these values were taken from the sports field out into the community.

Bailey (2005) states that when planning for education into values for citizenship it is important that teachers do not take a too didactic approach. It is not simply a matter of training pupils into certain kinds of behaviour that can be replicated like a physical skill. Life often requires ethical choices to be made: between truth and loyalty, self and others and long- and short-term benefit. The teacher, when educating in the affective domain, should create situations where pupils have the opportunity to (or not to) display values such as respect, responsibility and trust. It would be interesting for a teacher to observe their class, for instance, playing a game of football without a referee and note the different choice of responses to any disputes that may occur. This would be an example of what Hellison and Templin (1991) refer to as a 'built-in dilemmas/dialogue' strategy. Once these sorts of divergent activities are facilitated, it is important for the teacher to observe for pupil behaviours and not intervene, unless events are potentially dangerous. A period of reflection that focuses again on relevant values should follow. This can be initially led by the teacher but with the intention of fully involving the pupils in discussing and identifying examples of positive values behaviour. Once these 'teachable moments' (Beedy 1997), examples of behaviour that embodies positive values, are reflected upon, they are reinforced with recognition and praise. The teaching cycle when dealing with values might be referred to as: facilitate–anticipate–observe–record–reflect–reinforce.

An example of a divergent activity which has 'built-in dilemmas/dialogue' would be as follows:

- A group of pupils is asked to select two equal teams in order to play a game. The teacher makes no interventions and merely observes.
- The pupil behaviours that might be expected are: negotiation over the criteria for selection (numbers, ability), conflict over who selects the teams and how, some leadership skills from certain pupils, discussion, compromise and co-operation.
- The teacher makes a mental note of the 'teachable moments' that take place in relation to individual pupils and their behaviour before and during the game.
- At the end of the lesson, the teacher reflects, with the class, on the social behaviours that they have observed with an emphasis on what, now what, and so what.
- The teacher reinforces any positive values demonstrated by certain individuals with recognition and praise. The pupils are encouraged to discuss their reflections on the whole process.

To adopt a pupil-centred teaching style that requires little intervention and places an emphasis on personal values may require a shift in approach that initially may not feel comfortable. It is a model that has been adapted in Football4Peace, a project involving Arab and Jewish children which uses football and outdoor education as a vehicle for co-existence and conflict prevention in Israel, one of the most divided societies in the world (Sugden and Wallis 2007; Stidder and Haasner 2007). When the choice of learning activities is right and the teacher is confident enough to facilitate and then reflect upon teachable moments, the effect on attitudes and ethics can be very apparent. The following have proved to be valuable strategies for teachers of values-based physical education:

- modelling the values themselves: show respect, inclusion, equity;
- effective questioning: allowing time for reflection and considered answers;

- use of rewards: this may be praise and recognition to reinforce behaviour;
- developing positive relationships: listen and give time to pupils, establish social boundaries, reinforce the positive;
- observation and reflection: be prepared to stand back, observe and remember teachable moments.

The teaching methods advocated are based on well established learning theories. Social-learning theorists advocate that social skills, attitudes and values can be learned by observing behaviours of others and adopting and demonstrating those behaviours. In other words, pupils copy their teachers and peers. Structural-development theory claims that pupils behave in a certain way because of the reaction of others and the environment. Changes in behaviour are as a result of the actions and reactions of others. It is likely that physical education lessons will offer opportunities to learn behaviours in both ways. The teacher as a role model will influence young people and an environment where positive values are encouraged and reinforced will impact on the attitudes of pupils. Success is measured in terms of behaviour rather than athletic performance. Practical learning activities that centred in such learning theories and delivered through the associated teaching strategies are described in the next section. Below is an example of how one secondary school has developed and piloted a module designed to facilitate the teaching of citizenship values.

Theory into practice: Helenswood School

The adoption of values-based teaching and the transfer of that knowledge and skill to their physical education lessons have been adapted from activities included in the Football4Peace coaching manuals (Lambert *et al.* 2004; Stidder *et al.* 2006) and have been used in physical education lessons in order to develop positive citizenship values through a cross-curricular approach. The examples of activities in this section demonstrate how this school has developed a module for Key Stage 3 pupils covering key values under the heading of 'Conflict resolution' through classroom, football and outdoor and adventurous activities.

Helenswood School, a comprehensive school for girls, has included a module on 'conflict resolution' in order to contribute to fulfilling the requirements of the statutory Citizenship National Curriculum (QCA 2007). The module, delivered to Key Stage 3 pupils, briefly looks at arguments and leads on to looking at examples of conflict in their own lives, their surrounding environments, and in various contexts around the world. Throughout, strong reference is made to how to resolve conflict with use of actions and words that embody the values of a good citizen. Parallels with their own life situations are then made so that pupils are given a 'toolkit' for preventing and dealing with conflict.

The module provides opportunities to carry out debates on topical issues surrounding conflict and conflict resolution, sometimes in relation to their own lives. The module includes the development of citizenship knowledge and application of the personal and social skills. Pupils take on various roles in order to meet assessment criteria and to be successful in practical situations, working both individually and in groups. They participate in decision-making exercises, considering the moral and social dimensions of some political problems and issues. The module encourages the study of school, local, national and worldwide topics. The module incorporates some information communication technology (ICT) through the use of DVD clips and PowerPoint slides, which are used as an aid to lay the foundations for the acquisition and application of citizenship knowledge.

Outline of the module

The conflict resolution module is delivered over eight one-hour lessons. The first two lessons provide the grounding for pupils to acquire knowledge about issues resulting in conflict, in relation to their own lives and other people's lives around the world. The third and fourth lessons look at outdoor and adventurous activities, focusing on team-building and trust games. Lessons five and six utilise football as a practical medium through which to develop positive values. The final two lessons allow assessment opportunities and application of cross-curricular knowledge.

Lessons one and two – classroom-based

Starter activity

All pupils are included in the starter activity, which is the issuing of a red or blue ticket to every member of the class, at random. Once learners have their ticket, all with red tickets are invited to enter the room and sit down. Once settled, all pupils with a blue ticket enter and sit somewhere on the floor. The pupils with blue tickets are asked how they feel. A discussion is facilitated and comments are teased out relating to division being created between the groups. Feelings of segregation, discrimination, of being the minority or majority, of empowerment, anger, being made to feel different, feelings of division even though it has nothing to do with personality but merely the ticket that they receive are all expressed and analysed. Pupils are then all invited to sit on chairs to begin the lesson.

Presentation

A PowerPoint presentation on conflict resolution is shown which looks at the nature of arguments. It covers how pupils themselves may have been involved in arguments, with whom and how they resolve them. Pupils get the opportunity to discuss their experiences. Definitions and examples of conflict are studied. These are related to the pupils' own lives and are discussed in small groups where they are asked to list as many examples of sources of conflict in the wider community, between neighbours, in families and between friends. Leading on from this, pupils are made aware of various examples of conflict occurring in the world, including in Northern Ireland, Cyprus, Georgia, Russia and South Africa. The main example used to explain how conflict can arise and present itself is through the ongoing problems in Palestine and Israel. The history of how the conflict arose is presented, the people that it affects are described and some vivid images of the conflict are shown to bring the problems to life and help pupils relate to it.

Peaceful co-existence and conflict prevention: the Football4Peace model[1]

Football4Peace, a project that incorporates the practical elements of team-building and teamwork provides a powerful, realistic and age-related stimulus to link the theory with the practical. The aims of Football4Peace are shared with the pupils. These are to provide opportunities for social contact across community boundaries, to promote mutual understanding, to engender in participants a desire for and commitment to peaceful co-existence, and finally to enhance football skills and technical knowledge. Football and outdoor and adventurous activities are used as practical situations where young people have to learn about each other's personalities and lives, gain knowledge of each others' cultures and learn to work together to achieve practical tasks set. They become part of a strong team based around a set of shared values. Pupils are told they will be experiencing the same process that young people of Israel will experience when participating in the project, by carrying out some of the practical activities encompassed in Football4Peace. Pupils are given certain values to discuss with each other and come up with their own interpretation of what the values mean to them and how they can demonstrate that value. The values shared are neutrality, trust, equity and inclusion, respect and responsibility.

A Football4Peace DVD is shown to provide the visual context. Pupils are asked to look for examples of the values being shown and write them down once they see them. The points are discussed as a whole-class task after the DVD has finished.

A second DVD is shown: *Children of the Jordan Valley*.[2] This is a trailer clip that captures the deep divisions between Arab and Jew in the Middle East. It also, through a series of on-field scenes and interviews, demonstrates the effect that the project has on the young people that take part. It provides some strong examples of how the practical tasks had brought young people together across a religious and sectarian divide.

Pupils experience values-based activities which are all practical tasks set to encourage teamwork, communication, trust, responsibility, inclusion, equality and neutrality. Teachable moments are noted when pupils demonstrate them and are then shared with the group because they provide useful examples of the values that the project is based around.

Lessons three and four

The next two lessons focus on the use of physical education in the teaching of the citizenship curriculum, with reference to curriculum opportunities, key processes, range and content and key concepts. Physical education constitutes a large part of the conflict resolution module taught to Key Stage 3 pupils at Helenswood School, since the curriculum opportunities necessary to the physical education national curriculum (QCA 2008) have obvious links with those of the citizenship national curriculum (QCA 2008). The physical education opportunity requirements include being involved in a range of different activities, experiencing a range of different roles, performing as individuals, in groups or as part of a team and making links between physical education and other subjects. These opportunities are fulfilled in the citizenship module. The practical side of the module allows pupils to become leaders in their groups, mediators, creative thinkers and peacemakers, depending on the situations they are faced with. There is no teacher input into how they should meet their challenge apart from the outline of what they are to achieve.

The use of physical education in this module also supports the key processes of the citizenship national curriculum as both subjects should encourage pupils to reflect upon their work and their different ideas while expressing their own opinions to others in order to improve their work (QCA 2008). Both physical education and citizenship require pupils to explore creative approaches to taking action on problems and issues to achieve success when meeting the demands of their activity (QCA 2008). The 'electric fence' (Photo 11.1) gives opportunities to be creative as pupils are of different sizes and strengths and are also unfamiliar with others in the group, meaning they have to place trust in people they did not know and make physical contact of a close nature. Pupils become very aware of each other's safety while being creative in order to get all members of the group through the hole in the fence. Once achieved, this activity seems often to produce a clear morale boost as pupils cheer, smile and reflect excitedly on what they have just done.

Citizenship requires pupils to 'work individually and with others to negotiate, plan and take action on citizenship issues to try to influence others, bring about change or

Photo 11.1 'Electric fence' activity

resist unwanted change, using time and resources appropriately' (QCA 2007: 12). The practical nature of physical education in the citizenship module – using a large working space, dividing pupils into groups and setting tasks to complete, with emphasis on taking responsibility for the organisation of others and equipment, and making decisions on how to best achieve the tasks set – allows pupils to fulfil this key process. In some activities it requires all pupils to be alert and take responsibility for each other's safety and success. Pupils take on individual roles of communicators, equipment monitors, guides to their partners or anticipating safety monitors, for example in order for the blindfolded performer to get across an imaginary minefield (see Chapter 7). This activity can bring out motivational skills in pupils because those who fear walking while wearing a blindfold need reassurance and encouragement. Particular members of the class can show empathy with their peers whilst instilling a feeling of trust in them and that they would be safe in their hands.

A comparison of the range and content of citizenship and physical education shows that there are similarities in exploring and communicating ideas, concepts and emotions with freedom of speech and diversity of views (QCA 2007). All activities that pupils had to participate in had a brief outline set but how each group met the challenge was up to them in how they thought best to tackle it. Some groups communicated before trying to complete a task, others threw themselves straight in and learnt from mistakes and explored new ideas; some groups found challenges tougher than others. With the activities being laid out in a circuit format, it was possible to briefly discuss, between rotations, some common errors made or examples of good practice in order that the groups could learn from the past experiences of their peers.

The key concepts of both citizenship and physical education underpin the conflict resolution module delivered. Citizenship requires participating actively in decision making (QCA 2007), as does physical education. Both subjects allow pupils to investigate how individuals have responsibilities to weigh up what is fair and unfair, understand how rights can compete and conflict, and to take part in situations that require social cohesion. Physical education encourages pupils to use practical situations in order to learn the key concepts; pupils show competence by completing tasks that require selecting and applying skills which are applicable in group situations, and by responding with body and mind in order to look after the safety of themselves and others when completing problem-solving activities. All tasks involved problem solving, which gave the opportunity for pupils to respond to situations accordingly.

Pupils are responsible for their own decisions, which could potentially, and sometimes will, lead to conflict with others in the group, who may have a differing view on the pathway to success. Learners have to adapt to a widening range of familiar and unfamiliar contexts as they work with people they have never worked with before and do not know. They will not know the individuals' personalities or work ethic, which may lead to a conflict with their own ideas and practices. Pupils must work out the most effective ways in which to communicate with others, take a lead at appropriate times, and also be patient in order to work effectively with others in order to avoid conflict or, when necessary, resolve the conflict.

Lessons five and six: the use of football to bring out values and work on conflict resolution.

Ball sit (trust, responsibility)

Pupils stand approximately 10 metres apart from their partner. One pupil rolls the ball along the ground to their partner, who has their back to them, and calls out 'sit' when they think their partner should squat down to sit on the ball. Pupils must trust their partner's judgment on when to sit down on the ball so they do not fall to the ground, therefore demonstrating the responsibility of the caller to keep their partner safe. Distances can be increased once partners increase their trust for each other (Photo 11.2).

Photo 11.2
Ball sit

Head-to-head relay (responsibility, respect)

Partners balance the ball by facing each other and pushing their heads together with the ball in between. They can balance by having their hands positioned on their partner's shoulders. Pupils then move sideways together to touch a line 10 metres away and come back to their starting position while keeping the ball balanced at all times. The activity can be progressed by getting the pair to lower to their knees when they get to the line before returning, then the next time they can lower to the ground and try to lie on their front, while maintaining the balance of the ball. Pupils need to communicate to regulate the speed at which they move and to adjust their heights if matched with someone shorter or taller, therefore achieving equality. Pupils need to respect that some will find this activity very difficult and therefore try and help the other person to feel included by wanting to meet the challenge even though they may not be successful every time (Photo 11.3).

Photo 11.3
Head-to-head relay

Human bridge (trust, responsibility)

One pupil forms a bridge with the whole of their body and their partner passes the ball to go under the bridge. The partner in the bridge has to trust their partner to kick the ball with good direction and at a speed that will not hurt their partner. Pairs communicate to allow their partner to pass the ball faster if they feel they can trust their partner to get the ball through.

Treasure chest (equity, trust, respect, responsibility)

A square is set out with an equal number of pupils at each corner to form a team. A number of balls are grouped in the middle of the grid. One at a time, pupils run into the middle, dribble a ball back to their corner, and then the next person can go and collect a ball. Once all the balls have gone from the middle pupils steal balls from the corner either side of them. When the whistle is blown to stop, pupils count their balls up and the highest number stolen wins. This creates situations where cheating could occur if pupils do not abide by the rules set out. Pupils cheat by taking more than one ball at a time, going to get a ball before their team member has returned, blocking players from taking balls from their corner, hiding balls so players cannot see them to take them and passing the ball to their corner rather than dribbling. This can lead to arguing and conflict. Opportunities to discuss the rules that should be in place arise, whereby pupils can take responsibility for putting in place their own rules, ensuring the game is played fairly. References can be made to lessons one and two, where pupils discussed ways that arguments start. If arguments have occurred or conflict has arisen, a teacher intervention can help to facilitate ways to resolve the issues.

Football – own referees/substitutions (equity, inclusion, responsibility, trust)

Games may be conditioned, but because the emphasis is on values and not the skills in football, the games can be played without conditions. Each team is responsible for making their own substitutions; therefore pupils must be inclusive and involve all team members, with even times of play to meet the equality value. Teams must referee their own games; the teacher will not intervene unless it is necessary, therefore pupils must be responsible for following the rules. Pupils make up a team huddle and chant to bring the team together before playing, and they must invent their own goal celebration to include all members of the team. It is a chance to listen to people's ideas and select one that they all agree on.

Lessons seven and eight: assessment

Pupils are given two lessons to meet their assessment tasks. Pupils work in groups and decide the roles they wish to take in order to demonstrate what they have learned and how they will build on what they already know in order to demonstrate clear understanding of the material delivered. Pupils must write a proposal letter to a millionaire, asking for funding for a project they have thought of that is similar to Football4Peace. They can use their own interests, such as music, theatre, fashion, dance, food or any other area of their choice. They must explain how it will bring people together, how young people are integrated, how pupils will have to communicate with one another, what problems they may face during the project, what materials they will need to make it work. They also have to complete an assessment reciprocal sheet giving examples of how each value could be met through their project. For example, respect may be met when young people talk about their likes and dislikes about what clothes they wear before their new friend from another community has to shop for an outfit based on what their partner likes. Another example pupils came up with was to present a fashion show which integrates the colours, trends and materials of another country or group of people and mix the fashion trends together to create new outfits to put on a catwalk.

Pupils divide themselves up so all have responsibilities to write a letter, an information sheet outlining the aims and content of their project showing how they will help bring together people from any society fractured along racial, religious or political lines. A plenary is then conducted in order to summarise the module and to consolidate pupil learning.

A values-based approach to swimming

Student volunteer coaches who have worked with a values-based teaching model within Football4Peace have often become converts to that pedagogical approach and find ways to integrate values teaching into the physical education programme at their school. In her swimming lessons Yolanda Dashwood-Brady has devised 'values-based contrasting games and activities' which provide a divergent stimulus.[3] They are an effective teaching strategy sometimes used to re-engage or maintain the focus of the swimming class. Two example worksheets are set out in Figure 11.1 and Figure 11.2.

Values-based swimming activities: **trust**

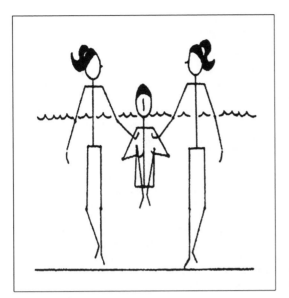

Activity no. 1
Carrying the bucket

This 15 minute contrasting games activity promotes trust through the wellbeing of team mates, and is split into 4 parts.

Part 1: In the shallow end of the pool, divide the class into groups of 3. In their groups pupils practise carrying each other as 'buckets' (see picture).

Part 2: Keeping pupils in their groups of 3, split the class into 2 teams to perform a relay race. Team A start from one side, team B from the other.

Part 3: Within each team, pupils discuss and select a more efficient way of carrying an individual through the water.

Part 4: Pupils perform a second and final relay race implementing the teams newly agreed technique. This activity is carried out within the shallow end and no equipment is required.

Learning Objective	Learning Outcome (*Most pupils*)	Learning Outcome (*Some pupils*)	Learning Outcome (*Few pupils*)
To develop an understanding and appreciation of trust through contrasting games activities.	Will have sufficient trust in their carriers and will happily be carried by any member of the class.	Will experience limited trust resulting in reservations about being carried through the water.	Will have complete trust in their carriers and may choose to perform the task with their eyes closed.

Teaching Points/ Values	Differentiation	Progression	Teaching Styles	Key Processes
Carriers work together to provide a secure grasp, ensuring the carried pupil feels safe. This feeling of safety will enable the carried pupil to place their trust in the carriers. Carriers to ensure that the carried pupil's head remains above the water at all times.	**Easier:** Supporters to carry a lighter pupil. **Harder:** Carried pupil to hold a float vertically half way out of the water to increase resistance.	Progression is demonstrated throughout all parts of the tasks. However, it is most notable in parts 3 & 4 where the teams implement an improved method.	Command Practice Guided discovery Divergent Inclusion	DSPA: 2.1b M & A: 2.2a, b, c DPMC: 2.3a, b MICHAL 2.5b

Figure 11.1 Worksheet: Carrying the bucket

Values-based swimming activities: responsibility

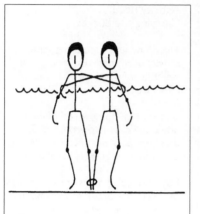

Activity no. 2
Three-legged race

This 15 minute contrasting games activity encourages pupils to be responsible for themselves, their actions and others around them. The activity is split up into 4 parts.

Part 1: In pairs, at the shallow end of the pool, pupils' ankles are loosely bound together with the use of a dive ring (see picture). Pupils practise moving around whilst being attached.

Part 2: Keeping pupils in their pairs, split the class into two teams to perform a relay race. Team A starts from one side, team B from the other.

Part 3: In preparation for a final race, divide the pupils into groups of 3. Each group needs to have 2 pupils attached in the 3-legged formation, plus one assistant. The teacher then sets the problem, being for the group to devise a way of getting the assistant to safely help the pair cross the pool width, using only two floatable aids and without their feet touching the bottom.

Part 4: With their agreed strategies pupils perform a relay race, team A vs. team B. This activity is carried out in the shallow end. Equipment: Dive rings, woggles, floats, balls.

Learning Objective	Learning Outcome (Most pupils)	Learning Outcome (Some pupils)	Learning Outcome (Few pupils)
To develop and practise responsibility for one's own actions and the actions of others, through contrasting games activities.	Will realise that their actions through consideration and communication impacts others.	Will demonstrate a basic level of responsibility and may require some teacher intervention to identify the need for communication.	Will quickly learn that combined responsibility is key to controlling actions. This will be evident even when paired with a less able pupil.

Teaching Points/ Values	Differentiation	Progression	Teaching Styles	Key Processes
Responsibility is promoted through understanding that one's actions have a direct effect on your partner. Take turns to communicate instructions to enable you and your partner to move in time. Tightly hold onto one another's shoulders. Similar heights are preferred.	**Easier:** Performed without a dive ring. **Harder:** In pairs, pupils hold an item of equipment in their spare hands. Or perform in 3s.	Areas of progression are demonstrated throughout, for example: parts 1 and 2, pupils learn to walk, communicate, then race against one another whilst being attached.	Command Practice Problem solving Divergent Inclusion	DSPA: 2.1a, b, c M & A: 2.2a, b, c, d DPMC: 2.3a, b E&I: 2.4b, c MICHAL: 2.5b

Figure 11.2 Worksheet: Three-legged race

Curriculum planning

The focus of this chapter has been on the development of personal values, such as respect and responsibility, through physical education. That is not to assume that this is the only area of the citizenship curriculum that can be developed through physical education. However, the physical and competitive nature of the physical education curriculum, and the relationship that physical education teachers typically enjoy with their pupils lends itself to values-based teaching.

The draft Key Stage 2 curriculum (DCSF 2009) under 'Essentials for learning and life' states that pupils should:

- manage their feelings using appropriate strategies, becoming increasingly aware of their own and others' feelings;
- reflect on past achievements and experiences to manage future learning and behaviour;
- adapt their behaviour to suit different situations;
- take turns and share as appropriate, stating their own views and needs;
- negotiate, respecting others' rights and responsibilities, and use strategies to resolve disputes and conflicts.

Physical education has, potentially, a great deal to offer in contributing to the development of such 'essentials for learning and life'. There is a natural link between physical education and citizenship in relation to the selected learning objectives above. It will be the task of teachers to identify how these objectives are taught and a cross-curricular approach is seen by the QCA as the way forward.

It is possible that some secondary teachers may take the view that they have enough physical education programmes of study without adding citizenship. However, those teachers that have spent time in physical education lessons on developing the social and moral behaviour of their pupils have benefited in terms of the attitudes and ethics of their classes and they themselves have developed into teachers who take a wider, holistic view of their subject.

Summary

The National Curriculum 2008 has as central aims the creation of successful learners, confident individuals and responsible citizens. The pedagogy advocated in this chapter will contribute to these aims. It demands that teachers take a holistic view of their teaching and adopt a humanistic approach to their pupils. This may not be seen as a new direction for many physical education teachers. However, there is a persuasive case for developing personal, social and citizenship skills and positive values in a more explicit way in physical education. Within a crowded physical education curriculum there may initially be some resistance from pupils and colleagues to adding organised teaching of socially desirable citizenship values. Nevertheless, there is a responsibility to explore how curriculum planning can take into account ways in which physical education can contribute to the development of attitudes and behaviour associated with good citizenship, as there is without doubt a role to play for physical education. Teachers who have taken this step have reaped the benefit in terms of the quality of both their teaching and the learning experiences of everyone involved.

Notes

1   www.football4peace.eu
2   *Children of Jordan Valley*, a documentary film about Football4Peace by Simon Joecker (Magic Hour Productions). http://www.youtube.com/watch?v=GgZ7CryO56c
3   Yolanda Dashwood-Brady is currently a Year 3 BA PE (with Qualified Teacher Status) student at the University of Brighton's Chelsea School.

References

Bailey, R. (2005) *Teaching Values and Citizenship across the Curriculum*. London: Routledge Falmer.

Beedy, J. (1997) *Sports Plus: Positive Learning Using Sports*. Hamilton: Project Adventure.

DCFS (Department for Children, Families and Schools) (2009) *Independent Review of the Primary Curriculum: Final Report*, DCFS Publications, Reference: 00499-2009DOM-EN.

DfEE (Department for Education and Employment) and QCA (Qualifications and Curriculum Authority) (1998) *Education for Citizenship and the Teaching of Democracy in Schools: Final report of the advisory group on citizenship*, 22 September, Reference: QCA/98/245.

DfEE (Department for Education and Employment) and QCA (Qualifications and Curriculum Authority) (1999) *Citizenship: The National Curriculum for England*, DfEE and QCA, www.nc.uk.net

Gardner, R., Cairns, J. and Lawton, D. (2000) *Education for Values*. London: Kogan Page.

Hellison, D. and Templin, J. (1991) *A Reflective Approach to Teaching Physical Education*. Champaign, IL: Human Kinetics.

Laker, A. (2001) *Developing Personal, Social and Moral Education through Physical Education*. London: Routledge Falmer.

Lambert, J., Stidder, G., Sugden, J. and Wallis, J. (2004) 'Football for Peace on-pitch coaching manual', University of Brighton, unpublished.

QCA (Qualifications and Curriculum Authority) (2007) *Citizenship Programmes of Study Key Stage 3*, QCA, www.qca.org.uk/curriculum

QCA (Qualifications and Curriculum Authority) (2008) *The Physical Education programmes of study Key Stage 3*, QCA, www.qca.org.uk/curriculum

QCA (Qualifications and Curriculum Authority) (2009) 'Understanding physical development, health and wellbeing' – Draft for consultation, http://www.qcda.gov.uk/22284.aspx

Stidder, G. and Haasner, A. (2007) 'Developing outdoor and adventurous activities for co-existence and reconciliation in Israel: An Anglo-German approach', *Journal of Adventure Education and Outdoor Learning*, (7), 2, 131–140.

Stidder, G., Haasner, A. and Spacey, G. (2006) 'Football for Peace off-pitch manual', University of Brighton, unpublished.

Sugden, J. and Wallis, J. (eds) (2007) *Football for Peace? The challenges of using sport for co-existence in Israel*, Oxford: Meyer and Meyer.

12 Thematic learning and teaching through physical education

Gary Stidder and Sid Hayes

Introduction

The aim of this chapter is to demonstrate how physical education may contribute to the teaching and learning of cross-curricular themes and whole-school concepts such as literacy, numeracy, science and information and communication technology (ICT) from a learner's and teacher's perspective. There are many opportunities for teachers to apply knowledge, principles and values to more than one curriculum subject at the same time and relate them to one central topic or issue. In most cases teachers can organise their units of work and lessons to reflect a particular theme in terms of what pupils will learn from the experience within the unit or lesson. This can enable the transfer of learning and teaching and provide a more relevant physical education curriculum to pupils across Key Stages 2 and 3.

When they are developing cross-curricular teaching and learning through identified subject areas there are many themes that teachers can integrate into physical education lessons. It is essential, however, that the main focus of the lesson remains on education through physical activity. For example, whilst there are many ways in which teachers can enhance and support the development of literacy and numeracy, this should be permeated within the lesson rather than seen as a bolt-on extra or by-product to the learning outcomes. In this respect, the revised National Curriculum for Physical Education (NCPE) (QCA 2008) requires all teachers to provide opportunities for pupils to develop the functional skills of English, mathematics and ICT which can provide pupils with the skills and abilities they need to operate confidently, effectively and independently in life, their communities and work.

Personal learning and thinking skills

The revised NCPE also requires teachers to develop in pupils essential skills and qualities for learning, life and employment. These include skills that relate to learning in subjects as well as other more generic, transferable skills. In this respect the framework for personal, learning and thinking skills (PLTS) provides a national framework which schools can build on in order to meet the needs of their young people and broader communities. There are opportunities for teachers to develop innovative approaches to physical education and enable pupils to become *self-managers, creative thinkers, reflective learners, teamworkers, independent enquirers,* and *effective participators* learning across the curriculum.

Alongside the functional skills, PLTS are a fundamental part of the overall educational development of pupils. They are embedded in the new programmes of study ensuring that all young people become successful learners who enjoy learning, make progress and achieve: confident individuals who are able to live safe, healthy and fulfilling lives; and responsible citizens who make a positive contribution to society. The development of PLTS within the physical education curriculum can enable schools to achieve these aims.

There are many opportunities within physical education to develop PLTS within the key concepts, processes, range and content and curriculum opportunities of the revised NCPE. Teachers can provide pupils with problem-solving and decision-making tasks. Pupils could, for example, act as coaches and provide other pupils with strategic or tactical advice. In other circumstances, pupils might make independent decisions related to the risks involved in a particular activity whilst evaluating their individual and team performance. All of these tasks can help to develop the key skills of reading, writing, communicating and listening. Teachers can also provide pupils with opportunities to become self-managers, creative thinkers, reflective learners, team-workers, independent enquirers, and effective participators according to the style of teaching they adopt in physical education lessons. There are many different ways to teach, known as *styles*. Mosston and Ashworth (1986; 1990) suggest that teaching and learning are essentially about decision-making: what to teach/learn and how to present/acquire the skills/ideas. Their model suggests that at one end of the spectrum the teacher makes all the decisions and at the other end the learner makes them all. In between is a range of styles in which the teacher and learner are both involved in decision-making. Below are examples of how teachers could extend their teaching styles to achieve various outcomes.

Command style

Pupils:

- follow instructions
- respond as a class
- conform in their response
- achieve high levels of activity
- undertake numerous repetitions of various tasks.

This style is used mainly in the interests of safety in the teaching of high-risk activities such as trampolining, swimming, vaulting in gymnastics and throwing events in athletics. See Table 12.1.

Table 12.1 *The command style of teaching*

Style	Characteristics	Outcomes	Example
Command	Teacher makes *all* decisions.	Conformity Uniform behaviour	Dribble a ball over a set distance, at a set time, in a set
	Pupils follow all instructions exactly and perform immediately.	Accurate replication	direction, with a set hand.

Practice style

- Teachers take most of the decisions about what is to be practised and in what way.
- Pupils choose the timing, pace, location and level of difficulty.

This style is used mainly when groups are working to improve basic skills. It is also used when the teacher wants to retain a strong control over the activity and/or if the teacher feels that the pupils are not ready for responsibility or capable of working independently. See Table 12.2.

Reciprocal style

- Teacher hands over all contact with learners to the *observers*.
- Worksheets with explicit instructions are used to set the task.
- Teacher helps observers with their teaching.
- Learners receive a great deal of feedback from observers.
- Pupil activity may be reduced but pupil learning will not be.

See Table 12.3.

Divergent style

- No one solution is assumed.
- Outcomes cannot necessarily be predicted.
- Encourages creative thinking and exploration of new ideas.

See Tables 12.4 and 12.5.

Table 12.2 *The practice style of teaching*

Style	Characteristics	Outcomes	Example
Practice	Teacher makes most decisions. Pupils make some decisions about when, where, how at their own pace.	Refined skills Development of new skills Independent practice Some decision making	Dribble a ball anywhere in a grid area, in any direction, using either hand or foot, change in your own time.

Table 12.3 *Example of a worksheet for a reciprocal style of teaching*

Task	Teaching points
Perform a forward roll along a mat	*Diagram of the various phases of the action along with teaching points:* *Starting position*: Crouch, Eyes look forward, Fingers point forwards, Palms face down, Arms at shoulder height, Feet slightly apart, Remain still. *Performance*: Hands reach forwards, Palms placed on the mat, shoulder-width apart, Fingers pointing forwards, Head tucked into the chest, From two feet push the hips up and forwards, Tuck and roll along the mat, keeping knees and ankles slightly apart. *Finishing position*: Roll to the feet without using the hands to push from the mat. Hold a straight position to finish.

Table 12.4 *The divergent style of teaching*

Style	Characteristics	Outcomes	Example
Divergent (or problem solving)	Teacher presents a problem. Pupils are asked to find as many alternative solutions as they can. No definitive answers. An infinite number of possible solutions.	Develops planning and evaluative skills Develops compositional and tactical skills	Make up a competitive game using a large ball. What is the aim? What are the limits of playing area? How do you start? How do you gain possession? What kinds of passes are used? How many per side?

Table 12.5 *Example of how teachers can use a divergent teaching style in the context of gymnastic activities*

Task	Teaching points
Find and practise a variety of balances:	On three parts On two parts On one part
Find pairs of parts on which to balance.	Forearms Hands Heels Knees Toes
Find various parts of the upper body on which to balance.	Shoulders Head
Find various ways of travelling into a balance.	Jump Roll
Find various ways of moving from one balance into another.	
Perform a sequence of movements that involve a selection of balances.	

Cross-curricular teaching and learning through physical education

Ofsted (2009) found that less than a fifth of the schools made strong connections between physical education and other subjects to help pupils understand the context of their learning better. In planning, teachers looked for ways to link subjects in order to make pupils' learning more relevant and seamless. The examples cited by Ofsted (2009) included the following:

- Good links between physical education, science and PSHE to explore 'leading a healthy lifestyle'.
- The use of command words in French, such as fast, slow, up and down, as the stimulus for a warm-up in dance.
- When studying other cultures or periods in history (for example, Mexico or the Tudors), pupils learnt dances related to the particular theme.
- Using a topic on the Greeks to explore the ancient Olympics and athletic events.
- Linking physical education to mathematics by studying, recording and analysing performances in athletics or personal fitness.

Ofsted (2009: 20)

The contribution of physical education to the broader development of pupils across the curriculum should not be underestimated. Pupils can develop communication skills such as speaking, writing, reading and – one that is often forgotten – listening through physical education. This might involve giving instructions to others in the group, such as how to set up gymnastic apparatus, providing feedback on a performance or technique in athletics, interpreting a reciprocal task sheet on how to perform a layup in basketball, recording information such as the technical requirements for serving in badminton, identifying key words or repeating patterns in dance or acting upon advice in terms of tactical formations in netball: all of which are included across the range and content identified within the revised NCPE (2008).

Pupils may also be provided with opportunities within physical education to make numerical calculations and evaluate the data with respect to performance or develop this through a range of multiple scoring systems across a range of games, for example. Pupils can also develop numerical skills in orienteering by estimating distance and calculating time to complete a set course or developing their understanding of angles by taking compass bearings. Within the context of teaching and learning in physical education there are many forms of ICT that can be used by pupils in the various environments in which they learn, such as the classroom, sports hall, gymnasium, dance studio, swimming pool, athletics tracks and playing field. The resources include computers, the Internet, digital cameras, portable multimedia players, pedometers and timing devices alongside other more traditional and established types of technology such as televisions and video (see Chapter 13).

Teachers may also provide opportunities for pupils to develop their knowledge and understanding of the effects of exercise on the body during an athletics lesson or the range of physical and skill-related fitness, such as strength, flexibility, speed and agility, used in certain activities. The importance of maintaining a healthy, active lifestyle in terms of nutrition and sleep can also inform pupils' understanding of science and health-related issues (see Chapter 10).

Developing FUNctional skills through physical education

The BBaLL FUN Programme is a Key Stage 3 cross-curricular resource that uses basketball in physical education lessons to teach the functional skills of literacy, numeracy and ICT. It can be applied across the range of invasion games. The flexible scheme of work can be easily moved into the curriculum for Years 7 and 8 and can enable pupils who have little or no prior experience of basketball to enjoy and learn from the lessons.

Each lesson involves five teams of five or six students working as players on the court (physical education), and coaches and statisticians (numeracy), commentators and journalists (literacy), television camera operators and sports photographers (ICT) on the sidelines. The FUN Pack provides all the task cards for pupils and the lesson rotation plan for teachers to switch teams through the different subjects for the next lesson. Teams of pupils rotate on a weekly basis and take on the roles identified above. Within the lesson pupils take part as performers within a structured game either as players or officials. Other pupils act as scorers, timekeepers, coaches or match analysts recording the number of passes or shots. Using video and still cameras other pupils record the game and download the footage or visual images whilst another group provides recorded match commentary and match reports, all of which can contribute to the production of a newsletter or be added to the school's website. The West Kent eLearning Group has provided eight schools with the essential ICT equipment including camcorders, MP3 voice recorders and digital cameras to enable them to develop the lessons.

The FUN resources are also available for use with rugby and with new curriculum links for Year 8. See the resources section at the end of this chapter for more information.

Developing cross-curricular themes through the range and content of activities

In previous chapters our contributors have all identified relevant tasks and activities that can develop numerical and literacy skills through the range and content. This can enable pupils to develop their skills of *communication, application of number, working with others, improving their own and others' performance, problem-solving and information technology*. Below is a summary of the ways in which cross-curricular teaching can take place.

Outwitting an opponent

- Match analysis (*communication*)
- Scoring and umpiring (*application of number*)
- Feedback to the teacher, individual pupils or whole class (*improving their own and others' performance*),
- Deciding the best way to individually outwit an opponent or the most effective pass/shot to play (*problem-solving*)
- Deciding on tactical strategies (*working with others*)
- Using digital still cameras (*information technology*).

Accurate replication of actions, phrases and sequences

- Identifying key words (*communication*)
- Filming a group performance (*information technology*)
- Group sequencing (*working with others*)
- Deciding on symmetrical actions and/or group balance (*problem-solving*)
- Reviewing and evaluating an individual or group sequence (*improving their own and others' performance*).

Exploring and communicating ideas, concepts and emotions

- Filming and editing (*information technology*)
- Key words (*communication*)
- Counting beats (*application of number*)
- Group choreographed performance (*working with others*)
- Choreographed dance relating to a set theme (*problem-solving*)
- Reviewing and evaluating a group performance (*improving their own and others' performance*).

Identifying and solving problems to overcome challenges of an adventurous nature

- Human alphabet and numbers game, map symbol word games (*communication*)
- Mobile camera phones to record controls on an orienteering course (*information technology*)

- Using a compass, estimating distance using a map scale (*application of number*)
- Orienteering relay (*working with others* and *improving their own and others' performance*)
- Score orienteering event (*problem-solving*).

Performing at maximum levels in relation to speed, height, distance, strength or accuracy

- Timing, measuring, averages, rank ordering, pacing (*application of number*)
- Filming and using data from pedometers (*information technology*)
- Effects of exercise on the body: pupils decide how to run a 400-metre relay in groups of four as quickly as possible without any predetermined starting points (*problem-solving*)
- Performing in a relay (*working with others*)
- Providing feedback to other pupils (*communication*)
- Analysing their own and other pupils' running, jumping and throwing techniques (*improving their own and others' performance*).

Exercising safely and effectively to improve health and wellbeing

- Recording resting heart rates (*application of number*)
- Compiling graphs (*information technology*)
- Writing key words (*communication*)
- Explaining and interpreting (*problem-solving*)
- Designing training programmes (*improving their own and others' performance*)
- Performing a set training programme (*working with others*).

Literacy through physical education

The focus of a gymnastics or dance lesson could be related to understanding verbs. Pupils are given a list of describing words such as leaping; quivering; striding; running; reclining; perching; slithering; prancing; flying.

In pairs they create a weight-bearing phrase or dance that shows three or four verbs and then show this to the rest of the class.

Numeracy through physical education

The focus of a health-related exercise lesson could be related to multiplication or division. Pupils are divided into pairs and given some equations. They then decide who will perform the answers in the form of exercises.

1. $32 \times 0.25 = ?$ press-ups
2. $4 \div \frac{1}{4} = ?$ sit-ups
3. $(16 \times 3) \div 4 = ?$ squat thrusts
4. $(16 \times 6) \div 8 = ?$ star jumps
5. $0.25 + 5\frac{1}{2} + 3\frac{1}{4} = ?$ straight jumps
6. $144 \div 12 = ?$ 'burpees' squat thrust to straight jump

1. Now work out how many exercises you have performed individually and in a pair.
2. Take your heart rate for 15 seconds. What is it? Now multiply by ? = heart rate for 1 minute.
3. If you exercised for longer what would happen to your heart rate? Explain in pairs.

Information and communications technology through physical education

The focus of a gymnastics lesson could be related to using digital still cameras and downloading photographs onto a laptop computer. Pupils divided into pairs. One pupil performs a series of balances whilst the partners take a series of photographs. They change over and repeat, then download the images and provide each other with feedback. (See Chapter 13 for more details.)

Personal and social education through physical education

The personal and social development of pupils can be enhanced through a series of get-to-know-you exercises, ideally introduced during the first week of the new academic year in order to build up relationships and encourage group cohesion. This should be taught in mixed-sex groups, and pupils should be encouraged to work with a different partner or group each time a new activity is introduced.

Ice-breakers – starter activities

Get as many answers to the questions below as possible – each pupil has to remember their partner's answers because they will be asked about them once completed.

Number and names of brothers/sisters
Any pets (Names)
Hobbies
What they think makes a good teacher
Favourite subject at school and why
Their favourite sporting personality and why
Their favourite physical activity and why
Favourite food
Favourite colour
The animal they think they are most like and why
Their favourite television show and character from television and why.

- With whole group ask quick-fire questions about each person in turn.
- Pupils must speak about their partner.

Circle exercises

Pupils sit in a circle on the floor. Explain the ground rules: everyone is of equal value in the circle; pupils must sit with their hands on their knees to indicate that they are ready to start each new activity; everyone must look at the teacher; everyone has the right to pass.

Name games

- Say your name and pass to the right.
- Go around the circle, point at someone and say their name.
- Tell the group something about yourself (hobbies, favourite colour, etc.) and pass to the right.
- Go around the circle, point at someone, say their name and repeat something about them.
- Happy clap – say your name to the sound of two finger clicks. Two hands down onto knees, clap and two clicks.
- Say the person's name on the right three times and pass on. Repeat to the left.
- Change places with someone and repeat the above.
- Change places with someone whenever the leader clicks their fingers.
- Walk and freeze when the leader claps.

Group exercises

- Roll a ball to someone and call out their name.
- Walk inside the circle, shake hands with three pupils, telling them your name. Sit down and say the names of pupils you shook hands with.
- Think of a signal. Walk in the circle and show three pupils your signal. Sit down. Point to someone on your right and show the rest of the group their signal.
- Walk inside the circle. When the teacher claps their hands and calls out a number get into groups of that number.
- Pupils find a new partner and face them as if looking into a mirror. Take it in turns to mirror the other's actions. Repeat with a different partner.
- With a new partner, one person is clay and the other is a sculptor. Take it in turns to mould a person into a different shape showing a different emotion (happy, sad, frightened, etc.).
- As above in groups – do a group sculpture.
- With a new partner, leapfrog over your partner and pass back through their legs.
- With a new partner, face each other in the press-up position and try to grab your partner's hand.
- With a new partner, one person takes the press-up position. As that person goes down their partner jumps over; as he/she goes up they go under.
- With a new partner, kneel on all fours at opposite ends of a mat. In a clockwise direction try to catch your partner without touching the mat. Repeat anticlockwise.
- Crouch opposite your partner and now try to touch their knee.

Extension activities

Back-to-back walk

Pupils stand back-to-back and lock arms together. One person leans forward, turns and stands upright. Partner then repeats this action moving closer to a finishing line. Pupils continue this until they have rocked all the way to the finish.

Under and over

In teams of ten, pupils place themselves on the floor on all fours in a line one step apart. On the signal to start the last person goes under the person in front and then over the person after that until they reach the front of the line. This continues until everyone has completed the exercise and the group are back in the order they started as. This can be repeated in a circle with pupils facing into the circle.

Circle relay

Pupils stand in a circle an equal distance apart from each other. One person runs a complete circuit around the outside of the circle and then tags the next person. This continues until everyone has completed a circuit. Progress to weaving in and out of each person in the circle and getting everyone to lie down so that the runner has to step over them. This can be further progressed by tagging a partner who must then attempt to catch the person in front.

Foot push

In pairs, pupils sit opposite each other with the soles of their feet together. Push feet together until both partners have their bodies off the ground with only their hands on the floor supporting their weight.

Group hopping

In groups of ten, pupils stand in single file. Then, holding the right leg of the person behind they attempt to hop as a group to a finish line.

Forward and backward circle

In groups of ten, pupils form a circle holding hands and facing inwards. Alternate pupils either lean forwards or lean backwards with their feet shoulder-width apart (Photo 12.1). Now repeat but with everyone facing out.

Photo 12.1 Forward and backward circle

Circle trust

In groups of ten, pupils stand in a circle and link hands. All lean backwards at the same time keeping their feet closely in contact with the floor. Repeat, but this time everyone leans forward with only their shoulders touching.

Back-to-back figure of eight

Pupils hand the ball to each other by moving it to their left and then to their right, then in a figure of eight, standing back to back.

Back to back under and over

Stand back to back and pass a ball to your partner in an under and over routine. Now repeat with one person blindfolded.

Wall walk

Pupils get into pairs, one blindfolded and one sighted. The blindfolded person stands 2 metres from a wall and walks towards the wall. The sighted person must guide their partner as close to the wall as possible.

Group press-up

In groups of four, pupils lie in a press-up position on the floor to form a square. Each person places their feet on the next person's back. Once complete the group attempt to push up so that all their feet are off the floor (Photo 12.2).

Photo 12.2 Group press-up

Small-sided games designed to promote personal and social development

The following activities provide fun, enjoyment and variety, and keep attention in a way in which learning is taking place subliminally.

Tag

Pupils try to tag other pupils without getting tagged themselves within a pre-set boundary. Pupils must attempt to tag as many different pupils as possible and keep count. Pupils cannot tag the same person twice in a row. The teacher should check to see which pupil has scored the highest.

Stuck in the mud

Two pupils attempt to tag as many other pupils as possible. If they are tagged they must stop and put their hands above their head with legs astride. They can only continue when other pupils who have not been tagged crawl through their legs.

Chain tag

The same as above but the 'catchers' must hold hands. Once a pupil is tagged he or she joins the pair to make a threesome. As soon as another pupil is tagged they split into two pairs, and so on until one pupil remains untagged.

Heads and tails

All pupils move around a pre-set area. When the teacher says 'heads' they put their hands on top of their heads. When the teacher says 'tails' they sit down. This is then changed to opposites, i.e. heads = sit down, tails = hands on top of the head.

Traffic lights

Pupils jog inside a grid. The teacher gives the commands 'red', 'yellow', or 'green'. Red = stop; yellow = jog on the spot; green = continue to jog. Then move to opposites (red = go; green = stop).

Bib change

Players carry a bib inside a grid. When the teacher says change they swap bibs with another pupil and continue to jog inside the grid.

Shirt tails

All pupils insert a bib inside the back of their shorts and then attempt to pull out as many bibs as they can while moving without getting their own bib pulled out. Move to 'fox and rabbits', where two pupils are foxes (without bibs) and have to pull out the other pupils' (rabbits') bibs. Pupils who have not had their bib pulled out can pick up bibs and return them to other pupils.

Round the circle

Pupils stand in a circle. One pupil runs around the outside in a clockwise direction and tags another pupil, who has to attempt to catch that pupil before they can return to the empty space in the circle. This is continued until every pupil has been included. Move to two circles (inner and outer circles) and repeat, but with one group moving clockwise and the other moving anticlockwise.

Rats and rabbits

Pupils stand in two lines, one for rats and one for rabbits. The distance between them should be an arm's length so that their fingertips can touch the fingertips of the person in the opposite line. The teacher calls out either rats or rabbits. If rabbits are called, the rabbits have to get beyond a pre-determined line before the rats can tag them and vice-versa. This can be changed to crows and cranes.

Left and right

Pupils stand in two lines, an arm's length apart so that their fingertips are touching with a partner. The teacher points either left or right. Pupils on the side pointed to have to get to a safety point before their partner catches them. Now reverse the command – left means right and right means left.

Indoor obstacles courses

Using a range of equipment, set up an obstacle course that encourages pupils to balance, crawl, jump, step over, step under, navigate, etc. These can be referred to as tunnels, streams, rivers, fences, etc. This is only limited by your own imagination. Alternatively, a string trail or obstacle course could be set up. Pupils work in pairs, with one blindfolded and one sighted. Pupils must use non-verbal communication to guide their partner around the course from start to finish. (This could involve carrying an awkward load which must not get wet or touch the ground. Carry this through a difficult maze, over a height or a series of obstacles, up and down difficult slopes and retrieve a 'key' from a difficult position.) This should take place indoors, using a gym or sports hall. Equipment can include:

- benches
- beams
- crash mats
- cones
- hoops
- gymnastics boxes
- tarpaulin
- hurdles.

Raiders of the Lost Ark

Pupils are divided into pairs. One pupil is blindfolded whilst carrying an object (referred to as a precious jewel) that cannot touch the floor. The sighted person must lead their partner through a series of obstacles set out as a course in a gym or sports hall. This can be completed using verbal or non-verbal communication.

As an extension activity, teams of four pupils must decide the best way they can complete the course whilst holding hands as a team.

The Crystal Maze

Pupils can complete the course as a pair but at each obstacle they must solve a problem and retrieve a key or crystal. The more crystals or keys they retrieve the more points they score.

The jungle survival challenge

Pupils must collect coloured stars each time they successfully negotiate a particular obstacle during the course.

Parachute games

The parachute is a useful way of involving a large group of pupils in an activity and the parachute games encourage co-operative, non-competitive play and reinforce turn-taking and sharing (Strong and Le Feuvre 2006). The games are a lot of fun for pupils and allow participants to share learning experiences with each other and generate a group spirit or sense of 'togetherness'.

Safety

- Check the ground underneath the parachute. If you are playing outside on a grass surface, the ground needs to be dry, not slippery.
- Inside, check you have a clear, splinter-free floor if pupils are barefoot.
- Make sure there is enough space once the parachute has been pulled out to its maximum circumference.
- Give clear warnings about head bumping and looking where you are going.
- If you are to advance to games where people need to be on the parachute, make sure the group can sustain their weight. There must be no letting go, dropping or kicking.
- It is a good idea to have an adult present who is not holding onto the parachute so that they can help pupils, field balls, give instructions, etc. when necessary.
- Most parachutes are highly flammable and need to be stored in a safe place and used in flame-free areas.

Getting started

Remove the parachute from the bag. Everyone takes hold of an edge with both hands (knuckles on top is best) at waist level. Once everyone is holding on, move everyone out backwards slowly until the parachute is fully stretched and participants are evenly spread out. Everyone slowly moves the parachute up and allows it to fall into place rather than tugging it down.

Practise getting everyone in time. After a short while, try to get the parachute as high as possible. Develop this by taking small steps in to create a mushroom shape.

Odds and evens

Pupils are given a number. Each time the teacher calls out 'evens' all the even-numbered pupils must change places. Repeat using 'odds'. This can be extended by calling out 'multiples of two, three, four, etc.

Mushroom sit

On your command, pupils raise their arms, lifting the parachute over their heads. Then, pulling the parachute behind them, they sit down with their bottoms on the edge of the parachute. Everyone will end up inside the parachute as if in a tent. One person can move to the middle and become the 'tent pole'.

Mushroom hunt

On your command, pupils raise their arms, lifting the parachute over their heads. While the group allows the parachute to fall down, you select a group of people to let go, leave their space and move to another position (Photo 12.3).

Merry-go-round

Everyone holds the parachute with one hand and walks around in a circle. On your command the group can start jogging or running. You can also instruct pupils to bob up and down or to jump as they run. You can instruct the group to change direction. Pupils then swap hands and then walk or run in the reverse direction. Pupils can be told to travel in different ways: to hop or skip, etc.

Tug 'til still

The idea of the game is for everyone to be balanced at the same time. Everyone holds the parachute at waist height and slowly leans back until they are in an unnatural position, only being held up by the parachute. The game can be made harder by everyone having

Photo 12.3 Parachute: mushroom hunt

their back to the parachute, reaching back and then leaning forward face to the ground in the unnatural position. The nature of this game often means that participants fall down. A suitable floor space is needed and participants need to be aware that they must warn everyone if they are going to fall and also to use their arms to cushion their fall if necessary.

Chase and catch

Place two balls, ideally of different sizes or colours (or both), on the parachute. Divide the participants into two teams. Teams can be either side of the parachute or mixed up into quarters (so that opposing quadrants work together). One ball is made to chase the other in the hope of catching it. It is helped by one team. The other team is helping the other ball escape from the first.

Raise the ball

Place a ball in the middle of the parachute. The idea is, through teamwork, to see how high the group can lift the ball into the air and then catch it for another go (Photo 12.4).

Summary

Teaching physical education across Key Stages 2 and 3 presents opportunities for teachers to extend the learning of pupils in many ways other than through physical performance. The examples provided can be adapted to suit different circumstances, facilities and resources and can enable teachers to develop and extend much broader themes.

Photo 12.4 Parachute: raise the ball

References

Mosston, M. and Ashworth, S. (1986) *Teaching Physical Education*. Columbus, OH: Merrill.

Mosston, M. and Ashworth, S. (1990) *The Spectrum of Teaching Styles: From command to discovery*, New York: Longman.

Ofsted (2009) 'Physical education in schools 2005/08: Working towards 2012 and beyond', April, Reference number: 080249.

Strong, T. and Le Feuvre, D. (2006) *Parachute Games with DVD*. Leeds, Human Kinetics.

Useful resources

Midura, D. and Glover, .D (2005) *Essentials of Team Building: Principles and practices*. Coachwise Publications.

Newstrom, J. and Scannell, E. (2007) *The Big Book of Team Building Games: Quick, fun activities for building morale, communication and team spirit*. Maidenhead: McGraw-Hill.

More information about the BBaLL FUN Programme can be found at www.bballfun.com

13 Using information and communication technology to support learning and teaching in physical education

Gary Stidder

Introduction

The purpose of this chapter is to highlight the breadth of information and communication technology (ICT) available to teachers across Key Stages 2 and 3 and how it can support teaching and learning in physical education. The revised National Curriculum for Physical Education in England (NCPE) (QCA 2007: 195) suggests that pupils should be offered curriculum opportunities across seven distinct areas (a–g). One of the areas identified within curriculum opportunities is the use of ICT as a means of improving individual and group performance and tracking progress. The NCPE states that ICT should be used by teachers and pupils to: 'Record and review performances and record data for the purposes of personal improvement' (QCA 2008: 195).

With ICT fast becoming a key feature within education across all subject areas, physical education has the opportunity to take the lead in developing a number of initiatives and innovative approaches in using ICT to support and enhance teaching and learning. For the purpose of this chapter I will group technologies under three main headings: cameras, software and gadgets. The intention is to highlight ways in which each of these contributes to pupil learning in a practical context; highlight its strengths and weaknesses; discuss its contribution to lesson planning; demonstrate the use of ICT across a range of activities; and highlight some of the best forms of ICT in physical education.

Cameras

There is a range of hardware applications that can be used in physical education departments. Video cameras can provide footage of experienced performers in action and can be used to inspire, to demonstrate correct techniques and to develop pupils' understanding and knowledge of the subject. By reviewing their own actions, for example, pupils can evaluate and improve their own games strategies, gymnastics sequences, trampoline routines or dance compositions, particularly if they are able to look at their performances in slow motion or from a different viewing angle. Cameras can also be used by non-participants, who can take a series of photographs which highlight the learning objectives of a lesson and then explain how each photograph demonstrates the learning objective(s).

Within practical situations the use of still and video cameras can highlight personal achievement within lessons. Video footage and photographic images can be cropped and edited and used either as a slideshow or highlight DVD. Cameras can also be used as an assessment for learning tool and as a form of classroom management. They can help to create activity cards, worksheets and presentations. Furthermore they can enable a teacher to break down a particular skill or technique in order to reinforce learning and demonstrate good practice. One example of a useful camera is the Sanyo Xacti video camera, which is waterproof and captures footage as a regular video camera would. The storage is through SD memory cards and this allows for easy transfer of data. Footage taken can be observed through a PC, on an interactive whiteboard. The camera is incredibly simple to use and it has a reasonable battery life. Other types of cameras include the Novatech flip camera, which is a simple battery-operated video camera with a USB cable that can be plugged directly into the USB port of a computer. Thus video footage can be automatically downloaded to the PC and can be uploaded onto YouTube if wished.

Mobile camera phones

The use of mobile phones in schools is a contentious issue. Some schools may allow pupils to use their mobile phones within physical education lessons. For example, during an orienteering unit of work pupils could take photographs with their phones of the items they are trying to find and use the picture as evidence of completion of the course. Pupils could also set up their own orienteering courses, using pictures taken with their phones and transferred to the computers within the lesson. Other groups can then have the opportunity to attempt different courses, which could be an excellent way to integrate ICT and literacy into physical education. This could especially work well if there is minimal ICT equipment within the department.

The use of motion analysis software

The use of motion analysis software within physical education is becoming a more mainstream means of evaluating pupil performance and enhancing learning. There are many software packages available. Software such as Dartfish can provide pupils with visual images of their performances that can be slowed down and also enlarged. It allows teachers, using a digital camera, to split the screen into progressive frames and is therefore useful for highlighting techniques in some of the athletic field events or trampoline routines. Freeze framing and overlay facilities are also a useful application. The footage can be saved and stored for moderation purposes. Whilst there are certain advantages in using this type of software there are also some disadvantages. For example, it can be time-consuming to set up the software and any associated hardware such as video cameras if the user is unfamiliar with them. In addition, the initial cost of purchasing the package may deter some schools from implementing this type of technology into the physical education curriculum.

Fewer than one in ten of the schools visited by Ofsted between 2005 and 2008 used ICT to stimulate pupils' interest and support learning in all age groups. Of these, most had purchased commercial software for movement analysis. This offered pupil opportunities to observe, analyse and evaluate their own performance and that of others to bring about improvements. For example, pupils in one school observed and evaluated work very effectively through using digital camera recordings of performance and peer assessment sheets (Ofsted 2009).

Film editing in physical education

There are many film-editing software packages that teachers can use to support and enhance teaching and learning in physical education. They enable teachers and pupils to study individual and team performances across a range of activities. Video footage taken in one lesson can be edited and used at the beginning of the following lesson to highlight the achievements of pupils but also to identify common faults. Teachers and pupils can compile footage taken from all the different lessons and use the film to show other pupils in different classes what to expect using film-editing software.

The popular package iMovie, for example, imports video footage using a fire wire interface on most MiniDV format digital video cameras. From there, the user can edit the video clips, add titles, and add music. Effects include basic colour correction and video enhancement tools, and transitions such as fade-in, fade-out and slides, as well as travel map functions for marking locations where a video was shot.

There are other editing software programmes such as Final Cut Express and Final Cut Pro which may be appropriate for more experienced users and advanced work. It is imperative, however, that you understand the issues involved in using moving and still images of pupils and that school policies and protocols are adhered to when using ICT to record pupil performance. This includes issues associated with parental permission; filming for a purpose; dress; angles; management of images; and access and security of clips. The Association for Physical Education has published guidance for safe practice (AfPE 2008). See in particular the sections on 'safeguarding children and young people' (55–72) and 'photography, digital imagery, filming, internet and mobile phone misuse (61–63).

Gadgets

Interactive whiteboards

An interactive whiteboard is a surface onto which a computer screen can be displayed through a data projector. As it is touch-sensitive it allows teachers to use a pen or finger like a mouse to control the computer from the board and save any changes for future lessons. Multimedia resources can be used, and access to the Internet and websites can give support to teaching and learning. Interactive whiteboards are a useful teaching aid in classroom-based lessons because they can support learning through presentations, demonstrations and modelling, actively engage pupils and improve the pace and flow of lessons. A laptop computer that is linked to a data projector can also enable this type of resource to be used in a sports hall or gym. Teachers can use interactive whiteboards for showing a whole class a particular technique from video demonstrations taken immediately beforehand or in a previous lesson (DfES 2004a and b).

Voice projection systems

Voice projection systems can provide an innovative way of communicating with pupils specifically within physical education. The Front Row To Go system is one example of a portable voice projection that can be used wherever you teach. The system includes a lightweight, wireless hand-held radio microphone and head microphone which transmits a teacher's voice to a base-station. This then amplifies, enhances speech frequencies and broadcasts it from speakers to the whole class. It is simple to set up and very effective. The system can be used either from a mains electrical socket or rechargeable batteries which give over six hours of power. The system can increase pupil attentiveness and concentration, improve teaching and learning and reduce voice strain.

Nintendo Wii

Nintendo Wii games consoles are being used in schools to encourage disaffected pupils in physical education lessons in order to increase fitness levels. Some schools are using the consoles to simulate actions of certain activities to improve pupils' behaviour and teamwork skills. Whilst some may think that the use of computer games is contradictory in raising activity levels and attainment, there is anecdotal evidence to suggest that with rigid structures in place and using specific games, pupils can be physically active without realising it. In one case study project teachers identified pupils between the ages of 14 and 16 who had often missed physical education lessons. A Wii console was bought for each school, along with heart rate monitors to show how much physical activity the teenagers were getting from using the consoles (*Guardian* 2008). It is too early to tell whether this type of approach to the teaching of physical education is potentially a useful means of engaging young people in physical activity and whether the physical education profession will themselves accept this as way of increasing participation rates in physical education lessons.

Nintendo Wii Fit

The Wii Fit is a video game that has been designed by Nintendo for the Wii console. The game focuses on exercises which involve an individual using a Wii balance board. The board is a wireless accessory and contains multiple pressure sensors which measure an individual's centre of balance. This can be applied to activity games such as skiing, for example. The Wii Fit package includes a Wii Fit game disk for the Nintendo Wii console containing fitness training related games and activities. The balance board measures a user's mass and centre of balance. The software can then calculate the user's body mass index when told of his or her height. The game consists of different sub games and activities – some of which are not available until being unlocked by building up credits in the 'Fit Bank' – including yoga poses, strength training, aerobics, balance games, and other exercises. Furthermore, Wii Fit allows its players to compare their fitness by using Wii Fit's own channel on the menu.

Dance mat systems

There are several multi-player wireless dance mat systems which allow pupils to activate panels on a dance platform in sequence with projected images and the beat of music. Dance steps are projected on to a wall or screen; users follow the steps displayed by arrows on their individual dance mat. At the end of a song or session, users and instructors can see instant feedback on how well they performed, and a leadership board can provide motivational competitiveness. Interactive fitness equipment offers many benefits at a time of growing concern about pupils' lack of participation in physical activity. Amongst the benefits to pupils is that they will burn off energy, boost their overall fitness, and improve their co-ordination and cardiovascular health. Physical activity can be more enjoyable and fitness and co-ordination is improved.

DanceMachine offers a twenty-mat system for schools. It has been developed to improve fitness levels through hi-tech sound and visual equipment and is suitable for all Key Stages. This interactive range of equipment is designed to improve fitness through a large video screen and the latest hi-tech sound equipment. It tests both mental and physical activity through a wide choice of games and music and offers unlimited hours of physical activity.

The iDANCE multi-player system offers up to thirty wireless dance platforms, simultaneous play, and three levels of difficulty which can be seen at the same time and is ideal for mixed levels of ability.

Pedometers

The FitLinxx ActiPed is a next-generation pedometer that clips to a shoe and records the wearer's walking, running or jumping and measures the distance travelled, calories burnt and total time of active minutes. This data can be stored and sent wirelessly and securely to an ActiPed account for the wearer to view their achievement and compare with their peer group.

Another innovative development using ICT in physical education is the Nike+ iPod system. This allows pupils to monitor their progress with regard to their levels of exercise in a similar way to other pedometers. It requires an iPod, Nike+ shoes, sensor to fit in the shoes and a receiver for an iPod Nano. As pupils run, their iPod indicates their time, distance, pace, and calories burned. It gives them feedback at the halfway point and in the final lead-up to goal, and also records the details of their workout. On selected workouts sporting legends such as Lance Armstrong and Venus Williams give periodic motivational help.

Pupils can upload all the run information onto the Nike+ website, where they can see a timescale indicating all the information about their run and review their workout. Pupils can store all the runs completed so they can compare them and gain advice and help with training/coaching for any distances. The website also has an interactive community of participants all over the world. Pupils can challenge other people, view their racing times, and interact with other runners. The Nike+ website motivates pupils to access learning outside school, increases their running and fitness, improves ICT skills, supports the teaching of appropriate techniques, and motivates their learning through self-pacing calculations and estimating distances. Pupils are encouraged to undertake courses appropriate to their levels of skill and fitness, set targets to challenge themselves, and assess their learning.

Qwizdom

Qwizdom is an interactive pupil response system designed to engage and motivate pupils whilst giving the teacher the tools to monitor and record pupil progress. Qwizdom is sometimes referred to as a classroom voting system which utilises advanced radio frequency technology and integrates with Qwizdom curriculum software. Qwizdom adds increased interactivity into classrooms through its interactive writing tablet or wireless slate, which presents a cost-effective alternative to interactive whiteboard technology. Qwizdom is essentially a series of handsets that interact with additional software for Windows PowerPoint which allows pupils to interact with the teacher's presentation. This could be in the form of a quiz or formal assessment. Each pupil has access to a handset. If required pupils can remain anonymous throughout the activity, or handsets can relate to each pupil individually. The results from each question can be highlighted to the group, via a graph or table, and pupils can compete against one another with a marking system or a time limit that can be adopted by the teacher.

At Seaford Head Community College in East Sussex, Qwizdom has been used to develop material. It has also captivated pupils' interest, particularly in areas that may be more academic or literature-based. It has been used with all Key Stage 3 pupils to evaluate the physical education course. This has allowed physical education staff to make changes to the curriculum throughout the year in order to enhance the learning environment for each pupil. In addition, Qwizdom has been used within an orienteering unit of work. The lessons were designed to include a strong theme of numeracy and literacy and included clues that pupils could answer using the handsets. The teacher was able to collate and save results, as well as to observe the progress of the pupils as the handsets interacted with the laptop used on-site by the member of staff.

Portable multimedia players

Portable multimedia players (PMP), sometimes referred to as portable video players (PVP) or Internet Media Tablets (IMT), are capable of storing and playing digital media. Digital audio players (DAP) that can also display images and play videos are portable multimedia players. Like DAPs, the data is typically stored on a hard drive, micro drive or flash memory. Other types of electronic devices like mobile phones are sometimes referred to as PMPs because of their playback capabilities. Below are some specific examples of multimedia players and how they can be used in physical education lessons to support teaching and learning.

Archos

Archos is an MP4 mass storage unit that can access the Internet and transmit video and still images and music through an external source such as a speaker system or an interactive whiteboard. Its main function within physical education lessons is its ability to record video footage. The player has a small camera attachment that can film any type of activity, such as a dance performance, and it can be instantly played back on the 4-inch screen. The screen size allows for students to observe their technique and make comment, or watch the performance. During the playback mode, there is also the opportunity to slow the action down to several variable speeds, as well as pause the footage. This is ideal when illustrating areas for improvement, or highlighting good technique and also incredibly visual for the pupils observing. Playback can instantly be transferred to a PC or laptop, and therefore be viewed on the 'big screen', or even edited to make into a video. It is a reliable back-up for pupils' written assignments and can make the course content far more interesting and challenging. At Seaford Head Community College, pupils have created videos of good technique during outdoor and adventurous activities whilst using the climbing wall using the Archos to capture the footage. They have then used the school's ICT suite to edit their footage together to make a short film.

Archos can save video footage which can be used for starter material at the beginning of a lesson: for example, footage taken from the previous lesson, or information from the Internet, or digital television. Clips can be related to the lesson focus, or learning objectives. Information can be stored on the device that will relate to the lesson planned, such as a good technique or performance. This could be observed at any stage throughout the lesson by pupils in order for them to enhance and compare their own work against the work of others. Music can be used at any stage and can play whilst the Archos is performing another feature. For example, it would be possible for the Archos to be plugged in to speakers for a dance or gymnastics performance while filming the performance itself.

Wireless Internet (Wifi) is also a useful feature, because pupils can use it to access the Web in order to aid their research related to the work being covered. This does require a licence from Archos and involves a fee.

Filming is easy with the Archos helmet cam. Pupils can gain instant feedback on what they have performed and develop work as a result. They can use the slow-motion tool on the device to illustrate an action or to evaluate their own and others' performance. This information can then be stored on any computer system that has the software installed (this will take three minutes to install). Footage is downloaded via USB and can then be used in various ways. For example, it can be added to Movie Maker and edited into a movie. It can also be added to presentations (PowerPoint). To view the footage on a larger scale it takes moments to plug the device in and illustrate the work on the interactive whiteboard. This works via USB again. The film can then be watched and paused a number of times. Slow motion is not available at a larger scale as the footage is being played through the computer, rather than the Archos unit itself.

Other recordings can be taken from digital television, terrestrial, video and DVD by linking the device up to a DVR station (which is also a charger). Using a DVR station alongside the Wifi allows the teacher to set a timer on the Archos to record programmes. Data is stored directly onto the device and can be played back. Alternatively, highlights of programmes can be recorded by hand using the record and pause functions.

The iPod

The iPod is a brand of portable media players designed and marketed by Apple Inc. The products include the hard-drive-based iPod Classic, the touchscreen iPod Touch, the video-capable iPod Nano, and the compact iPod Shuffle. The iPhone can function as an iPod but is generally treated as a separate product. iPod Classic models store media on an internal hard drive, while all other models use flash memory to enable their smaller size. As with many other digital music players, iPods, excluding the iPod Touch, can also serve as external data storage devices. Storage capacity varies by model.

The iTunes software can be used to transfer music to the devices from computers using certain versions of Apple Macintosh and Microsoft Windows operating systems. The use of iTunes and its alternatives may also enable transfer of photographs, videos, games, contact information, e-mail settings, Web bookmarks, and calendars to iPod models supporting those features. There are a number of potential benefits of using gadgets such as iPods to engage and motivate pupils through analysis of performance. Pupils can rip and upload videos to their own iPod. A dictaphone can allow pupils to provide commentary to moving images. For teachers it allows practical forms of assessment to take place and provide immediate results and feedback. Clips can be stored in pupil files, allowing for reduced marking and paperwork for both teachers and pupils.

Podcasting

A podcast is a series of audio or video digital media files which are distributed over the Internet by download, through Web feeds, to portable media players and personal computers. A podcast is distinguished from most other digital media formats by its ability to be syndicated, subscribed to, and downloaded automatically when new content is added. Like the term broadcast, podcast refers either to the series of content itself or to the method by which it is syndicated; the latter is also called podcasting. The host or author of a podcast is often called a podcaster. Podcasting is becoming increasingly popular in education and is currently being used at Hayesbrook Specialist Sports College where it has enabled pupils and teachers to share information at any time. An absent pupil can download the podcast of the recorded lesson. Podcasting is also being used as a tool for teachers or administrators to communicate curriculum, assignments and other information with parents and the community. Teachers can record trampoline and gymnastic routines, dance performances, swimming techniques, post-match interviews, and pupil debates for example. Podcasting can be a publishing tool for pupil oral presentations within accredited physical education courses at Key Stage 4 and beyond.

The virtual learning environment (VLE)

The virtual learning environment (VLE) has transformed the way in which pupils learn and teachers teach. The virtual learning environment is a global website that allows pupils to access their work and their curriculum from anywhere in the world. It is rights-protected and therefore only parents, students and staff are able to log in. Pupils' work can be set, collected and marked via the VLE, saving on a great deal of paperwork and collection and deadline dates. This, in turn, can empower pupils and inform their own learning. Pupils are able to make more decisions, as tasks will be completed at their own pace and potentially in their own time.

There are many ways in which physical education teachers can optimise pupils' knowledge and understanding through the use of this technology, with significant advantages. For example, pupils are able to join subjects (known as courses) and from there they will see the tasks, homework, quizzes and forums linked to the teacher, from home and school. As a teacher you are able to post work for your pupils that will be available around the clock. Your pupils will be able to submit work online and you can feedback to them from anywhere in the world. This allows teachers, parents and pupils to monitor their work and current attainment in physical education.

Using the VLE, pupils are able to post their work for others to see and comment on; parents will be able to participate more fully in their children's learning; learning can continue outside the school day; pupils will be able to participate in collaborative work involving other schools locally and internationally involving external experts; and learning can be more personalised to suit pupil needs. As many pupils make use of interactive online services (such as blogs, messaging and virtual worlds) at home, the VLE allows them to make use of these services in a controlled and safe online environment.

At Hailsham Specialist Sports College in East Sussex, the VLE is being piloted to enhance collaboration with feeder primary schools by having online mentoring of Year 6 pupils by current Year 7 pupils, helping to ease the transition to secondary school. Cross-curricular learning is also facilitated through use of the VLE. Current examples of this working are the science and physical education project run in Year 7 by physical education teachers. Pupils are able to interact online with teachers and each other to discuss and formulate answers to questions relating to learning objectives from lessons 'out of school time'. This type of learning environment and this specific cross-curricular work has been recognised as a model of good practice and is growing rapidly. With many schools moving toward a more interactive way of teaching and learning it is likely that these types of practices will be commonplace in many schools by the start of the next decade.

Video conferencing

A video conference can take place anywhere in the world, provided that the technology is in place. Video conferencing involves a set of interactive telecommunications technologies which can enable two or more schools to interact through a two-way video and audio transmission. Teachers and pupils are able to see and hear each other at the same time. In schools, video conferencing can be used for formal teaching, using guest teachers, multi-school projects, and community events. Once connected, pupils can see the other person on a TV screen and ask questions. The equipment required includes a television monitor, camera, microphone, speaker and a compressed video system which can be transmitted through an Integrated Services Digital Network (ISDN).

Video conferencing can provide pupils with the opportunity to learn in different ways, which might include a focus on a particular topic being covered in physical education. This could be arranged with another physical education department where teachers can offer particular expertise, thus allowing for the sharing of information. This interactive approach to teaching can be highly motivating for pupils and improve their communication and presentation skills. In addition, memory retention can potentially be improved and a range of different learning styles can be catered for and can provide a much broader forum where learning can take place. Video conferencing can be arranged by using Skype, a software application that enables users to make voice calls over the internet as well as instant messaging and teleconferencing.

YouTube

YouTube is a video-sharing website where users can upload, view and share video clips. It uses Adobe flash video technology to display a wide variety of user-generated video content, including movie clips, television clips, and music videos, as well as amateur content such as video blogging and short original videos. Most of the content on YouTube has been uploaded by individuals, although media corporations including the BBC offer some of their material via the site. The wide range of topics covered by YouTube has turned video sharing into one of the most important parts of Internet culture. YouTube is fast becoming an effective medium for gaining and presenting images in schools. This has many advantages for a physical education teacher wishing to visually describe a sport, an action, a skill or technique to a class. Most schools now have facilities for Internet access to be shown and the use of large spaces such as the school hall for assemblies to present images from YouTube can be hugely effective.

YouTube is beneficial because it is fast. Teachers and pupils can type in the sport wanted and a variety of differing images is displayed. It is possible with appropriate software to download videos from YouTube and save them onto a computer, which would cut out the need for the Internet when showing the class. However, using YouTube effectively requires knowledge of the Internet and in some cases an Internet connection is needed. There also needs to be clear guidance on its use by teachers and pupils and in some cases this will require forms of governance in terms of access. The website at Seaford Head Community College currently utilises YouTube for publicity, promotional and marketing purposes as well to highlight pupil achievements and experiences in areas such as performing arts and physical education.

Ofsted (2009) cited one school where ICT was used very effectively. In particular:

> Video clips from 'YouTube' on the boxing match between Mike Tyson and Oliver McCall were used to discuss somatic and cognitive impact on physiological

arousal when participating in sport and its effects on performance, following the breakdown of McCall in the ring. This led to discussion of the importance of temperament under pressure, drawing on examples such as an England versus Germany penalty shoot-out and the missing of an easy conversion which would have won the rugby league challenge cup. The teacher then led a session expertly on the impact of confidence, peaking in performance and self-talk, comparing performances of Usain Bolt and Asafa Powell. The use of visual cues, contemporary examples and discussion combined with the teacher's excellent subject knowledge helped to consolidate students' understanding of a complex topic very well.

Ofsted (2009: 36)

Summary

This chapter has looked at using a range of ICT to support and enhance teaching and learning and administration in physical education. There have been many new innovations that have particular relevance to physical education. The first step in assessing the application of ICT in physical education is for you to decide when to use it and whether it is suitable in supporting good practice in teaching and learning. An overemphasis on using ICT in physical education lessons at the expense of the 'physical' and 'practical' aspects of physical education potentially can do more harm than good with respect to pupils' learning. Your professional judgement should be used to make decisions about the use of ICT to support and enhance the achievement of learning outcomes and provide opportunities to explore and enhance understanding. Nonetheless, ICT does have many advantages in enhancing learning in physical education in schools.

The use of ICT within physical education will continue to be an integral part of many future developments and initiatives that are likely to emerge as technology becomes more advanced and accepted as part of mainstream teaching and learning. Key questions for you to consider in respect to the use of ICT is whether pupils might achieve or learn something different or more effectively by incorporating this into your lessons and whether this may challenge, stimulate and engage pupils to a greater extent. If it does, use it; if not, don't.

ICT can only be a useful tool for enhancing teaching and learning if used correctly and effectively. This means that you will continue to need to learn new skills. Changes to working practices and technology can sometimes be uncomfortable but are, nevertheless, inevitable and there are many opportunities for you to develop your professional ICT skills and enable pupils to improve their learning.

Acknowledgements

I would like to acknowledge the help and support of Kevin Morton (Seaford Head Community College), Craig Bull (Hayesbrook Specialist Sports College), and Andy Gore, Sam Carter and Ben Gould (University of Brighton) for their assistance in researching certain aspects of the chapter.

References

AfPE (Association for Physical Education) (2008) *Safe Practice in Physical Education and School Sport*, Worcester: Coachwise Publications.

DfES (Department for Education and Skills) (2004a) *Key Stage 3 National Strategy: ICT across the curriculum, ICT in physical education*, Ref: DfES 0184-2004 G.

DfES (Department for Education and Skills) (2004b) *Key Stage Three Embedding ICT @ Secondary Physical Education: The use of interactive whiteboards in physical education*, Ref : DfES / 0801 / 2004.

Guardian (2008) http://www.guardian.co.uk/education/2008/may/06/link.link7

Ofsted (2009) *Physical Education in Schools 2005/08: Working towards 2012 and beyond*, April, Ref: 080249.

QCA (2007) http://www.qca.org.uk (accessed June 2009).

Useful resources and websites

Motion analysis software

www.dartfish.com

Interactive whiteboards

www.whiteboards.becta.org.uk

Voice projection system

http://gofrontrow.com/

Nintendo Wii

www.nintendo.com/wiifit

Dance mats

www.pulsefitness.com/kids_dancemachine.htm

Actiped pedometer

www.actihealth.com

Nike+

http://nikerunning.nike.com/nikeos/p/nikeplus/en_GB/

Qwizdom

www.qwizdom.co.uk

Video conferencing

www.skype.com

Index